S0-AWU-549

Frank,

a good friend
and a great contributor
to the school district.

Hoover Liddell
5/17/11

Journey from
Kilimanjaro

Journey from Kilimanjaro

Hoover Liddell

Writer's Showcase
presented by *Writer's Digest*
San Jose New York Lincoln Shanghai

Journey from Kilimanjaro

All Rights Reserved © 2000 by Hoover Liddell

No part of this book may be reproduced or transmitted in
any form or by any means, graphic, electronic, or mechanical,
including photocopying, recording, taping, or by any
information storage or retrieval system, without the
permission in writing from the publisher.

Published by Writer's Showcase
presented by *Writer's Digest*
an imprint of iUniverse.com, Inc.

For information address:
iUniverse.com, Inc.
620 North 48th Street
Suite 201
Lincoln, NE 68504-3467
www.iuniverse.com

ISBN: 0-595-00487-3

Printed in the United States of America

For my wife, Margaret
my mother, Bernadine
my daughter, Maleka

Contents

Preface
The Journey

I went to Africa millions of years after the earliest humans living there emerged into an unknown world and a hundred years after white explorers were attracted there in search of the source of the Nile. The river begins both in Ethiopia (the Blue Nile) and near Lake Victoria (the White Nile), and the two come together at Khartoum and travel hundreds of miles to the Mediterranean Sea. Human life, like a river, flowed from a source beginning in Africa in the world of Kilimanjaro and the Rift Valley. The earliest human inhabitants left this place not knowing or understanding how far we could go across the earth or into space, or how intelligent we could become, or what we could make of this earth. Human life is a river of impermanence. That is its actuality. We live in a vast and unknown universe which reveals itself through us. Our journey is profound.

Human life in its travel encounters new adventure and moves on without surrender. There are such planetary journeys occurring in climbing the mountains of the world, from human expeditions in the California wilderness, and in schools and classrooms when students encounter mathematical frontiers to border crossings to new worlds. In these adventures we learn, discover, and understand things which connect us to a larger world. We all live diminished lives when the environments that we exist in do not challenge and deepen our capabilities.

This is a book about my journey through life. As a teacher and a traveler I am writing this book on how I see life through this beginning adventure of humankind which is still present in us. We are driven by curiosity to observe and to understand the world. As a teacher and a traveler I am interested in my own learning and that of others, the rich investigations that come from their own questions and finding things out for themselves. Though no one told me or instructed me to inquire into things or to pursue my curiosities, I probe and explore and I find things I never knew existed.

Acknowledgements

I am deeply grateful for the dedication, tireless support and serious attention over the years from my wife, Margaret, in the writing and publication of this book. I am also grateful to Herb Kohl, who as a writer, encouraged, shared ideas, and diligently worked with me. I am grateful and fortunate for the editing and proofreading contribution of Lorin Oberweger. Her thoroughness, expertise, and writing insights were invaluable. I am grateful to the students, teachers, scholars, friends, thinkers, and writers with whom I have dialogued, learned, traveled, read, and explored over many years. These people and their lives make this book possible.

Introduction

Our schools are now sustained places from past ages. We perpetuate these schools of the past because the previous ages of humankind are not extinct. They continue on in our lives. One day none of our schools will exist, and youth will go on learning of freedom and live free by good teaching (which includes teaching oneself), rigorous challenges, and being amongst other motivated and serious individuals. Our schools will no longer exist because the thinking that created them is incapable of solving our problems.

Much of my working life has been in schools and freedom has profoundly fascinated me. I am not in this world to change its youth. Let them be who they are, understand who they are. That is the beginning of freedom.

This book is an expression of a life and journey that I live and discover in being a black person in the world at this time. **My vision of schools is that they are places that must stand for personal and human freedom.** I see the world as a place that challenges us to be free as individuals and as a society. We are all part of a universe and we are connected to everything else, but the prison of our consciousness isolates us from the living state which is a flowing and rushing river. The content of our consciousness is the past, and freedom is now, in the present. Life is not a matter of achievement but of moments and adventure.

I find life to be exciting because I am challenged and fascinated by living and learning with youth and others whose spirits seek to free themselves from life's traditional battles and to face the adventure in the world.

Early Years

CHAPTER 1

Prologue

I am a teacher, first in Africa and then later in America. As a youth Africa is unknown to me and I never imagine myself working in a school, but it is a life that I do come to live.

As a black youth growing up in inner-city Memphis, Tennessee and Toledo, Ohio, the world is both smaller and larger than it is now. It is smaller because places like Africa, Europe, and South America are distant, abstract, and non existent to most of us. We are fragmented and isolated in our own worlds from these places. The world today is more accessible, less vast. Africa, South America, and outer space are now part of everyone's realm. What is distant and unknown to us as youth now seems as close as our street corners. I do not know as a black youth that I am ever to leave America. I never know that I am one day to live and work in Africa and journey to places that are for us beyond thought and mind. My world as a youth lacks the technological presence and complications of today. Now technology makes the world smaller through travel and global communication, but in those days, there were fewer networks and interacting agencies. These linkages and connections also enlarge the world by providing vast seas of information and by allowing us to see previous areas in greater depth, with greater possibilities for exploration and discovery.

Also the half-life of information is continuously shrinking. If the half-life of information is now three years, in three years from now half of everything we now know will no longer hold. Many things become obsolete very rapidly. It is the way of our world today. We do not know what we are to encounter when we are born. What will be there? Today, it is often said that now is a time when black youth lack strong role models. While I am growing up I never have a need for role models. Teachers and others around me are not role models because I never want to be a teacher or to do the things that others are doing. I do not know what I want to do in life. It is not important to me. I am unambitious about the future. I love being young and free and I am fascinated with the world and my life in it.

All youth long for deep meaning in their lives. There are obstacles that they all face. For many it is a world of neglect, dehumanization, poverty, ignorance, and violence in which they exist. Some make it out; others do not. Getting out is an endless conflict for many. There are no lasting or sustained answers or solutions to their problems. There are youth in many places seeking an education to deepen their lives. Many hope for distinction. Some of them chase significance and the distinction they are denied. Those who are unmourned and forgotten seldom are moved to cure themselves. Is it important that one cures oneself? It is important because, in a school, devastated lives are not fixed by others. We cure ourselves if we are to come back at all, by confronting the challenge of strengthening ourselves from within. For many students schools as they exist have no effect on them. For most African American students, schools are not places that reward them with reasonable and worthwhile problems to solve. They are not environments that inspire them to hold themselves and others in high regard. Many of them do not value learning. Our society and our schools do not value them or their existence. The problem is that there is no shared vision with them and society, with them and school. **Our schools lack the vision and the ability to reach all students. As a nation we are so far ahead, so far**

behind. For so many students the process of inquiry is limited, disconnected, and lost which does nothing to deepen their existence.

Youth and teachers in a school who inquire about the natural world and about themselves, and who share deep goals of learning, sustain challenge for themselves and others. They give the school a purpose, they have compelling reasons for being there, and they are absorbed in the life of the school.

Most schools and other such institutions exist because we are not a light unto ourselves. Most youth are conformists and live mediocre lives. We are accustomed to going halfway to the top. We lack discipline and order in our lives. We seldom reach our full capabilities. We live secondhand lives. Our being is filled with someone else's state of mind and another's vision. We continue to live in the light of other beings and events. We seldom awaken to understanding, to freedom.

Life, for me is lived in still and quiet places that perpetually shift states. My life awakens when I begin to communicate about the world in my own way and terms. As a youth I struggle to speak of existence, and I reflect on the things I find in the world.

I work in schools where I experience amazement and fascination. Schools represent temporary states in society where individuals gather for learning. Most schools never recognize that there is no need for everyone learning the same thing at the same time. In all schools there is variety, uniqueness, and monotony. Is it possible for a school to profoundly challenge its students and teachers at all times, to not need to present artificial situations, and to let each student learn and contribute in his or her own way and to find his or her own path to self-discovery? I never consider this question, but one day I find myself in a school in the Sierra mountains in California. It is a wilderness school that lasts for fourteen days. It unexpectedly impacts me in ways that no other schooling experience has. For me personally, it makes unimportant and insignificant all of my prior years of education and schooling where I traditionally learn of life through knowledge. In the wilderness, we are souls driven by life who never yield or surrender to any tradition. We all participate in and contribute to a school that deeply changes all of us in it as we reach our mission and move on.

Life is sometimes a raging storm. It is also a battlefield and a nightmare from which I am hardly able to awaken. Much of my life is spent working in schools, which are astonishing places to observe human activity. At times, they are compelling worlds to free oneself of life's prejudices. Schools fill the earth. They are diverse and plentiful. A school is an earthly invention. It is a place to live through the winter and the rain. It is a way of life that has been maintained through darkness: tradition and conformity (surrender and slavery). It contains information and knowledge that capture and hold our minds and are believed to be important. What is learning? Learning is above knowledge, time and ourselves. It is a fire that lives in us and makes us deeply alive.

For many students, poverty smothers their educational opportunities. Some are part of a lost generation that is left behind by the schools. For others poverty and social disadvantage do not stop their educational journey. Nothing and no one can stop them from learning. What does it mean to be human on earth? It is we who are determining this; we who are living now. Life stays a mystery. The beginning of a school year everywhere on earth surpasses time. Each year when school begins, the time is new. It has not happened before. It makes going to school a spirited time and a special occurrence like the coming of an earthly season. Some students enter school and become imprisoned by past knowledge that brings them deep pain. School for them is a life of deep sorrow and pain because it demands conformity that dominates their day, and as followers, they never learn.

Schools are places in society in which I have long dwelled. They are places of deep tragedies and profound challenges. Schools are challenging places when there are people in them who have goals with great depth and it is important to them that they question all conventions of the past. The thinking of those who perpetuate schools is to keep the past alive. We work to convince others of the importance and relevance of our prejudices, ideas, and wisdom and to bring these things into others lives. The conformity of these beliefs maintains schools. Past knowledge is held to be important, valued. This belief makes schools trivial places. Masses of beings are imprisoned because of situations that happened thousands of years ago as well as those that happened moments ago. All is the dead past.

A great challenge for schools is to exist in the world as it is where learning is alive and profound. My years as a youth and a student in school are of little personal significance. In a lot of ways they are a non-event. The schools are quiet and lost places. They are lost in the past.

As a youth I one day travel to New York City. It is a great adventure. I am overwhelmed at how alive it is and it seems to be driven by unique earthly forces. Its life is my life. I do not know that one day I am going to live in New York. It is an interesting life of learning. The schools in New York are like the schools everywhere else. It is the rivers, the people coming and going, the buildings, and the unexpected life which are so fascinating about being in New York. It is a great place to pass through. After passing through, I never look back. I never long to return. As important as we want our life on this planet to be, it is not. The earth is a place we are passing through.

Before I come to live in New York, I finish school in Ohio. Travel and adventure are in my heart. I travel to New Mexico, Minnesota, and to an Indian reservation in Wisconsin on my own and for a while I live in Wisconsin.

I reach New York. I live and study there but there comes the time that I can no longer accept an existence in a society where one worships success, progress, and a better life than others. However, while in New York I am excited by chess and other games and life in the parks. I read books of adventure, struggle, and life on the sea. I learn of the conflicts of race and being black. I learn much about life in Harlem. There are days along the Hudson River of reading and observing life on the river and the sea. I am fascinated by human freedom and I leave the city and go to sea. It is not easy getting seaman papers to be a merchant marine. There are two black men at the National Maritime Union (NMU) who realize the energy that is in me to be on the sea. They help me get a letter of commitment from a shipping company on Wall Street. From there I go to the seaman's hall to see the scheduled ships that are set to sail. I am selected to sail on a Mediterranean cruiser to Portugal, Spain, France, and Italy. It is my first journey.

I work on the sea before I begin my life of working in schools. I love the sea which to me is vast, still and deeply alive. Everything about it is magnificent. I recall sailing the earth for the first time and how my life is filled with joy. After days of sailing I see land burst forth from the sea; I see quiet, green peaceful places with men in seaworthy crafts in the Azores drifting through the silence from place to place. They ride these uncertain waves through whatever winds are before them, never capsizing. How vulnerable they seem.

I learn much from the sea. It is a timeless place. Because it is such a profound life being there, it never leaves me. The sea is a great frontier for those with a passion for exploration and discovery. It is a place of quiet, peace, hard storms, great strength, and silence. I am always fascinated by those who live through the harshness and relentlessness of the sea; those who drift thousands of miles alone living with its mercilessness and gifts. We learn of those who survive and we perpetuate their stories because rising to the challenge are the adventures that move us. We live in the light of the adventures of those overcoming adversity. Some of us do not become attached to the heroic past. But few of us transcend the need for strong individuals and special events that are publicly accepted and we are unable to awaken and to discover our own lives.

When I first sail on the sea it is the most spectacular place I have seen. The sea and the ship that hold us are the greatest symbols of freedom that I have ever encountered. They take me to a new world. We are leaving New York City and the known world, breaking away to a new world of learning and freedom. The ship moves on through the sea, bound for freedom, the unknown and what adventures are before us. In facing the new, the difficult, and the unfamiliar we are challenged to bring forth strength and perseverance that we do not know even exist. In life's real and dramatic situations I learn that we are called on to do the impossible and I learn that we are all more capable of performing in more serious ways than our thoughts and past experiences of success, failures, and greatness lead us.

I sail with men who are absorbed by life on the sea and men who are illiterate and can not write home to their families. I am young and life on earth is an adventure for me. On my first trip I travel through the strait of Gibraltar and I see Europe on the left and Africa on the right. The actuality of seeing Africa overwhelms me. It captures my total attention and how much more interesting the world becomes. From the first moment I see it, it is a quiet, strange, and vast land that we sail so far to reach, then it is gone.

From life on the sea I get the chance to live in Africa and to work there. I am filled with excitement and wonder when I walk in Africa and see the beauty of the earth there. Being there is so significant and meaningful to me. The earth, the sun, the heat, the trees, and the wind cry in quietness. They are new to me and they are timeless is their existence.

These are some of the things I have lived through and I tell to students when they are curious about what I have done and how I have lived. Though these things happened not many years ago, I realize they are events of history. They are dead. They are no more alive than things that happened fifty million years ago or what happened five minutes ago. All is lifeless stored information and the memory of these denies freedom. Memory is invention and has a life of its own in its own contrived time. I find a way to deepen the lives of the students and my life as a teacher is through life's adventures. Our adventures connect us. The learning from our heart and soul comes from our inner life and adventure.

My experiences with students and their concerns, curiosities, frustrations, tragedies, success, understanding, and enthusiasm begins in Africa. I am not excited about being a teacher. I have never taught and I have never thought about it until I am told it is my assignment in Africa. I have little idea of what I want to do in life and never have I considered what encounters a teacher faces. Living and working in Africa are great events to come into my life. It is a new life for me. It is a significant contrast to living in America. Africa is to America as the village is to the city, that faraway in stillness and quietness.

I have never thought about how to teach children or how to deal with discipline or other matters. Teaching in the classroom is a challenge. I have few materials with me and I do not know what I am teaching. Teaching mathematics is good for me because I like doing the work as much as the students do. Teaching science is also good because since a youth I was intrigued with astronomy and chemistry books. I am still strongly interested in learning about them. I was challenged at an early age by their mysteries and their internal connections which allowed me to systematically explore them. I do not really look forward to teaching English, but I am here to do what is needed. I am willing to teach any subject there is. It is why I am in Africa. I find that there are few books at the school. The school, indeed, is always searching for more books for its students to use.

Classroom discipline is not a problem here. Students seem to be grateful for the opportunity to be in school. It seems as though their families and others are counting on them to do well and to be successful. There exists a single minded dedication to working hard and finding school success. Some of the students are brilliant individuals and are fascinated about learning all that their minds are able to process. Most of the students memorize what they are told and struggle hard to comprehend all the knowledge that is presented to them.

I am enthusiastic about being in Nigeria and this new life.

CHAPTER 2

The First Days

The land shows few signs of life. It is the middle of the day and the fire from the sun is inescapable and penetrates into the earth. The heat matters. It is a life of surrender because the sun's strength devastates all that exists. I love the African land.

Deep down it is not clear to me why I am in Africa. I have no idea of what to expect in my life here or in my job as a teacher. Though I am unable to determine what my life will be, it is still an exciting time because I find myself moving further and further into the unknown. This is a new life for me and it is the first day of my seeing school as a teacher. I am unable to see that these early days will impact how I teach and learn in profound ways. I want to learn. There is an inner quest. I know there are many thing that I have to teach myself. I have to know my subject and love to explore it. It is not possible for me to put things aside for a future moment and to work for success (now is the time), nor can I be disappointed in those things that I have not learned or brought with me to this lonely, distant, and strange village. I have to learn everything now. The world as I have always known it is breaking up. The possession of all that has defined me and made me safe is suddenly dead and non-existent.

Early in the morning I awake. Like always I had slept like a dead man. I awake to the light, the heat, the stillness, and to an unknown world which begins a new day. I am living in Africa, and for me everything about the land, the people and their energy, their hopes, misfortunes, and daily lives are of profound significance. It is good being here and it is good being black in this place and at this time. It is a new time in my life. I feel grateful to be alive seeing and meeting people and going places, and living the life I am living. It is where I am to live some great days on earth. It is also the place where the darkest days will be.

On a quiet, dusty Nigerian road stands the house where I live. Further down the road is a government secondary school where I work. It is a lonely bush town surrounded by rain forest where we all exist. Perhaps this is too romantic a description because there are people from the town who will say that I am putting them down, calling the town bush. It is true that it is not as primitive as a lot of other places for thousands of people live here. (I am told they do.) There is a seemingly timeless social structure and there is true sophistication. But there still exist dusty roads and mud huts with thatched roofs. There are also stone houses with rusted corrugated tin roofs, passed by people walking barefooted to their farms. There are bare chested women who struggle with their loads through the wind, dust, and mud. They walk for miles. The school stands on a dirt road as does our house which is nearby. I share the house with another teacher, Sam, who is African.

Sam sees me as I am. He does not anticipate my actions nor predict my feelings. He does question my being alone. Two other Africans from the University of Ibadan later come to teach at the school. Like Sam they are young and both are Yorubas. They too are enthusiastic and capable teachers who know and love their subjects. They work hard and they deeply enjoy life with their friends and relatives. It is a great life, working and traveling together and staying in our stone house on the road.

There are several Americans in other villages in my early days, but I seldom see anyone. There is a girl from Pennsylvania in a village forty miles away who came when I came, and she is beginning a life of teaching just as I am. I also have another American friend from Minnesota who lives thirty miles away along another road. He is also a teacher. In the beginning days it is important to Sam that I am among friends, and I have a good time because I am far from home and away from my family. Still he knows I do like quietness and he doesn't always visit me. He has two brothers and a sister who live with him and whose schooling he is responsible for. Since his father died the year before he is now the responsible person in the family, which means that he is called upon often. It might be to replace a roof blown off by a storm, to pay for someone's journey, to buy a pair of shoes, or to entertain visiting relatives. Sam and I travel together to places in town and to other nearby villages. I love Africa and Sam's friendship and going places. One day we travel to the town where he was born to visit his mother and other relatives. It is a great place and a great time. I sleep on a hard cot and suffer from mosquito bites. The night is miserable as I struggle to rest and sleep. The people, though, graciously welcome me and they display such strong feelings about my being there.

The African towns are unique places to me as a stranger. Their organization and structure are filled with life. The animals, the smells, the local foods, life of the children, and the work of the people capture my full attention. Towns are much like schools to me in that I once wondered why they came into being and their purpose on earth. I know both towns and schools are complex. I later learn in life that they are reflections of our own mind and thought. When I look at a town or a school, I am really looking at how the human mind and brain works. The questions I ask about the towns and schools are questions I am asking of my own existence and being.

My first days of living in Nigeria are strenuous. I don't think strongly about the school in these early days because the heat, the mosquitoes, the sandflies, the sun, the miles of walking and urinating and defecating in the grass and in the small latrine behind the house, cause a peculiar disorientation that consumes my strength. I am good at going days without eating. It is difficult taking the food. I can't eat and

I don't care to. I never drink water. I never do. I seldom bathe because the muddy water seems incapable of being clean. The people around me are always bathing and cleansing themselves. They are as clean as any people in the world. I feel that about them. In these early days, I am so overwhelmed with learning to live in this world that I don't think about the school which is yet to be of meaning to me. The school is less significant than the day to day encounters in which I am continuously involved. They form my life.

The children whom I meet are dedicated to the attainment of knowledge. They feel it is important. It concerns me that they are not questioning this acquisition. Why do they want it? When I first arrive in the country, I am in Oshogbo in this hotel and school children are all about. They learn that I am a teacher and they eagerly approach me. They want knowledge and to be told things. It is a tradition that holds them. I give them several arithmetic and algebra problems to work. It is interesting that nobody arrives at the correct solutions even through intense effort. I try to tell them about inaccurate, invalid, and misunderstood assumptions. They are not interested in these things. Not yet. They prefer more problems, another chance. I do not question them for not wanting to listen to me because if they cannot understand my language how can they understand my reasoning? Nigeria is a former British colony so its national language is English. Though it is English, I find it to be a strange sounding language spoken in peculiar sentences. Some letters lack sound.

I remember one day I am asked by Sam to name a puppy he has acquired. "Call him Texas," I say. But there is no 'x 'sound in Yoruba so they can not say it properly in English, though still the dog stays Texas. I do not know much about Africa before I arrive. I possess no knowledge nor understanding of the life, the land, or its people. My beginning feelings for Africa are perhaps similar to those of Africans and others going to America for the first time. People in America want to know how life is in Africa. They are curious about the food, the people, the schools, traveling about, the weather, and the day to day existence here. I write them what I am learning in being here. I write to my family and a friend in Ohio and to a friend in New York. I also write to my grandmother in Memphis. The last time I saw her and talked to her she told me, "Write me now so that I can tell people my grandson wrote to me."

Neither one of us knew that I would be writing her from Africa.

I have no way of knowing what I say to those whom I write has meaning. I do love telling others about Nigeria. It is a land filled with contrast: beauty and harshness. It is a place of desert and sand, inescapable heat, and Harmattan winds. The north touches the Sahara desert and one exists in intense heat. There are also plateaus and elevated land making it cool there. Nigeria is a place where the Niger and Benue rivers meet and flow south and form a multitude of tributaries that break into a profuse channel of waterways descending into the Atlantic Ocean. There is also the rain forest and its life. People in Nigeria do live differently in each part of the nation. In the various places one finds such foods as fish, beef, rice, corn, cocoa, coconuts, and groundnuts. Language varies from place to place as do types of dress, local customs, games children play and the practice of religion.

I live in a town called Ijero. It is 150 miles north of Ibadan and 250 miles from Lagos and the coast. Because it lies in the rain forest it is like a lot of other places in Africa and in the world, like Brasil. (I had been to Brasil before as a seaman and the town and the jungle and the rain and the palm leaves here smell like the Brasilian coast towns of Bahia and Paranagua.)

I am fascinated by the life in Nigeria. It is said that the Nigerian nation consists of several hundred different ethnic groups. Of the hundreds of groups that are here, I live amongst one of them, the Yorubas, who number many millions. Other large groups are the Hausas in the north and the Ibos in the east. The school where I teach is in the southwest. The entire southwestern region is the home of the Yorubas who have their own language, customs, traditions and social structure. The people are filled with spirit. Their language is rich, proverbial, and so alive.

Oba bi Olorun kosi.

(No king is as God.)

Eni a fe ni a mo. A ko mo eniti o fe ni.

(We know whom we love but not who loves us.)

They eat a lot of yam, cassava, and bush meat. In this town dwell ancestral spirits, hunters, blacksmiths, and the god Ogun. The blacksmiths labor and hammer back and forth, back and forth. It is a town of farmers, teachers, and herbalists. Some men live exemplary lives and become chiefs and all honor and respect them. In the center of the town is the palace and the market place. In the palace the king lives with his wives and children. It is there that he exists in all of his greatness.

It is difficult to say what a school stands for if it stands for anything at all. The school, for some time, has become an accepted place. What has the school become in Nigeria? It has become a way of life for me. I am paid to be here, not a lot but something. Indeed, teaching provides international possibilities such as work in other places and working and learning with others with different educational thought and background. It can take one to many places in the world. As to the other teachers at this Nigerian school, teaching is a way of life for them also. It is a reason why they are here. The headmaster is African, who studied at Forabe university in Sierra Leone. He was born right here in the same town where the school is, so he is a local man. He is competent and fair and well thought of. Only one other teacher is from the town; the remainder are from different places. All the rest of the teachers at the school are African except for an Indian couple from New Delhi. A teacher is respected and well thought of in the community, which is another reason why people come to the school to teach. I learn in these first days that teachers who love and understand their subject and who conduct their classes in a businesslike manner can offer something profound to their students. Doing what we say we are going to do in a school can be a miracle. Teaching is sometimes intense and is a life of self-education, wonder, and sometimes exhaustion.

Now what is a school to an African child? In many ways it is much like it is to a non African. It is a building that exists in his lifetime. You never know what is going to be there when you are born. It might be a famine or other natural catastrophe, a war, or a fabulous machine, but it's there. In the beginning days I am in Nigeria, it is a time of peace. It is a time of earthly struggle, dancing and singing and the enjoyment of local festivals. These are enthralling times that surpass ordinary earthly events. They are uplifting to the spirit. In Nigeria, schools exist in the cities, towns, and villages. They are everywhere. Still there is not an abundance of schools, particularly secondary schools. So it is a privilege to attend them. It is unlike in America where education has become an often abused right. In America, the masses are educated, here, the few. In Africa, students are more serious about learning than the students with whom I grew up. The African students are grateful that they are here. Some travel several hundred miles for their chance to acquire knowledge. A trained teacher is a respected figure. The first day of school I recall awakening and walking the dirt road to the school. It is January and the rainy season has not yet begun. The rainy season is from April to October while the dry season is from November to March. In my walking I pass several early rising villagers. They see me as a stranger, a mystery. Later I would be a friend to many.

I am fascinated by Africa's roads and the people who come and go. The road from our house to the school is a place at times busy with those who travel to the town, the local farms, the school, the market-place, and the main road. (One day I would travel to East Africa to see where earliest African roads and people began, which was hundreds of miles and thousands of centuries away from our village.) Those who come, travel with their families, friends, and classmates. Sometimes they travel alone. The life and days of the road is sustained by streams of men, women, and children whom I would greet and hardly know but sometimes do meet. Some would become friends and special persons in my life because of a particular moment or serious event or a story we share which connects us. One day I take a man on the road by motor-cycle to a nearby clinic because he has severed his finger with a machete while working on his farm. I am able to hurry him along the road, all the time seriously wondering what is to happen to him. We travel on a road surrounded by the rainforest and its growth. The trees quietly stand as though they are observing each moment of the journey. Beyond them are hidden huts and dirt roads and fires in the hollow of trees. There are lonely wildflowers that are beautiful. On the side of the road, now and then, is a light density of people. They do not know of the urgency of our mission as we are just another passing vehicle on the road for them to be aware of and to avoid. At the clinic they are able to attach and reconnect the finger. It is a miracle. He endures great pain but how fortunate he is. This event makes us special friends.

One day down on the road men are working to build a house. They need to finish their work on the house roof. It is important to get it done so that the things inside the house will be protected. They are seri-ous about their work. Rain is imminent. They say they have the power to stop the rain. They labor until completing their job on the roof. The skies are dark and the rain is threatening. The men finish their work and leave. All the while I doubt if they can complete the roof before the rain comes. They do. A flood then inundates the road as a great storm deluges the countryside. Is it coincidence or do they have the powers they say they do to stop rain? I never know. But I am so impressed by these men and their actions and the powers they say they have.

Another day I travel along the road coming from a nearby town and I see an insane person living there. I notice the person and think to myself how unusual it is that such a person in Africa is living alone, along a road. I am unable to see if this person is a man or woman. A few days later on the road I see the same person lying there dead. An auto-mobile kills the person, who is dragged and crushed along the road and the body is defaced, lifeless and devastated. Life is violently thrust from the body. I am struck by life on the road and the abandoned corpse. Inside I have a quiet sadness and I cry from absurdity and insaneness.

On this first day when I reach the school, two students—one is called Obasa Samuel and the other George—come and take my books and all else that rests in my hands. "Good morning, sir," they say, bowing their heads as they speak. It is evident that respect is strongly learned and seriously carried out. The king is the most respected person in the town. It is the unexpected genuine acts of respect that I receive that cause me to so honor them as people. My books and other materials are taken to the classroom by the two students dressed in short khaki trousers. I am told that I am expected in the assembly hall. There all the teachers and students are gathered. It all starts with a prayer. Inside of me I strongly protest this school practice. I least expect this formality. I suspect that prayer and meditation have their places but this particular morning routine is one in which I refuse to conform to. Indeed it happens that I rarely come. Though these are required meetings, the headmaster agrees to release me from having to attend. It is something that I talk to the other teachers about. Most of them defend these meetings. The Yorubas are sometimes described as the people of four hundred gods. It surprises me at how dedicated they are to becoming Christians and how important these meetings are to them. It is said that they are a developing nation and one day it is going to be necessary to abandon primitive beliefs, so many are becoming Christians. Besides, they say, Christianity is a religion for all people of the earth, and it speaks the truth. To me, a religion is only one view of the universe. It is final, not alive. When we agree on how the universe is we agree to a reality that is fixed and frozen, and we do not understand that it also will pass away. Freedom and understanding come from the movement of one's soul and its emerging views of life and from the questioning of one's concept of reality. Religions bring conflict and violence because the people in them separate themselves from others. Our world deepens itself through the individual and not through religious systems. It is not my intention to tell them what to believe in. However, this morning religious practice is an unexpected event that I encounter on my first day in the school that I do discuss with them in the beginning days. It seems that Christianity has become necessary here just as Islam has become necessary in the north, maybe for the same reasons that religion has become necessary in the first place. Let me not dwell on analyzing causes. It should not disturb me because they are like other people in other places. I am curious about living here and I am anxious to investigate the things that enter my world. Already the land and the people fascinate me.

Outside the assembly hall it is hot. It is going to be several years of enduring this heat. There is verdant growth and crawling insects seeking shade. There are people going along the road. I think about everything that is born and is about to die beneath this hot sun. This is the first day of school and the children are excited. They are young, and full of health and life. They are all wearing school uniforms. The girls wear short dresses and some are very beautiful. In fact, one day I fall in love with a school girl from another school, but it never lasts nor becomes serious. I never let it grow. She writes me letters which I seldom answer. One day I am going to leave this country so I decide to let things die and to prevent complications.

It is still the first day. I walk over to my first assigned classroom. I guess this is my first teaching job. I was a practice teacher for several weeks in a Boston suburb where there was not one black face. I didn't mind being there, but it was not an interesting assignment. The children are quiet and from rich families and indeed I can hardly remember their names or faces. I prepare diligently for each lesson. We study the changing states of matter. It is very dramatic witnessing a solid metal, with sufficient heat to reach its melting point, become transformed to its liquid state. We absorbed ourselves in such observations.

I momentarily think about that singular teaching experience which is so distant that it soon fades away. I don't know what is on my mind as I enter the room. All stand erect and quiet as I enter. One day I am going to accompany some of these students to their villages and farms, but that time is down the road. I know I am strange to them. Nobody stirs. And though I am as black as they, I realize that my presence is something mysterious. Every movement I make is noted and interpreted. It hardly seems as though these weak walls can provide a comfortable setting, but there are going to be days that I shall be grateful that they are here with their protection. When the heavy rains come, I am going to love the sound and the way it overwhelms the earth. The students stand there, curiously until I tell them to take their seats. (That seems what I say to them, but I am not certain.) From the moment of my first spoken word they listen intensely. Most are listening in ignorance because, for one thing, I am speaking so fast to them. I begin to hear noises from among them. They must be discussing my absurd ways. I am different, but I am also similar to them. They, the heat and the rain, make me feel a part of me that is not new in being here. There is a sameness of planetary substance. And though I face new moments here, somedays, I comprehend all things; some days I find confusion and mystery and I wonder at life, which is complicated by the fact that humans are momentary beings, living now. It is in the present where we are vulnerable and where we are free. This moment is my first day in an African school that we are passing through. The headmaster has already given me a new name "Omowale" which means the child comes home. So I am back. I am standing in this classroom. The time is now. Nothing else matters.

It is a crude room. The books are old. Some are older than any person in the school. It is a classical and traditional system of learning, unmistakably British. In this bush, books are precious and indeed there are those who worship knowledge. Some students are known to study religiously. They study intensely in order to sit for their school certificate examinations. These examinations become the only things in their lives. Indeed their importance seems almost unreal. They study with weak kerosene lamps throughout the night until morning comes. And I suppose I am as much a victim of this system as they are because I work as hard as they do in it. We would all focus our greatest efforts to preparing for these examinations, and as a group the students perform at a high level. The students work hard to learn the subject deeply and we achieve much together. I wipe the sweat from my head. The heat in this room is killing me. Heat is something you don't know until you exist in it. I don't know if this way of learning destroys people. At times there does seem something indestructible about these students' enthusiasm and wanting to learn. They are spirited and filled with life. The schools as such hold no particular excitement. Memorization, struggle, success and failure monotonously dominate. Few of the students are mathematically inquisitive and many find numbers to be more magical than real. And this is justifiably so because mathematics is a man made, secondhand universe and a lot of facts seem to disagree with their reality. It is a difficult task to memorize a mathematical proof if you can't understand it. How does one convince oneself of its validity? To allow these things to exist within you, even though they could be untrue, often requires struggle and faith. Many people can never believe in mathematics. A thing about teaching here is that you can teach down. You don't have to teach up. In Nigeria you don't have to start from simple truths and facts and construct or justify some elaborate structure of knowledge. You can start with the most difficult of facts and go from there. You can do this and they will struggle to learn and understand everything you say because a teacher's function is to prepare them for their examinations, therefore they cling to the things you tell them. They don't require that a school be immediately justifiable, that it show itself to be related to their day-to-day living. They are not used to the questioning of all things. They are like students everywhere in that they like a teacher who is fair, who presents difficult and profound problems, and who is enthusiastic about the subject. The school can be a place of monotony and reiteration which may or may not pay off. The whole system consists of examinations. It is a residue from the colonizers.

*   *   *

It is inevitable that I learn how it is to grow up in Africa and about the lives of the students who fill the classroom. Every day of living in Nigeria means further familiarity with the forces that are defining their lives. In a lot of ways the life of the village is the life of the children. They tend the sheep and the cows, and they carry various loads. The children sometimes plant and harvest yams and groundnuts and kill small animals. They cook the food, clean the houses, travel to the market and care for the younger children. They do the jobs they are told to do, and they contribute in a real way to the life of the family and the village. Life in so many situations means the child is the one to get the job done. The children are needed and loved. Those who are able to study in the school are believed to be fortunate. As for the women, they carry the water, the firewood, and other loads. They seem forever pounding yam, vigorously laboring to prepare the main food Yorubas consume on many occasions. I do not immediately enjoy eating it but later I come to appreciate it. I never like okra until I eat it here in Nigeria. The women run the marketplace and they love their children. The men rule and administer the affairs of the estate and the village; they are respected. I find it interesting observing this life and sometimes being immersed in it. A familiar concern among the students however, is how we live in America. How is life there? All of these students who fill this room wonder and for as long as I am in Nigeria I talk about it. Preconceived notions and ideas are abundant. I recall an African in America telling me about a white woman who had asked him if it was true that Africans lived in trees. Did they live and swing like monkeys? She didn't know so she had asked him. All she knew were her secondhand and fragmented thoughts. He told her they did. This added more secondhand knowledge. It also perpetuated her ignorance. Many of us die ignorant, unaware that the events that are occurring in the world and in the universe are happening also to us. The world is no stranger than we are. Who are we and what do we seek? Few of us realize that we are capable of changing our own lives. We do not question our own ignorance and we have no impact on the world in which we exist. We are controlled by what we receive. We give nothing of ourselves to the world or to others. I know of a German girl who lives in a small village. Most of the Africans have never seen a white person and she has never lived among black people before. She is a nurse; she loves her work, and she loves Africa. One thing I know is that she will never accept, or practice, racial ignorance or discrimination because her life has been seriously changed in living here and her experiences here have deepened her life. There are a multitude of encounters that enter one's life in the world. How man has feared his life on this planet. I am reminded of a Yoruba boy who came from this same place and his journey to an unknown world. It was a frightening experience. The incident happened several hundred years ago. The towns were much the same as they are now. (The Yoruba towns seem as though they have always existed.) He lived a quiet life and he never left his town. He had heard of other places and other kings, but he himself knew of but one town, one oba, and one palace in which he lived with his many wives. One day he was snatched away by a band of European men. After days of travel they reach the coast. He has never seen the ocean before. After having reached there, he is crowded together with hundreds of others. The journey there has been painful. His life is a living nightmare. And what is he to think of these strange **oyinbo** (white) men except that they are evil spirits who are going to eat him. Their talk is strange and they treat the Africans mercilessly. Nothing makes sense to him. There are men with red faces and long yellow hair, fires burning in the furnaces of the ship, and Africans in chains. He cannot eat. What would they feed him? And when the boat comes to take him away, he faints. When he awakes he is down in the hole of the ship. He looks around and knows no one. He is in chains. He wonders why he has awakened. Why hadn't these **oyinbo** men eaten him yet? When would they? All around him is despair and uncertainty, and he is waiting to be killed by these ugly men. Through his mind run thoughts of killing himself, of starving to death, of jumping into the sea. His dead corpse would be in the sea, cut off from his family. He wills himself dead. He never reaches America or Brasil or wherever it is he is destined to be taken. He never lands as a slave. Upon the mad sea the slave ship is attacked in the afternoon in plenty of sun, plenty of light. White men fight white men and all seemed confused. The boat eventually reaches Sierra Leone and all are freed. He is able to reach home again and to tell his story. Through conversation and discussion with Africans and others, and through reading accounts of slave journals, I am able to tell this story. I make this same journey every time I go to Lagos and the coast. There is only a change in time. The earth probably has not changed much, so the journey across it is similar in many ways. Do the same roads exist? There is no evidence of them as slave routes. The people and the towns along the way still carry on. They endure.

Now it is a new day to wonder about the world and the lives of those beyond us. In this classroom I am going to encounter notions about how people live in America. It is believed to be a nation where everybody owns a gun and shoots and robs and murders. Everybody is a cowboy in the days of the wild west. There is particular concern for the American Indian and how he lives. There is fascination with America's great material wealth. There are questions about American blacks and how they are treated. Why are the racial minorities not treated as other humans and individuals? Why are they so oppressed? The domination and perceived racial superiority of the white world was everywhere. It oppressed people in Africa and America. But we also imprisoned ourselves. It is seldom that the oppressed ever fight to be free.

It seems unlikely that I ever add much to their understanding in these matters, but I know it is more than how white people treat us. It is also how we allow ourselves to be treated. We accept oppression and racism when we lack a mission of freedom.

The Nigerian students are fascinated with America and the Americans. They are abstractions that are not real to them. The root of their interest and inquiry is that of America a century ago when it was a nation where people fought for land and a future for the taking. The persistence of this time forever drives Americans and others to invent this future from the past. This future is the American dream.

My life as a youth is in a different world. With me and those around me, race is our destiny because of how the dominant white society views it. This society sees race as a single cell organism and in its struggle to survive finds it necessary to determine whether what is moving toward it or the group is a friend, enemy, or food. One is accepted or excluded based on this criterion. It sees race in all of its cells which make up its existence. Therefore, it programs and constructs a closed society for itself. It does not understand that race is a human conditioning that has existed and been accepted for hundreds of years and is allowed without question. When we do communicate with alien or with extraterrestrial intelligences from deep space how do we know who is friendly and who is not? We are not born to hate but to question and to doubt. One who is free lives in the world without any conditioning.

Some African American youth hold a deep anger inside of them. They are unable to move beyond the racism that oppresses them. They know that as black Americans they are the least accepted people in American society.

As an African American youth I am challenged to learn about the world, but I am not a follower of others. I refuse to accept others' definitions of how the world is. Though I live an ordinary life just as the others around me do, I do not yield to those who are moving counter to the way the universe is. In these times I work out problems in my own way, and it makes the world an unusual and fascinating place. In these times I discover a life of learning and freedom.

This black dilemma is not new, but instead, a chronic condition. In San Francisco there are records of documents that are more than one-hundred years old. They are written before the civil war when slavery is a part of America. White school superintendents view colored students as ignorant and inferior. In some ways San Francisco schools have changed. Now, more than one hundred years later, there are no colored or racially segregated schools. Indeed, black and white students are only two groups among the Vietnamese, the Filipino, the Spanish speaking, the Chinese, and others. In many ways though, the schools are not changed because the way white people thought and wrote about us has not changed. The way that we think about and speak of each other has not changed in many ways. As a people we are imprisoned by our own predictability.

In America there is an absence of respect for black people by others and as black people we lack respect amongst ourselves. We find ourselves struggling against white domination as well as black disorganization. As Black Americans we continue to be destroyed and to destroy ourselves. Black students in America will refuse to attend urban inner city schools because they do not yield to the oppression that these schools sustain. Refusing to surrender to oppression and injustice is what gives us hope to freely create our own lives in the world and to have the capability to change ourselves and to change the state and the direction of society. In the schools and in the societies where I have worked and lived I know that when you are learning, nothing can destroy you.

As I now exist in this African classroom I am not thinking much about war and dying because it seems like we are in an unlikely place for that. But as we are sitting in the classroom, one day a war is going to begin. The war comes in July. It is a civil war and there are strong feelings throughout the country. In May the Ibos declare themselves dissolved from the Nigerian nation. Everybody, it seems, hates the Ibos. The Ibos are referred to as the rebels and nobody expects them to be able to struggle against the federal troops for long, but it is to be a very long and hard war. My feelings about the war are unclear. For one thing, it is difficult to know what is occurring. One can read the papers and listen to the radio which inevitably turns out to be biased and prosaic propaganda. It seems as though the Ibos are to die quickly. Certainly no one believes that they will fight for several years. Each side wants to kill the other. Like every war, it seems senseless because every time you kill one of the enemy, you are not just killing one of the enemy, you are killing someone's father, brother, or cousin. In a war we are always killing ourselves. Because I am not a part of the fighting and having nothing to win or die for, I am able to be rational. Being rational, however, may have little to do with what is going on at a given time.

It is said that it is in war that we learn war, or it is in a revolution that we learn to carry out the revolution. As I sit in the classroom, I think about how the war has not gotten to our village yet. Our school is a place of comfort. We are removed away from the struggles of life and are not driven to fight for survival. I have American friends who are captured or taken to jail for security reasons and then later released, but we do not know war in our village, only the talk of it. At one time the school vacates to make room for the soldiers who are fighting, but it never becomes necessary. As I look around the classroom, I again realize the protection and comfort these modest walls provide. Few leave this village for the war. In the east there are no classrooms, no books. The fighting is in their land where they learn of war and revolution. Though they are young their lives are filled with first-hand encounters with life and existence. These things cannot be taught, planned, or anticipated. How artificial our lives here in this school sometimes seem. The Ibos say that it is the Nigerians' aim to commit genocide and wipe them from the face of the earth, so they are fighting to save the race. They have this in mind as they fight to endure. I think in the beginning of the war that this feeling of their profound struggle, more than anything else, gives the Ibo the edge. In our village students walk to school with books in their hands, in the east they carry guns, and are soldiers.

It is easy to speak out for the Ibos and be sympathetic to their cause. At school they call me the rebel because I do speak out at times for the Ibos. I am accused of being obvious in my views. Nobody bothers me. There are certain things that make me respect the Ibos in the beginning. They build their own tanks and make their own bombs. I can respect the Nigerians more if they fight their own war. When the war first starts there are outsiders from other nations assisting them, so in the beginning I respect the Ibos. Most of the Nigerian soldiers are Hausas, who are from the north. They are almost all Moslems. I once met an American who taught school in the north. He said that few of the people there valued an education. They were Moslems and most of their time was spent in prayer, idleness, and living a religious life. He said that if Britain or America really wanted to help educate them they should stop building schools. All of that money should be used to convert them to Christianity so that they would strive more for knowledge rather than be held back by their changeless life of prayer and idleness. Such was one man's opinion in the north. Who is to say that a striving nation is better off than a religious nation?

From among the Ibos and those people sympathetic toward them, certain myths are circulated. The Ibos, they say, are a special people, blessed with a certain greatness. It is said that it has been the Ibo effort that sustained the Nigerian nation before the war.

I remember a journey I make to Uganda. I meet an Ibo there who refuses to return to Nigeria. He is a quiet and honest man who tells this story. Among the Ibos, he says, it is told that there were three men: a Hausa, a Yoruba, and an Ibo. They are all sitting under a palm tree. The Yoruba says I wish I had a palm nut. The Hausa says if God so wishes I shall have a palm nut. The Ibo climbs the tree and pulls down a palm nut. And indeed this is the picture of the Ibos that many people paint. I too, initially believe this to be the case. After the war starts and people begin to be killed and suffer from starvation and sickness, nothing one sees, hears or learns about seems strange. We who live on earth sometimes are victims of darkness and absurdity. Wars are absurd. They are also an actuality. Until there is order throughout the world, wars will exist. It is understandable that people outside the country wish great things for the Ibos. Indeed, they become the chosen people, and even to the end it is said that they are achievement-motivated people and they can still win, but after the war is going on for a year I know they will be defeated. They have no special greatness; it is an absurd fallacy. After my first year in the school I travel to east Africa and encounter its diversity and wonder. I travel in the Congo, Kenya, Tanzania, and Uganda. It is a great journey. I would one day return there. I am happy when I return again to Nigeria. Shortly after returning to the school in Ijero, I become sick, and I have to leave. I go to the hospital in Ibadan. I am away from school for three months, and I am deathly ill at times. In the end I return. While I am there in the hospital, I meet Hausa soldiers, sleep beside them. They are all young and they have bullets in their heads and in their chests, and amputated limbs. Within them dwells an indestructible spirit. It is a burning military spirit that is unconquerable. They are not reluctant to die, and cowardice is an act of disgrace. They have just as much to die for as the Ibos and are just as great. They seem invincible. Suddenly I know that the Ibos are not going to be victorious in the war. It is these soldiers who are going to cause their inevitable defeat. In the end they do.

School is almost finished this day and the students are weary from the heat. A few find they have no resistance to it and surrender to sleep. I don't disturb them because the bell will soon ring and they can leave to perform their special duties and then later involve themselves in their social recreations. The classroom, I discover, is different from their social world where there is thick blood of friendship and unbreakable bonds.

The bell comes, and I walk out of the classroom. I cut across a wide field to the house. Jungle and thick forest surround the school and form the countryside. Already I am beginning to know the soul of the forest and how filled it is with spirits. The Africans say that these spirits are our ancestors. At first I wonder: are they alive? Do people fear them? I learn these things don't matter because even if they are dead we are still their children. It is not necessary to fear them. I learn an African proverb which speaks to us about our life with nature's creatures and forces. It says: if there is no enemy within us, then the enemy outside can do us no harm.

It is night and I must sleep. I always awake early. I love the early morning. It is the greatest time to be alive. It is when life seems most sacred. This has been my first day in the school, and I now find that the heat and the night make me weary. I'll sleep until morning. Will morning come? Will the earth be alive? Can I endure living here for several more years? Whatever may happen in my life I must first get through the night. I must live to work another day.

CHAPTER 3

Family Visit

As a teacher I occasionally visit families.

Three others are ahead of me as we make our way through the thick jungle. This is a great day for me as I have not penetrated the rain forest before. Thick growth crowds the path, and the two youth use their machetes to cut limbs and vines that impede our journey. The other person in the group is an old man, the grandfather of the two boys. It is to his farm that we all walk. The heat is strong, and the sun reaches through the labyrinth of growth. It is harsh and bright and challenges my effort to stay with the group. The others walk along in their barefeet. I wear sandals that I bought in a nearby town. The others are thoroughly familiar with the path. Their actions are without effort in situations that to me are obstacles. Every step I take is new and carries me deeper into what moments before were unknown and unimagined. The sun helps us get there because of the absence of mosquitoes. We get to the farm.

One of the youth, Obasa Samuel, is a student at the school. I have known him since my first day there. He helps me in many ways to learn about the town and travels to the market when I need things. The other youth, Obasa's brother, is younger and attends a nearby primary school. Obasa is a kind and respectful person and a serious student. He loves to learn. He is a hard worker who studies continuously and eagerly works every problem in the mathematics book that we use.

Many of the problems are difficult and challenging to solve. Some of the problems require rigorous and exhaustive effort to arrive at a verifiable solution. He is a fine scholar who is much the same person at this farm as in the school.

We reach the farm. I once visited the family house in town which was mud and simply made and I find this farm house much the same. Though the floors are mud it is clean. There are small wooden chairs to sit on. The grandfather has Obasa and his brother do tasks around the farm. They are busy cleaning, preparing food, collecting fruits and yams from the nearby trees and fields. They work together. Obasa joins me as I talk to the grandfather.

"Tell me," the grandfather says. "Are the people who live where you come from our masters?"

"I come from where I live, and I'm your brother. I'm your black brother." This response is one that I expound but is it convincing to an African who sees white dominance and power in tools, weapons, wealth and knowledge?

He asks how far away it is and I say that it means going from Ijero to Lagos and back thirty times before he reaches there. I also tell him that it is not only far but that there is much water to cross to reach there.

"You come by water?"

I have to tell him that I come by air, an airplane, which is a giant machine that is driven through the air across land and sea. I ask him if he has ever left Ijero. Twenty years ago he went to Ibadan and Lagos.

"How about Ikere? Have you been there?"

The girl I know from Pennsylvania lives there. It is forty miles away. Her name is Kathy Newcomb. She is a teacher who loves Nigeria and her life and her work here. I deeply respect her unusual spirit and her dedication in working with the Nigerians.

"I have never been to Ikere, but I have heard about it. There are many thieves there," he says.

"I have a friend there, and I would like to take you there."

"I shall go when you say," he says.

"One Saturday we shall both go there."

"How shall we go?"

"Lorry. We'll take a lorry, because you wouldn't like sitting on the back of my motorcycle. The lorry costs four shillings, but you will be my guest."

"What will we eat at your friend's? Does your friend eat pounded yam and bush meat?" he asks.

"Sometimes she does. I will tell her when we are coming and then she will have it when we get there."

It is a journey we never make together.

I do accompany him, though, on a trip to the Ifa (god of devination) church in the town. I am welcomed there. They tell me that they are not afraid of my being there because they speak the truth. They ask me if I wish to speak to their god or their messenger. I tell them their god. I am then told that it must be the messenger this day and that I can ask it any question I wish. I give a coin for good luck.

The diviner chants verses. He reads the information which comes from the palmnuts he gently drops to the floor. Obasa translates for me. My question to the messenger, "Why is Nigeria in this war?" I am being told why. There are two reasons. One is the greed that exists everywhere and the other is the failure of people to respect the elderly. These things are occurring in Nigeria and the rest of the world, and they are the reasons Nigeria is in this war. Before I leave them they wish that I reach home safely and not be struck by lightning.

Obasa's grandfather is now complaining about his taxes. I have a friend who is a tax collector, and I tell him that he is taxed on what he reports to the collector. He also pays for electricity, which is good for Nigeria.

His farmhouse is made of mud walls. They are ground from the earth. In the village his house has a corrugated tin roof. This roof is made of palm leaves. A fire burns inside, and I do not know which is worse: the mosquitoes or the smoke. It seems as though the smoke should drive away the mosquitoes but it does not happen. The mosquitoes devastate my flesh. Everything is cooked on an open fire, making all objects black. Life is harsh but simple. Palm wine is taken from the tree down the bush path and it is tapped high in the tree from a crudely synthesized ladder. The water comes from the stream brought by bucket on one's head. Everything in the world is either obvious or is a mystery. The world is here as it is, real and imagined.

The old man drinks palm wine and eats kola nuts. I cannot tolerate the bitterness of kola nuts but I do drink palm wine with him. It is when the palm wine is making him drunk that I decide to return home. Obasa guides me through the several miles of jungle back to town. We leave his grandfather at the farm.

The grandfather, in many ways, is as interesting a person as I meet in Nigeria. He is always generous toward me. It is in his genuineness that he invites me to his house in Ijero as well as to the farmhouse. He is open-minded and interested in me as a person and as a foreigner. He is more aware of my foreignness than of my blackness. He is a responsible person who pays his debts and who supports the education of his family, making him a conscientious citizen of the town. He invites me to be involved in African systems of thought as well as a life that is close to nature. Urban life in Ibadan, Lagos, New York, and San Francisco deal with complex and technical issues more than here in the village, and this can take us away from the basics in life and from the freedom to explore and discover things for oneself. Life in the wilderness is unpretentious and real. The grandfather, as much as any one else in Nigeria, shows me a distinct way of life absent of urban convention and thought.

Obasa is an exemplary student for the two years I live in Nigeria. Few are more intense or enthusiastic about their studies. Again, I am genuinely impressed by the dedication to learning that some of the students demonstrate. Many work hard out of conformity. Many students are independent. They all learn from each other. It is those who find learning to be meaningful that makes Nigeria worthwhile and a great place. There are interesting problems that challenge us. There are problems of motion, rates, areas, time, and clocks. One problem that involves time and a clock is the following: at what time after three o'clock do the hour and minute hands coincide? One approach is to determine how many minutes the minute hand gains on the hour hand in one hour, then determine how many minutes it takes to gain fifteen minutes. The time we arrive at is sixteen and four elevenths minutes after three o'clock.

We also prove theorems that have existed for thousands of years. What is important is constructing things on our own and building our own understanding. It happens or we do not learn.

CHAPTER 4

The Next Year

I now wonder about individual, as well as organizational, change. I pay attention to ways in which we systematically cooperate to pursue our goals as students and as teachers. Though I love mathematics, the first year I am not a very good teacher. I struggle for mathematics to be a worthwhile adventure for all students but it is not penetrating through all the minds in the class. As an individual I work endlessly to live in a world that is often strange and overwhelming. Though we all seem to work hard, only a few students profoundly understand the subject. There is frustration and disappointment from many.

Things stay difficult. It is the way we come to live and to accept the world. In the second year I discover new things as a teacher. I find more interesting ways to approach the Cambridge School Examinations. They are also called the West African School Examinations. These examinations reveal a serious pursuit of mathematical rigor and challenge. They represent mathematics from collective, creative, and shared thinking. I become aware of the limited individual knowledge I share with students in the beginning and am later able to think beyond my isolated world. In the second year I move beyond the boundary of classroom and personal knowledge to a richer learning community. I work with and learn from teachers who have studied in this system as well as from teachers at other schools who have taught in Europe, other African countries, and Asia.

This allows the students and me to pursue deeper dialogue and a deeper goal. We are challenged by the best thinking in England, Africa, and elsewhere. It is exciting as students evaluate themselves and assess their own work and preparedness from performances on previous examinations.

They work tirelessly and discuss many problems. Some students know they will do well because they master the concepts of the testing strategies. They acquire that intelligence. In the end each of the students sits for the examination. In the previous year the school did not perform well. It is a national exam that has consumed their existence since they have been in the school. Nothing else matters to them. We reach a high level of coherence and cooperation in our work. All students pass the examination. Some pass with honor and distinction. It is a collective effort. We all work hard, attain our common and shared goal and then move on to other places and other lives.

I do not know what makes a good teacher but I think that it has to do with the understanding that a teacher is a learner, just as a student is and there is no boundary between the two. A teacher is an advanced learner in some areas and is interested in learning to the limit of these subjects. He respects all of the students and where they are in their learning. It is going beyond the narrowness of one's life and self-enclosing needs. Interesting things happen when one moves beyond oneself. It is the way some men once held that the earth was the most important heavenly body, but replacing the idea that the earth is the center of the universe allows a much more exciting picture of space.

There are interesting days of teaching in Nigeria as we are young, free, and spirited. There is great energy for teaching and for life. Coming from America I recognize a strength in Africa; it is the ability to make do with less and to live with less. Our days are filled with life and challenge which make it a wondrous time in Africa, but then the war comes and we know of the daily deaths and killings and it effects all of our lives.

Nothing describes the difficult times I have in Nigeria better than the experiences that I have in traveling on the road. They are intense. For the first year I spend most of my time in Ijero and make local visits to other places. After my first year in Nigeria a close friend of mine (Shyaam Shabaka, then Willie Ellis) comes to visit me. One day I am cooking beans and okra, and he arrives in time for dinner. He has come from seventy miles away to visit me and to tell me of a journey to the Congo and East Africa sponsored by Nigerian University students. I decide that night that I am going as Sam, my friend and teacher at the school, releases me from attending his father's upcoming funeral. I never met his father because he died before I came to Nigeria. Sam was a student and penniless then and was unable to afford a funeral, but now he is properly burying his father. Regrettably, I am unable to attend.

It takes us several days to reach the coast, Lagos, where the trip is to originate. I make the entire trip by lorry. We are there several days when I realize that I have forgotten my health card which has a record of my immunizations. It is several hundred miles back to Ijero and two days travel, but I travel back, again by lorry. After getting back to Ijero I have to make a thirty mile journey to Ado. That evening I am returning to Ijero to set off in the early morning for Lagos again. The African roads are dangerous. One always needs to be aware of unexpected disaster. I have never had an accident, but I know that I have been fortunate. I have just left Ado and it is late in the evening. I know that I will not reach Ijero before night and, as a rule, night travel is unadvised. It is cooling off and darkness comes quickly. After I am out of Ado I remember that I should have bought petrol; I am now on reserve. I am certain there is enough fuel to get me to Aramoko, and I plan to fill up there. The motorcycle headlight has been turned on since I left Ado. This same road provides such a wonderful journey in the day but at night it always seems as though something dreadful is about to happen. But all one can do is to ride on. I am now hurrying through Iyin and Igede making good time. By the time I pass through Igede it is black outside. Night has arrived and a stillness has settled in. I have seen many such nights.

Black, cold, quiet.

There are now curves in the road that slow me down, and there are hills I fail to anticipate. Though I travel this road often at night I am ever a stranger to it. I hope the petrol is enough. Why can't I ever remember? I must be about seven miles from Aramoko, and I feel a strong chill in the night. Something bursts from the forest and runs across the road in front of me. I do not know what it is nor what my situation is. But whatever is there: human, animal, ghost, spirit, or nothing at all, I avoid it. Looking back I can see nothing, but I know I witnessed an orange creature streak through the night in front of me. Something was there. Now there is nothing but a black wall of darkness. Suddenly I am traveling too fast into a curve. I am unable to realize what exists in this darkness. In my attempt to avoid what I witness, I am now off the road. I know that I am going to crash. Furiously I apply the brake as my body desperately tries to control the machine. I am deeply confused and realize I can die here. Everything is now out of my control. I tell myself that I have to stay with the machine, go with the accident. A friend told me that. The machine turns over and over and its mass seems immense. When at last it rests in the grass, all movement stops. I am alive. I have somehow survived. When everything stops my first feelings are of pain. Blood trickles from my left shoulder and my left leg hurts, but nothing is broken because I walk and move all right. I am on the left side of the road, and I am aware of how the traffic moves. Walking is hard and it is damp out, which makes the earth seem alive, watching a drama in the night. Wet, quiet, dark and I am nowhere, maybe seven miles to Aramoko and I have to go on. I have to keep moving. I get to the machine. The headlight is busted. I am certain that the machine is dead, but the engine starts. I can move. I start toward Aramoko and however many miles away it is, but I cannot see and run off the road. I have to change the way I ride. I use my feet to guide me and I go dead slow, and I vigilantly look back for an oncoming lorry that might come from behind. When I reach the turn in the road, there is Aramoko. There is no light in the town, but I can see the houses that hold the people who sleep. I get to the mechanic's house. He comes out and I tell him my headlight is out. I know there is a good chance that he cannot help me, and I can be sleeping on his floor. The Nigerians are kind and welcome me to their houses. Luckily he has an old machine he uses for spare parts and is able to help me. He wonders how far I have come and I tell him seven miles. He is surprised and concerned and hopes I am all right. He tells me that it is going to cost ten shillings, and I gave him a pound, that's how elated I am. I did not really expect him to fix the light. I now have light and less than ten miles to go.

It is still cool, dark, and quiet along the road. I have forgotten the petrol. I don't know, but I think that I have passed the point of no return from Aramoko, so I keep on going. I expect the worst and know that I will not make it. Not too far down the road the machine slows down and dies in its tracks, and I abandon it on the roadside and walk until a lorry comes and takes me to Ijero. It is a hard night. I tell Sam what happened and he regrets the misfortune but is not overly concerned because I do not look that damaged in the dark. Besides, anything can happen at night on a road in the rain forest, except that nothing like this has ever happened to me. The next morning I collect the machine from along the road where it still rests, untouched, and then I travel back to the coast to Lagos.

The flight to East Africa is canceled. It never materializes. Shyaam, though, is so disappointed and is so seriously determined that the two of us to be allowed to make the trip, that he convinces the airlines (Air Congo) to send the two of us. It is a miracle. He is unsure how he convinces them, but he does.

We travel to Kinshasa, the capital of the Congo, and see its quiet streets. The Belgians leave an archaic colonial system and we see the battle for independence continue just as it is happening in so many other African, European, and Asian nations. It is the fight to have either an ethnically-focused decentralized government or a unitary state. In the end the governments formed seldom work for the mass of the people. Even though the Africans living here are in a free and independent nation, they remain oppressed and dominated by government corruption and by European ways and customs. We walk the city streets and are moved by the Congolese Highlife music and dance, and we are fascinated by the African marketplace. It contains food, clothing, jewelry, art and a multitude of other indigenous and imported articles and objects. With little money of our own, we are much like two poor Africans walking the streets. We are struggling as others around us are getting through the day. They do not hear us speak and have no idea where we are from or how we got there. Many probably never would think or believe that we are there from America. We are cut off from the material and the business life of the city.

Our path leads us from Kinshasa to the city of Kisangani, which at one time was called Stanleyville. It is a place of empty store shelves and social unrest. It seems as though somewhere in the area are a hundred twenty mercenary soldiers who are holding off the entire Congolese army. We are cautious in our movement. I am fascinated to learn about the conflicts that have occurred here since 1960, and the days of independence from Belgium, and the battle for copper and other resources. It is the exploitation of the nation's resources that make this country and others remainder places in the world-and Africa a remainder continent. The masses struggle for what those in power have not used for themselves. As the Nigerian elders have stated, it is greed and absence of human respect that perpetuates war, poverty, and struggle among the masses. Five hundred miles to the east is the Rwandan border. We fly out of the Congo and on to Nairobi, Kenya. How astonished we are upon reaching East Africa. It is so still, peaceful. Nigeria is vibrant, chaotic, alive, crowded. Kenya is such a reserved land. Still. The previous years of British colonization remains in many of its places. It is a distant and strange African nation to us. We join a group of Americans who are on a safari to Tanzania and the game reserves.

We cannot imagine the world we are about to enter. The road we are on brings us face to face with giraffes, elephants and other free-roaming wildlife. There are endless herds of zebras and countless wildebeest. Occasional Masai are along the road, sometimes with herds of cattle, sometimes alone. Everything we observe on the road is new to us but seemingly timeless. Giraffes, elephants, gazelles, ostriches, and vultures richly populate the land.

I am not aware of the significance of this valley. It is a spectacular place and a wonder of the earth. We have come in January, which is the dry season. The breathtaking presence of Kilimanjaro looms a hundred miles away. It is across the Kenyan border in Tanzania. Its presence penetrates us and dominates our attention as it stands alone in its massive and singular existence on the African plain.

I talk of climbing Kilimanjaro, but I have never climbed a mountain and have no idea what is necessary to make such an unimaginable journey. Besides, we have no money and are unable to climb it alone. We have no idea of what it takes to get to the top, but we know others have done it. We are told we can do it in five days. The idea does not persist because it is not deep inside of me at this time. It passes through me like so many other African thoughts and ideas that I do not, and cannot, seize.

It is interesting to learn that it is in this great Rift Valley around Kilimanjaro that individuals have communicated findings of the earliest journey of humankind, as beginning here and traveling across the earth. We now continue that adventure to journeys into space. The human journey is unimportant as it is imagined or projected. What is significant is what happens or occurs. Just as it is now beyond thought and the power of the mind to know what our present journey will be and what we will make of this earth.

The African world here is new to us, and we learn that where we find ourselves are the remains from humans who passed through here a million years ago. There are early stone tools that are a transforming force to those who were existed here. Sometimes the paths and technology we discover can seriously change us. Profound change is how the universe communicates with us and expresses itself through us. Life itself is serious and of the moment. It is free from past and future events. Profound events happen in this African world as the stone tools and the human mind empower and deepen our survival. They are a breakthrough in the beginning of our human journey.

From East Africa I return to my village in Nigeria. Just as the school term begins, I become seriously ill. I go to a nearby village hospital and the doctor gives me an injection of morphine that induces sleep. He diagnoses the case as acute appendicitis and says that I need to go to Ibadan immediately for an operation. The headmaster at the school has his driver, Lucky Boy, drive me from Ijero to Ilesha, a town forty miles away. He makes good time and we reach Ilesha at 3:30. After refusing to pay extra money to a Peugeot (taxi) driver, I take a lorry to Ibadan. There are seventy-two miles to go. I do not know the time. It is during the Biafran Civil War and we have to get there before the 7:00 curfew. I am an American, and they have me sit up front with the lorry driver. I often ride here. First the driver brings petrol. There are numerous stops and nobody is in a hurry. They buy oranges and kola nuts from the market people, so I buy an orange. I give the market lady a pence and she gives me a half pence change. We are on our way when a policeman stops us.

There is continuous corruption from the police and the soldiers at all of the check points. They are always questioning the drivers, and searching the passengers, and seeking bribe money. I think that we will never get to Ife, and I consider getting off there and taking a taxi. I have some pain but my mind does not dwell on it and for a while I forget why I am going to Ibadan. The lorry starts to make good time so I remain, knowing there is still more than fifty miles. The most serious problem is the time. We go along smoothly until we reach Ikire where we are stopped again by the police. Can we get there before the curfew? Will we make it? I seriously doubt it. The driver is certain we will. He knows that we would because he has made this run many times, he tells me.

We get to Ibadan. It is too late. Vehicles are lined up for miles. There are no vehicles allowed through until the next morning. Soldiers are everywhere with guns, acting suspicious. They have a duty to perform, orders to carry out. I tell them my situation. I always have a tough time with soldiers. I am black, and I am not African. They know this from how I speak. Was I Ibo? Where was my passport? Why did I wear a beard? The Ibo leader, Ojukwu, wears a beard. I am always warned about the problem that it symbolizes. I tell them that I am an American and that I am ill. I am a teacher and I need to be let through so that I can receive medical attention. After much discussion, I am allowed through the checkpoint. I walk up the road past all the other vehicles and soldiers until I walk through the gate.

Up the road I get a taxi, and the driver takes me to the hospital. The hospital is filled with 70% military, but they find space for me. They operate on me that evening and remove my impaired appendix. It had been in such a deteriorated state that I developed an infection in my abdominal cavity which leads to complications in my recovery.

I am away from school for three months. I am hospitalized in Ibadan and undergo three operations. I have competent and dedicated Nigerian doctors and nurses who work hard for my recovery, and I am fortunate to return to the town of Ijero to teach again.

There is one student, Remi, who understands mathematics profoundly. He is as bright as any student I ever teach. Most students struggle, but he is driven to discover the total human invention of mathematics and is fascinated with its internal order and connections.

The next year there are other new teachers with whom I travel, live, and discuss learning and teaching. They are Americans and Nigerians. I also meet a Canadian and an Indonesian with whom I travel and learn new things. We are all conscientious about our own efforts and the challenges that we share with our students and among ourselves. In many ways we live to teach. It is a time of pouring our soul into our work. We mainly teach mathematics and science. We are all challenged by hard problems, those that are complex and whose solutions are not obvious, solutions that may or may not exist. We realize that there is much that is unknown and that at times we must impose our own meaning in the world and tirelessly labor as teachers. Life itself is inviting and spectacular to us. We all love Africa and the lives we are living. Some of us are born into this system of education, others are driven to master it. Though we all live in small towns and villages in the rain forest, with primarily poor and rural students, we are diligent in working to make something of this system. I think what sustains us is that we each understand that we are responsible for our own learning and we are propelled by our own self-understanding.

It is the only teaching job that I have ever known. The books (by Durrell, I believe) are the only books we use for all levels of math. They are British, have been used for decades and they engross us. American teachers criticize this education as stagnant, inflexible, and a limited system of study. Some years later I would teach high school mathematics in America and the beginning and advanced math books would be written by a single author, Dolciani. I would find them to have provocative and engaging problems and ideas. So to criticize Nigeria is to criticize ourselves.

There is a national curriculum in Nigeria. I follow a national syllabus during my first year. In the second year I simplify the focus. I teach to the test. It is a rigorous examination. It is true that schools study artificial and abstract material in Africa and in America. We study hundreds of problems that sometimes have no meaning to us. Often they are not related to the here and now. This does not concern me. I love games and mathematics. I am absorbed in the game of Ayo which I spend numerous and countless hours. When I studied mathematics in New York there was a student named Shreekant Malvadkar from Poona in India, and he had done six thousand pages of Calculus problems before coming to America. He was a brilliant mathematics scholar. There are such students and teachers in Nigeria. Mathematics is as real and as interesting to them. I love mathematics and it matters to me that all students experience its truth and beauty. This comes in self discovery and learning things more than one way. It is enlightening and significant in the lives of students when they actually prove Pythagoras's theorem of the right triangle in several different ways. When we study it years later in America, students would find it as provocative and interesting. It provides a fresh understanding of the world to them. It illuminates their lives as thinkers. They are able to perform something that is extraordinary because reality has not changed, their thinking of reality has. They are making the most of their human experience. In the classroom there are profound times and ordinary ones. Outside is an absurd war of nationalities as well and sometimes a world of personal battles.

As I express the struggles in my life as a teacher, the last days and final battle in Nigeria is written. It is about the death of a friend which happens about fifty miles from the village in which I live. The death of a student, a stranger, or a friend deepens life's mystery.

It is the next year. I am going to be leaving Nigeria soon. Several friends I know are also leaving. Kathy Newcomb, who lives in another village, is leaving. She had visited me in the hospital in Ibadan several times. She brought me some interesting books to read. I was hospitalized for more than two months and it was always a special time when she came. I respect Kathy as a teacher and her selfless effort in working with, and helping, the Nigerians. She genuinely loves the country and its people. I have occasionally visited her since my release from the hospital and my return to Ijero. She had abandoned a project of trying to raise chickens as it had not proved as successful as she had imagined. Her garden is doing well, however, and she grows cucumbers, corn, tomatoes, and melons. She considered staying on in Nigeria for another year but decided that she would leave when the school year ended in December. I will leave in early January but probably stop in Spain first. I have always wanted to journey to India, but I would not get there this time. I receive a letter from my friend (Shyaam) who has left Nigeria and is living in California. He recommends coming to California to live when I return to the states. I don't know what I will do.

In these last days in Nigeria I meet a new friend. He is an Indonesian whose name is Sanmugam Thanapala Singam. He is a teacher in Ado, thirty miles away. He is a short, dark, carefree person who lived in England and Ghana before coming to Nigeria. He teaches chemistry. In my second year I teach chemistry and find him to be a good resource in discussions about preparing students for their West African Examinations, setting up titrations, and devising interesting experiments to perform at school science fairs, such as making nitrogen triiodide whose decomposition and explosion provide powerful fascination. We traveled a lot together. We make mostly local journeys, but we also travel as far as Ibadan.

One week the two of us ride to visit Kathy. It is a surprise visit, and she welcomes us. We decide that we will visit a friend in a nearby town. She first talks about traveling through Europe on her way home. She talks with excitement of seeing new places about which she has only read. After a month in Europe she will return to Pennsylvania. Going home is a significant time for those of us who have existed several years in small bush towns. Most look forward to visiting other places in the world on their way home to California, Pennsylvania, or Minnesota.

Kathy is the only girl in her family. Certainly her family must worry about her and her life in Africa during all of the days that she has been away. How happy they must be now that she is returning home after two years of their waiting, wondering, and worrying.

I suppose my family worries about me also, but my being thousands of miles away from home is not new to them. I have thought little about America during the last two years. Africa is my home, and I love being here. Kathy's life still has freshness and meaning. She is as enthusiastic, eager, curious and energetic as she was on her first day in Africa. She is as youthful and filled with life as then. There are several others living here who are like her in their exuberance. They are not many, but they are fascinated with the life here. Though I deeply love Africa, I have deteriorated. The war and illness sometimes exhaust me.

We finish our visit and the three of us get into Singam's small car, which resembles a Nigerian taxi. Sometimes people try to flag it down. We turn the car around and leave the house. Singam is driving. I am in the passenger seat and Kathy is in the back, directly behind me. We are on the road. It is dark out. Though the light of the car shines into the night, everything around us is covered in blackness. We all feel fine. It is quiet and we are surrounded by the multitude of stars that inhabit the still, black African night. No one says anything for some time. It is not deliberate silence but it just seems to happens. Anyway I am the first to speak and I believe that Kathy does wants to speak, but does not. She does not want to seem to give to panic, so she does not speak. That is the way it seems. I say," Slow down, man. You don't know this road."

He did not. Neither of us had ever been here before. We are into a curve. Nothing can penetrate the outside night. He is going too fast and can not negotiate the road. It is hard to say what is occurring, but we seem to be in trouble. He cannot respond to all the things happening. There is dead silence in the car. I am thinking that it is just another hard time in life that we will have to get through, again. It is often hard in Africa. We are probably telling ourselves if we can just get through this moment, then everything would be all right. It was just surviving this time right now. Suddenly it was the only thing in life that mattered. No one speaks. The accident happens. Everything seems to explode all at once. Some things flash through the mind. What is life? Suddenly it is a fleeting moment, hurrying by. Sounds and images thunder and explode and flash and crash and all thoughts are fleeting. Will this confused and entangled world ever rest? I am there in all the violence. All motion is swift as forces impact and change objects in the destruction. Our bodies are carried along. We were all destined to uncertainty. The accident is over. Here I lie in the stones on the side of the road. I stand up. I can walk. I know nothing else. I call Kathy. Nothing. I call Singam. Nothing. In the still black night I continue. The first body I see is Singam's. I try to move him, and there is no response. I keep on moving. I see the car up the road, not knowing how much damage it had sustained. It is flipped over and is standing on its top with its wheels still and facing into the night sky. Not far away on the road lies Kathy. She has lived through the disaster, for she is still able to speak. She has no consciousness of the world around her. I look about me to see where we are. There are people around us. They came from somewhere. They must have. They are amazed at what they see. To them it all seems beyond belief. They all stand in wonder. I think we must be close to Owo, that is the road we were on. But I learn that we are closer to Ikare. I know I have to get them to the hospital before they die. I hate to think about what can have already happened to them and I wonder about the state of their lives. My mind is filled with the great times I had with them before the accident. I want to remember all the good things I can about them. I think about how senseless life is and how imminent our extinction always is. I feel the absurdity of our time on this planet. A taxi comes down the road. It is filled with people, moving fast. I wave it down and it comes to a stop. I tell the driver I have friends who are dying and I have to have help. I need to get to a hospital now! Those in the taxi get out, but to get Kathy and Singam into the empty taxi, I need help. "Help me! Help me!" I cry. Help is not forthcoming. I cannot move them alone. I try. Nobody helps me until one man finally stepped forward, then another, and then we put them inside. Blood flows from Kathy's head as she is lying in the road. I hoped there was no brain damage, and as she is placed in the car we take particular caution to protect her head. The taxicab is on its way. We go to Ikare because that is the closest hospital. It is full of soldiers. The doctor seems uncertain of what to do and seems threatened and uncomfortable at the idea of having expatriates in the hospital. He is African. I look around the ward. It is dirty and poorly kept. We do not stay. We go to Owo instead. There they are both immediately hospitalized. It is a relief and a disappointment to arrive there. There is some comfort knowing that at last they are receiving proper medical attention. The disappointment comes when I realize how helpless I am to do anything else. All I can do is sit and endure the hardest moments I have ever lived through. An Italian doctor is in charge of the hospital. He is not immediately available and every moment it takes him to arrive emphasizes life's futility and its insurmountable limitations. Kathy is the worst. Her condition is critical. When the doctor arrives he immediately orders full emergency treatment for her. Fluids feed her arm and he fights into the night to sustain her pulse. He never tires, never takes his attention from her. A priest comes and gives last rites. I cannot grasp the full significance of what is taking place. This is my most tragic encounter with reality. I refuse to accept the possibility of death. I refused. I refuse it absolutely. The Italian doctor is a master surgeon and a relentless and untiring healer. He fights heroically throughout the night and into the next day. Just as courageous is the Irish sister physician from Ado who arrives the following day. They fight for her life. They want her to live. The Italian doctor tells me that it is because of her strong will for life and her unyielding spirit that she is able to barely hold on. They have done all they can for her here. They will have to move her to Ibadan. Singam, he said only sustained a dislocated shoulder and would be all right. I do not rejoice at the news for it seems a dark victory, for Kathy holds on ever so faintly. I can never forget the helicopter that hovers over Owo this day and all the wind it creates before setting itself down. Kathy is delicately placed inside and a multitude of persons witness her fly away. As the helicopter takes off there is such deep hope for her to live. God, I don't want her to die.

The helicopter carries her to the University College Hospital in Ibadan. Her personal strength and determination enable her to hold on, but she never regains consciousness. She is unable to sustain her battle to live. Her life ends. A military plane from the states flies to Africa to take her back to the states, but she dies before it arrives. It is her strength that allows her to remain alive for the week that she lives. If she had lived she would have been paralyzed from the waist down because she had three severed spinal nerves.

Nothing diminishes her death for me.

I know I am witnessing the death of my own life here. If I had died, a similar world would be going on. People would be talking about me and writing letters home about my life in Africa. Death is this way.

We had accepted as fact that Kathy was going to reach home safely. We had imagined and lived with the illusion that we could tell life what to do. We were dishonest in that assumption. We are powerless to dominate life. Life is no different from a person or a student. There is a difference between telling a student what to do and watching and observing him or her do it. As I observe life, it is a battlefield from which we never seem to leave.

Many Americans come to Africa and live dramatic lives here. Some have a profound presence. Some of them perform small miracles. Some learn African languages fluently and know more about these languages than the Africans themselves. Some grow plants that have never existed here before and some sail boats against the current, which has never happened in a village before. But Africa goes on after they leave. Much of the innovation dies in time. The memory of people's lives, former African kingdoms and empires, thriving rivers, and great herds of wildlife, all die in time.

I write a letter home describing to her mother and father all the details I can remember. It is a difficult letter to write but her family wants to know about her death. So I recall every detail I can about how she had died. I write how determined she was in being a serious teacher. Her life in Africa had been both spirited and undaunted. Her body was flown to Pennsylvania. A reason for her death is unimportant to me. She is dead. She is not coming back.

Being on the African road brings other severe times, even after the death of my friend. During Ramadan and the harmattan season I am on a crowded bus in northern Nigeria that is traveling from Kano to Kaduna, hundreds of miles from my village in the south. We are traveling fast and suddenly the left front tire blows out; the bus goes out of control and overturns. The driver struggles as hard as he can to keep control of the bus and to prevent the accident but in the end it flips over and everyone is trapped inside. It is chaos and panic as we break windows desperately struggling to escape. After things settle down, I crawl out through a window. I am still alive but not fully aware of the injuries and condition of others. Ambulances and other vehicles come and take people to hospitals and other places. I ride back to Kaduna, again lucky to have survived.

I leave Nigeria for the United States uncertain of what I will do. Nigeria was a new and great land as well as one of sadness and tragic journeys.

CHAPTER 5

The Ranch School

I return to the United States and move to San Francisco. I get married and became a public school teacher. My first assignment is at a ranch school for delinquent boys located fifty miles south of San Francisco in a small mountain town surrounded by a redwood forest, near the Pacific Ocean. There are no fences and students live in a minimum security environment. Though escape is possible, few run away.

As a teacher there I realize how schools damage children through racism, tracking by ability, and using authority to control minds. The lives of many of the students are filled with perpetual resentment of school, self-hatred, and deep anger.

There are six academic groups based on reading scores. Group one is the lowest. They are all black. They are unable to read and none are able to write letters home to their families. Someone else writes for them if letters are written at all or someone else reads to them if any letters are received. They are accepted as the dumb group. They see themselves as dumb, stupid. Unfortunately, most of them are in this group for life. They are silent witnesses to their own death and destruction.

A student in Group One tells me that a student asks a teacher, "How come white people are so ugly?"

"The same reason black people are so dumb," the teacher replies.

Group Six is the highest; they are the best readers and many of the white students are placed in the higher groups. The practice of sorting students out leads to a situation where intelligence is accepted as closely related to race. This view is perpetuated throughout the school. Intelligence, however, is not acting from what we know (knowledge), but what we do when we do not know something.

I teach mathematics to students in all six groups. I discuss the same concepts and problems throughout the classes. I am here to challenge every student encountered. It is my mission. All are capable of mathematical understanding. I present material on binary operations, mathematical games, modular arithmetic, and mathematical logic. I am fascinated with mathematical games, and those that question and probe the mind. I play the African game of Ayo with them. It becomes the school game. The students make game boards in woodshop and use marbles to play it. I brought my board from Nigeria. It challenges and engages them. They are also very curious about the Ayo seeds, which come from a Nigerian tree. It is a serious game that they take a strong interest in. The game is played by two players and is similar to Mancala. The object is to accumulate the most seeds through a series of player moves. There are strategies that one masters as one moves deeper into the understanding of the game. In their involvement they find something intriguing about African life and thought on their own, and because the game absorbs their minds, they get an insight into learning. In Nigeria I would sometimes play for hours a day and have played thousands of games. I never tired of it. Students challenge me all the time. There are games of NIM which win-loss situations can be established by binary patterns. The binary system and learning the code interests many minds. I work to impact the total school and to awaken the mathematical power in all our students.

I do not reach all the students. The Group Four class is interesting. They can all read. All do their work in the math class. Some push themselves harder than others. Some prefer to read more. One student is a quiet leader. His name is Ceda and he is Puerto Rican. He tolerates math but is much more interested in becoming a serious reader and wants more insight into the world of social thought. He is reading the *Diary of Che Guevara.* He sometimes discusses ideas with me. I read the book also. He is not deeply interested in math. There are books that I am reading that I want to share with him. They are about slave rebellions in Brasil, but we have never discussed them. One day I come to recognize his particular intensity and the way he deals with the world.

It is the day of the fight between Willie Stamp and Ceda. Willie Stamp is black and Ceda is Puerto Rican, though born in Hawaii. Willie Stamp is absent a lot and has had bad health. He is just about as tall as Ceda. Suddenly a fight breaks out and the room changes. I realize the chaos and confusion that suddenly exists. Ceda has much strength for his size and he is respected for that. There seems no fear in him. He is possibly the strongest boy at the ranch. Anyway, Willie Stamp gets mad at something Ceda says. It has happened before. One doesn't know what he will do. He moves unpredictably and he, like Ceda, is not bothered by fear. There is a force in Stamp, at times, that we recognize as something that can hardly be contained. Suddenly he is coming at Ceda with a chair. Willie Stamp is about to knock the living hell out of him and though others attempt to prevent his actions, nothing is to stop him from getting to Ceda. He is too determined. No one can contain him. He strikes Ceda with the chair. It crashed into Ceda's back.

It is too late to reach Stamp. It is all too quick as the blow lands and Stamp falls back. He has been hit and his nose is bleeding profusely. Ceda, who is still standing there, had hit him hard. But Ceda too has been hit hard. Everybody is still trying hard to hold Stamp and to tell him how much blood he is losing. He doesn't know. He touches his face and sees the blood but it doesn't seem to matter. He gets away out the door and runs out of the room. Before we know it Willie Stamp is back and carrying a baseball bat. He says that he is going to kill Ceda, and he is determined to knock Ceda's brains out if he can just get to him. Ceda stands there, never saying a word, waiting, but we stop Willie Stamp at the door. It takes two of us to wrestle him down and to get him outside. I suppose if Ceda were here now he would still have pains in his back.

After six months I leave the ranch school to teach mathematics at Mission High School in San Francisco. On the same day I leave the ranch school Ceda and several other students run away. So we leave there together. We have that in common.

That September in San Francisco, I don't remember the day exactly, Ceda comes. He discovers that I am teaching there. He is still on the run. I ask him if he has managed to stay out of trouble, and he says that he has. I would have helped him if I could. He never asks me for anything except for books to read. I am happy to lend him books, and I am pleased that he reads them. I once tell him to meet me at the library one Saturday afternoon to find some books that would interest him. He never comes.

One day Ceda comes to the school and brings his girlfriend to meet me. She hardly says a word. I am just glad that he brings her. We do not talk much and they do not stay long. Ceda never seems happy. He is too serious. The girl seems good for him. She makes him seem less alone.

Life is routine and quiet at the school, and one day seems like all others. One morning though is different. A student walks into the room. He comes quietly and without a word. I have not looked up from the desk to meet his eyes as a student's presence is usual and ordinary. He speaks my name. I look up and see Francisco Gamieno. I never knew much about Gamieno, but he had been a former student at the ranch school, as had Ceda.

"Good morning, Gamieno."

"Did you hear about Ceda?"

It is not a question I am anticipating.

"No I didn't hear."

"You probably didn't see the paper."

I haven't.

"Well," he says, Ceda was shot."

I hear him, and it doesn't seem so unusual to be hearing these words. I know Ceda's life is hard and I know he has been in trouble before, so I am not surprised that he might have gotten into trouble again.

"Is he hurt?" I ask. Already I am thinking this might be a serious situation, that I might be going to see Ceda in the hospital.

"He's dead," he says. He says it with complete coolness as though it is ordinary news. He seems strange in his coolness. He says that he died two days ago and thought I knew about it.

"He was shot in the head three times," he continues.

"How did it happen?"

"His body was found in a park."

He says that nobody knows any details.

Suddenly I am shocked and his coming has changed my world.

"It was murder," he said. "Somebody just killed him."

People who knew him said he would be killed one day. Teachers at the ranch school said his life would be filled with doom, and I suppose that the killing itself does not shock me as much as the realization that it has occurred. Gamieno says no more, but he seems to possess uncommon patience. Because of my silence I think he feels he should leave.

He leaves.

Later in the day he comes again. He tells me that he has been unable to find the newspaper where the death was written. I am glad he came back to tell me. Gamieno still seems unwilling to talk about the death, so I don't question him further, making it easy for him to leave. He is gone and the room is empty. I decide that I will visit the family and see the body. I have never visited a student's family before in San Francisco. I would tell my wife and then I would go. In the afternoon before it is time to leave school, a girl comes. She is noticeably attractive. She is quiet and has long black hair. I seem familiar to her. I am puzzled by her presence. I wonder who she is. I am thinking seriously about it.

"Did you hear?" she asks.

It is when she speaks that I remember her. She is Ceda's girlfriend. "Did you hear?" she is asking me. She shows no sign of emotion. "Someone told me about Ceda this morning."

It had been some time since we first met. I had only seen her once since then.

"Well I wanted to be sure that you knew," she says.

She doesn't seem to want to stay, for it seems as though she has just come to tell me this. I am glad she came. She is so quiet and indeed she is the girl I remember. I won't ask her for any details about the death because I feel her reluctance to talk.

"I am glad you came," I tell her.

"I wanted you to know," she says. She wants to leave. She seems to have nothing else to say. I tell her that I am going to visit Ceda's family and see the body. She seems pleased. She tells me exactly where the house is and where the body lies. I tell her when I am going and she tells me that the family will not be at home but with the body at the funeral home. She leaves quickly. Because she came, I know at the time of my visit that the family will be at the funeral home and I never visit Ceda's house.

After school I go home. That evening I go to the funeral home to see the family and Ceda's body. I invite my wife to accompany me, but being pregnant she has a certain reluctance toward death. She says that life is swimming all around inside of her, and she doesn't want to be touched by death. She goes there with me, but she doesn't go inside.

The body lies in a funeral home on the opposite side of town from where we live. It is in North Beach. I don't know what to expect, but the place is large and has a certain elegance. I am surprised at how large it seems. I walk off into some new room. A feeling of death and darkness dominates me. The floor on which I walk is covered with a thick and dark carpet. The rug is so soft that my feet become drunk. I feel like a strange wanderer. I come into another room and, upon entering, I see a young girl standing there. I wonder where her father is. She goes away and comes back with a gray-haired man in a black suit. His suit fits him loosely. He is an undisturbed and collected individual.

"Hello," I say.

"Good evening," he says to me.

I am certain he is Ceda's father because of the similarity of faces. I greet him.

"I am a teacher," I say to him. I tell him that I know about his son's death and that I wanted to come here to meet the family and see the body. I tell him that I was once Ceda's teacher.

"Yes, come in. Please come in. You are welcome."

I follow him into a very large room. He walks slowly. His black suit is no longer current and has not been stylish for sometime. The suit is large for his body but he seems a man beyond such mundane considerations. One wonders if he has ever given significance to such matters.

"Is there anything you would like?" he asks.

"No, nothing. I only came here to talk to you and see the body."

We stop at the front of the room.

"Please excuse me for a moment," he says.

He walks to the other side of the room where a small group of people sit. They are mostly children. He returns.

"I would like for you to meet my family," he says.

I follow him, and as I do I wonder about the life he has already lived. He is a short, quiet man with a slight accent. Nothing has disturbed him. We reach the other side of the room where his wife and children and his wife's sister sit. I am introduced as Ceda's teacher. He is glad that I came. The children are hardly aware of my presence, I am just a person visiting. The wife, Ceda's mother, is dressed in black. She speaks.

"You knew my Ceda?" She asks.

"Yes."

"When did you see my Ceda last?"

"Last week," I tell her.

"Last week," she says shaking her head. "Last week."

"How long did you know him?"

"For almost a year."

For a while it is dead quiet. She seems to be waiting for something to happen, for something to be said.

"I am sad that Ceda is dead," I say to her. I wanted to tell her that I knew him as a determined person who was always so serious, but that some people die young. It happens, and it is beyond us to save them, but she no longer seemed to be listening. She looks away and shakes her head. She doesn't want to accept the death or the fact that she suddenly finds herself in a universe that can never be the same. She is a small lady, and this death is causing a sickness in her heart. It is making her weak. She hardly knows how to act.

"Thank you for coming," she says. "Thank you."

The box where the body lies is not far from us. Ceda's father takes me there and presents the corpse to me. It is neatly dressed in a new blue suit that is stylishly tailored. Only the face and hands can be seen. Someone has delicately treated the skin and carefully combed the hair, but nothing is able to bring back life. I know it is true that he is dead and lying there; it is just such a strange and hard time, but I know it is Ceda there, dead. I notice Ceda's father maintains his ever steadiness and quiet strength. I talk to him. We move away from the lifeless body.

"Tell me," I say. "Are the brothers and sisters like Ceda?"

"My youngest son," replies Ceda's father, "is only ten, but there is much difference between him and Ceda. They are not the same at all. My youngest son never gives me or his mother any trouble. He's a good son."

"Did you find Ceda to be a bad son?" I ask him.

"He was hard to know. It wasn't easy to get close to him. He would pick his friends."

"Do you feel like you understood him?" I ask.

"I wanted to," he said. "He would miss school. When he ran away from the last school, I told him to give himself up and return to the school. He never listened, but I pleaded with him to return to the school."

I knew school never meant much to him and I know our schools are not for everybody. Sometimes schools only challenge a few who are there. We all learn different things at different times and schools can be obstacles and may not touch our lives.

I told him that some of us are driven by forces outside the school.

"Even so," he says, "it was better that Ceda was in school. He was always in trouble. He always was. He ran around with dangerous people. He had trouble with the police. I pleaded with him to go to school and change his friends."

"Did the two of you talk much?"

"He never needed me. You couldn't change him. Once he made up his mind you couldn't change him. He wasn't even living with us the last month. We only saw him sometimes. The way he died, it had to be that way. I would say to him, Ceda, let us help you. Tell us what your problems are. Tell me! I'm your father. But he picked his friends and didn't trust people. His life was hard. He had too many enemies to have a good life. He had to keep too many secrets. He was always hiding and running. It was the only life he lived."

What I remember about him is that he did not complain. He did not see life in those terms. And he did not blame anybody for his life. He was not selfish. That is what was so unusual about him. He did not cry or make a scene ever, and he did not hate life. He was serious for his age. He did not seem frightened of dying and he never expressed dissatisfaction. Though he probably worried about a lot of things, he was the most unemotional student I had known.

The father agreed but added,

"It was still a bad life because he lived like an animal."

"How do you feel about whoever it was who killed your son?"

"I just feel sad that Ceda is dead. Whatever the truth is about his death cannot surprise me. He was going to die like this," he says. I have always known this. I just feel sad.

I tell him I am going home.

"I hope you can come for the funeral," he says. It is certain that it will mean much to him if I can come.

"Perhaps if my wife is well," I say. I tell him that she is pregnant.

"I would like it very much if you could make it, and if you don't, I'll understand. You are always welcome to visit our home."

I thanked him and said good-bye.

This was my first visit as a teacher since I had left Africa. I was learning about men and women who lose their children.

Students, parents, and teachers are all driven by the idea that one must go to school and that one must be educated. It dominates our thinking and our society. We seldom go further in our understanding. Sometimes ones personal mission is deeper than that of the school.

After Ceda left the ranch school, I gave him three books to read that I never got back from him. I doubt if he ever read them. I know that I shall never see them again. Those books do not mean anything anymore. Living in the here and now ends the need for the continuance of things and the self. Those books are dead, and their possible impact on him is ended.

Ceda lacked formal education but was an independent learner. I am uncertain what level of learning he may have realized. No one knew. He did realize a personal power that was derived from what he read and understood. He was serious about his life. Sometimes schools are not good places to learn.

There are those who believe that to change schools we need the parents and families involved in a child's education. Schools are complicated in the way that parents, students, administrators, teachers, and the community interconnect. There are some strategies that come and go. Solutions, answers, and strategies do not change schools. The beginning of change in the school is through the individual and not through an outside system.

Most parents I have worked with stand alone and isolated in the education of their child, and it is difficult for them to know what to do.

The education of children is empowered when the members of the family share a common vision about learning. I do know that there are parents who strongly care about their children, and there are children who deeply love their parents. The success of the child's education is less important than their deep feelings for each other. I have seen cases of students new to formal education from Asia, Africa, Russia, Mexico, and other places whose dedication to their parents and family has been profound. There are families who as a group can internalize goals, and create a deeper life for their children. Such youth can become driven by forces that hardly seem human. In the end, however, some youth make it, others do not. It is the way of our world.

CHAPTER 6

Cry for Spring

I leave the ranch school and go to teach in San Francisco. After our daughter is born, travel is in our hearts, and so we leave San Francisco to go to Kenya. As a family we travel through a vastness of time and space around our planet, and late in the night, we arrive in a strange and quiet land.

Kenya
It is dark. The sky is a mystery that dwells in a strange silence. I hardly feel alive as we walk through the dead still night. What will happen to us? All past knowledge seems to be incomplete and not to pertain to us. We have come from half a world away and are here at last. It seems something to have made it. Every step we make is history that now stands behind us.

We traveled from San Francisco to New York to Athens. They would not let us leave the airport in Athens because of a dispute with Greek and American governments. We left Greece and came upon the ancient brown African earth. From the air the earth changed slowly. Brown timeless dust and sand and quiet orange fires characterized the earth as we witnessed it in our flight. We travel until at last we reach Nairobi, Kenya, and land in the night. I wonder how do my wife and daughter feel to be here. Do they remember those whom we left behind in San Francisco, who hated to see us leave, who were going to worry about our well-being, those who brought us small things to remember them by? My wife was pleased to be going to Africa even though it seemed so far to be carrying a one-year-old baby. We don't know how long we will be here, a day or for the rest of our lives. I had visited Nairobi before, but I hardly remember the place. I knew it had a kind climate and would be good for my wife who is of poor health. We would often talk about its fine spring-like weather that seldom varied. Coming here is a promise of spring to us.

I had wanted to get back to Africa for some time and we are finally here now. We have to be here. It is going to be good for my wife and daughter. I hope that it is going to be a new life for my wife. My daughter is going to be as excited and as curious as ever. She is going to go on learning; she is going to be in another place that she hardly realizes is any different. For her, living is no different from learning. Being here to her is just something she is passing through. Some day she is going to learn about school. I don't want to dwell upon it because I am living now. Besides, riding too hard on such suppositions may likely lead to the subdividing of things and times that may never happen.

Nairobi is quiet this night. It is we who are intruders into its stillness and darkness. The wind is full of free information. There is no news. Nothing is alive in the air. There is a deep silence everywhere. The earth is dead still, and nothing else seems to matter. The people who do move about are reserved, and though from them there is life, they seem to be going to appointments that are nowhere in time. There are strangers who reach here. We are strangers and half a world from home. Such is our entry into this new world.

Nairobi is an equatorial city so high up that it is hardly tropical. One must descend downward toward Mombasa on the Indian ocean or toward Kisumu which is on Lake Victoria, where it is hot, tropical.

We leave the airplane and we walk until we reach the airport. We get through the immigration process with no difficulty and find an unknown world awaiting us. If things happen as arranged there will be a person here awaiting us, and indeed there is. A man who is the cousin of a friend quietly greets us as we come into the space of the station. He is Edward Antao, an Indian whom we have never met, but whom we had written to. He is a small, quiet man who is well dressed. So quietly has he awaited our presence. As long as we were to remain in Kenya he would always be very kind to us. With gladness we greet him. In darkness we ride away.

The Nairobi night is pleasant. He does not talk much as we ride from the airport to the city. Nairobi is seven miles away. We pass the Mombasa road. Mombasa is three hundred miles down the road on the Indian ocean. It is a town of ocean winds, mango trees, white sand, and women whose gazing eyes penetrate through the black shiny cloth that surrounds their bodies and their beings. It is a town filled with shops.

One day, during a school vacation, we go there. We pass through Machacos and Tsavo and finally reach the coast and the Portuguese and Arabic ruins and the Moslem, Indian, and African streams of life. It is an exotic, tropical, and vastly different place from Nairobi. Mombasa has existed as a coastal town, some say, for thousands of years and has been occupied by the Persians, Arabs, Turks, Portuguese, and finally the British. The British were responsible for moving the life of Kenya inland from Mombasa. It is how Nairobi began, as a commercial center by the Europeans in the beginning of the twentieth century. Mombasa has a rich and varied history but is ancient and existing in previous ages. Nairobi is a place that still seems to be defining and finding itself. It is a crowded African city with shanty towns, crowded buses, wealthy neighborhoods, international hotels, an airport, flowering trees, souvenir shops, a central market, museums, and a national wildlife park. Many Europeans pass through here on their way to game reserves and safari expeditions. Our Indian friend takes us to a hotel in Nairobi where we stay for several days and then we move to another place.

Soon after arriving I begin searching for a teaching job. I interview for a job in Nairobi. A small man in a vast room looks at me in wonder.

I present him my hand, forcing him to rise and to reciprocate my greeting to him. He greets me with seeming suspicion. He seems anxious for me to state my business and he deliberately gives the impression of being a busy person. He knows that I am from some far-away place, and my presence is puzzling to him. I tell him that I want to teach in a school that is not far from Nairobi. I tell him that I have taught in Africa before. He asks a few questions. Of all the things we discuss, what impresses him the most is that I have taught in Nigeria, which is believed to be a rich, powerful, and sophisticated nation.

"How is it in Nigeria?" he wants to know.

I think of little to say about Nigeria and living there, so I only tell that my time there was worthwhile and that my life there was interesting.

"And why aren't you going back there? Why are you in Kenya?"

It is because it would be too hard struggling to settle there with my wife and daughter. We have come here because we know that life is less harsh.

Anyway, there are schools that need teachers he says. He isn't any more specific than that. He gives me an application to fill out and return to him. I take it and leave the office.

Even before we came to Kenya there had been the possibility of work in a small private school some distance from Nairobi. It is a school attended by the poor and others. The third day after arriving in the country we go in search of it. Our Indian friend drives us. He doesn't know exactly how to get there, but he brings a map. It is near Ruiru, which is on the map. The road to Ruiru is good, but from there the tarmac ends and it becomes dirt and dust with but an occasional road sign. We become lost several times, and the only things that sustain the journey are first, that we have the name of the school, and second the Indian's knowledge of Swahili. He is fluent since he was born in Kenya. There are some people whom we meet along the road who know no Swahili and no English. They only speak Kikuyu. We are in Kikuyu country. The countryside is green and richly alive.

It is open country, fresh air. The sky is blue and the white clouds exist like I have never seen them before. Clusters of round mud huts with thatched roofs stand on the hills. Small streams flow and people bathe and wash their clothes. It is a new world to us but to them it is probably the only world they have ever known. They seem used to their lives. Eventually, we find the school. A mud path leads to a small, stone building.

The school is a crude structure that stands alone. Somehow school buildings seem like insects that breed everywhere and in areas as peculiar as the people who pass through them.

It seems as though no one is around but a man does appear. He is European and that is surprising. He is short with gray hair. It seems a hard life for him in this place. There is no sign of running water, no sign of light. No electricity reaches here. He says he is used to living here. He enjoys it. He is the school's headmaster. It is a girl's school. We expected an African woman to be headmistress. She had written us about the school. She is gone, however, and this man has taken her place. He says there is a house for us and that we will love the country here. I realize the richness and the beauty here. He is very enthusiastic about our being here, just as he is about being headmaster and his responsibilities here.

"It is important what we are doing here," he says. "The school may not look like much to you right now, but it is an important place. It's important. If we weren't here there would be two hundred students who wouldn't go to school. They couldn't go. We make it possible for them to learn who otherwise would be unable to. So we need your services. (My wife is a teacher also.)" He has strong feelings about the school. He tells me things I will be teaching, but I have to stop him.

"We won't be coming." I tell him. "It's too remote. We have decided that we are going to be closer to Nairobi."

He is surprised and disappointed and he doesn't want to accept it.

"It is only thirty miles to Nairobi," he says. "There is a short-cut over these hills. You have come here in a roundabout way. You can go to Nairobi once a week, if you have to. Nobody here goes more than that."

But still we are going to stay in a place closer to Nairobi, some place that is less hidden away. We leave him at the school. He does not have a car but an old bicycle that stands outside the small stone building. He seems sad to see us go. We leave the hills.

After a few days, the Kenyan government assigns me to a school near Nairobi. It has a direct access to town. It is a school about twenty miles from Nairobi that hasn't had a mathematics teacher for several years. There are great needs there, I am told. We travel there to speak to the headmaster who is a priest from Ireland. He genuinely wants us there. It all seems possible. The school is an easy ride from Nairobi. The only problem is a house. There is a new place, not yet finished, where we can live. It is surrounded by the African countryside and stands deep inside of Kikuyu country. The men are still working on it. If we do decide to move there it will be ready when we arrive, we are told by the landlord. We agree to move there.

It is a new, enormous stone house. My wife loves a nice house; it is something she has always hoped for. She is never to love this house, though. It is big and cold and more than she can manage alone. The next thing for us to do is to find help to cook, clean, wash, and look after our daughter. There is too much of everything to the house. Time, space, isolation, wind, and cold dominate. How are we to manage? We need help to be able to get through the days here. Things are not easy for us. The Irish headmaster who has already been living the same highland life we are now facing knows the reality of the struggles here. His idea is to hire help from among the local Kikuyus. We agree. Now we must decide whom to hire. The headmaster arranges for interviews for the job to be held at his office in the school. He has a neat, well-kept office. The headmaster is known to run a strict school. Though there are those who disagree with his approach, he has a way with the Kikuyus. The time comes and three people are interested in the job: a young girl, a woman, and an old man. They all have letters of commendation saying that they have served well with previous employers. They all seem fairly comfortable speaking English, which is important. The old man hears English well. He doesn't do a great deal of talking but knows all that is happening. My wife appreciates the attention he gives to things. He has a kind presence. He stands in an old blue sweater, wrinkled gray trousers, and his bare, black feet. He seems wise, unpretentious, and unafraid. He says he can cook. My wife says that we should hire him. We do.

The next day he comes to work. From the very beginning it is evident that he is a peaceful man. His actions are clear and he carries himself with a quiet ease. He knows what to do. There is probably no more important decision my wife is ever to make in Africa than that of hiring Mr. Mungai. He is a fine cook and keeps the house in perfect order. There is so little water and so much that has to be washed and kept clean, but he rigorously conserves and expertly manages the resources that do exist. It is hard bringing up a child in Africa in a scarcity of water.

Mr. Mungai is a master fire maker. There seems such meaning in the fires that are formed from his hands in the order and arrangement of wood. For me, building a fire is still a trial-and-error process that often leads to failure, but none of his actions are forced and they always lead to successful results. Even when he makes errors he knows the proper corrections. I learn from him. He has an untiring nature. He knows Kikuyu, English, and Swahili. Sometimes he teaches me some Swahili and Kikuyu words. He loves to learn. Words fascinate him. My wife often tells him words and he is intrigued with them always. Reading and writing and chaining these words into ideas and statements is complicated and mysterious to him. It seems so hard for him to construct correspondences between these words and the symbols that represent them. Children make him happy. He loves them. He himself has two wives and eight children.

I ask him, "Do you find eight children too many?"

"They can make you angry," he says. "But you don't see me complaining because no man is happy without children."

All of the Africans seem to love children and the more children, the greater the blessing.

Life here is never easy. It is filled with chilling winds, water scarcity, fleas that attack our daughter, perpetual illness, rats in the ceiling, isolation, and cold, lonely walls. We came here to find spring, a place to settle down and live freely, but where we live it is never spring. We are so high above the earth. This land lies thousands of feet above the sea, and we know only cold days and cold nights. The sun is always quiet, never dominating the earth. Spring does not come, only its possibility. We buy firewood by the truckloads from an Indian in a small nearby village. It is mainly acacia and eucalyptus. Firewood is scarce in these parts. Part of the wages we pay Mr. Mungai is in firewood. He prefers it. We pay him one hundred sixty shillings a month and the firewood. We have a car and we drive to Nairobi several times a week sometimes. This journey brings tremendous joy to my wife. Occasionally, Mr. Mungai rides with us. To him it is always a special time.

The school is two miles down the road from the house. It made of stone like many of the other nearby schools. It is unusual also because it lies near the rim of the great rift valley. Some students come from miles away. I am not the first expatriate teacher to be here. There have been other teachers as well as other headmasters. Now there are also two Indian teachers at the school. One of the Indian teachers is leaving soon. He has been told by the Kenyan government that he must leave. He has been teaching for thirteen years in Kenya but has received a quit notice which means that he may no longer teach here. He must find some other work or some other country to teach in. I hear he is going to Zambia.

Schools mean so much to the Africans. Schools mean a chance for them to gain in image and materially, a way to prosper, a way overseas, perhaps to America. They mean the possibility of leaving the bush and a way to the city. So they maintain importance in Africa. Students know other Kenyans who have returned or are living in Europe or America. They desperately want to leave here just as Nigerian students seek Ibadan and Lagos and then a life overseas. So much of their lives rides on hope. They come to learn. Nothing is to deny their efforts and determination. I am paid to teach them. They expect it, demand it.

As to the teachers here, it is interesting to see how they grow old, to witness their seeming powerlessness to do otherwise. Schools as they exist can hold teachers in a state of changelessness. If one is a teacher it is hard knowing what happens to the time. One does not break away, and then one is old. All one can do is to look back. It always seems a looking back job when you work to keep the status quo.

I never feel any particular sorrow or sympathy for the Indians who are being dismissed from their jobs. Many of them do not seem to be people who care for, or show compassion to, the Africans. They have prospered here and slowly they are leaving, being driven away. I love Africa. I lack sympathy for them, perhaps, because I do not know them personally. Their lives are abstractions to me. The two Indians at the school have contrasting characteristics. The older Indian has lived for a long time in Kenya and is the more sophisticated. He resides in Nairobi and daily drives to the school. He is a Sikh and wears a neat beard and a turban, and he always comes dressed in a suit. These remain his symbols of dignity. I only speak to him in passing. I can scarcely understand his words. I make nodding gestures at him, or I say nothing at all when he talks, for his words seem so encoded and disguised that I no longer wonder about translations. How I must sound to him. I always think he talks in secrets because he doesn't want it known where he is going when he leaves the school. (I continue to hear that he is likely to be going to Zambia.) I don't think that anybody at the school feels sad about his leaving. And though he is not hated, he is not loved. But when I look hard at him, deep down I realize his loneliness. After all of his years here he is leaving and he isn't complaining. And the more I consider him the more he bothers me. He has a family. It is hard being jobless and trying to make a living in ones own country when one does want a job, but this man does not have a country, a society to dwell in. (Though we all have the earth.) He says that he has been away from India too long to return. Many of the Indians say this. He is soon to be adrift in the world. It seems such a hard life.

The other Indian at the school is younger, less sophisticated. He is unmarried and lives alone in a nearby country house that lies on a dirt farm road. It is a small stone house protected by a line of trees that overlook the rift valley. He lives a simple life. He wonders about his days in Kenya and if he too will one day be asked to leave. Whereas the Sikh was a fair-skinned man from India's north, George, the younger Indian, is from the south (Kerala) and is black like me. The headmaster takes special interest in him and tries to protect him from the immigration crises when they arise. He helps me also. My wife and daughter and I sometimes visit George in his stone house.

He offers us tea and cookies and exotic dishes that are so hot one cries to be relieved. My wife cannot eat the food. He never has much need to journey to Nairobi and usually spends most of his time in the countryside. One school vacation he traveled back to India. He said that he was going to get married there and did. He came back to Africa with a wife. She was quiet and humble and dedicated to George. She had problems with immigration which prevented her from taking up work. All she could do was remain at the house, but one day father Kelly, the headmaster, came to me and asked if I could take over some of the science classes for a while. I told him that I could. I really don't like teaching science, but I would do it again. I had taught it before in Nigeria. Then there were lectures to be given that tired and discouraged my interest. There were days in Nigeria when I did not lecture. Teaching by walking students through basic skills was just as important as teaching by telling. I like to tell students less and to ask them to teach themselves more.

One day I ask a student, "You have been studying carbon?"

"Yes, sir."

"Well, can you tell me what carbon is?"

Carbon is a material, he tells me. We then consider what a material is. It seems to be a substance with certain characteristics. But must it have any special characteristics?

Indeed, why is anything that exists special? Somehow it all just becomes words. Carbon, he then says is a material that possesses certain chemical and physical properties and he names several of the properties. He names them correctly, but what really is carbon? Does he know? Is it something real to him? Is it an artificial idea?

I ask, "Is carbon a familiar substance to you?"

"It is a compound that I have heard about."

"Why do you say a compound?"

"I don't know."

"What is a compound?"

"A compound is a substance made of elements. Salt and sugar are examples of compounds."

"Then carbon is like salt or sugar?"

"I don't know." But then he remembers that carbon is an element and cannot be like salt or sugar which are compounds.

"Well, tell me this. Is carbon something that one can see or feel? Has anybody ever seen it?"

"I am not certain. I have never considered that question."

Nobody in the class knows.

I light a match, and I tell them the black residue is carbon. I burn a piece of paper and I tell them the black stuff is carbon. I bring charcoal from a box in my house and I tell them that it is carbon. I ask them to touch and to feel it.

"This is carbon," I say to them.

It seems interesting to them that they were holding carbon and that this is what it is. They had already known about it, but had not until now realized it. Carbon, though, is still unexciting. It is dull and inert. It does not do interesting things when they touch it. They want carbon to be something more than it is. Except carbon is carbon and nothing else. One cannot change the facts. Though carbon is the building block of life, and is the stuff of which biological molecules are made, this has small meaning to a student who has not questioned and internalized carbon's properties herself or himself, or thinks about its unique significance on earth. Carbon, when combined with sulfur and potassium nitrate, makes gunpowder, which burns and explodes and may sustain wars and earthly devastation.

What do I learn from our carbon experience? It is to engage ourselves in the common and collective scientific learning of humankind, to question the atomic theory and those things human inquiry and exploration have discovered in the world. I learn, though, that the mind knows and understands what the mind does, not what the world does.

So I would again teach science in Kenya because, with no warning, George is leaving the school. He never complains about his life here, but suddenly he is leaving for Lesotho. He and his wife both have teaching jobs there. They leave and we never hear from them again. I sometimes think about them and their life there. How does Lesotho look? How are the people where they are? I still long to see the places in Africa. There are journeys in Africa that I want us to make. What about a boat ride from Kigoma to Bujumbura? The African teachers at the school are unlike the Indians in many ways. They are all young. They do complain. They don't like their situations and they often tell me their feelings. They seldom talk to the headmaster with whom they do not comfortably converse. They have material drives and they want things. Many study so they can sit for examinations to improve their positions. They all want to improve themselves and change their lives. They all are Kikuyus except for one. There is a Luo from around Lake Victoria. He takes life as it comes, but he is hopeful and active. The Kikuyus are quiet, reserved, hard-working and serious.

While I am at school my wife is sometimes at home, writing letters. Some days she assists me in my work at the school. In the English composition classes there are always countless composition books to be marked. She reads them all and, makes notes in them. She also works in a primary school several days a week in Tigoni, a nearby town. My wife is able to teach at the Tigoni School because the Australian headmaster there learns she is a teacher, and because Mr. Mungai is able to take care of our daughter while my wife is away. Tigoni was once a town of European wealth and still there are Europeans who continue to linger there.

To my wife there is probably nothing more interesting in that town than the Tigoni store. Two Indians run and own the store. To us they are men of stone who operate the store without emotion. They have rich and reliable European customers and every time we see them they just stand there, never speaking or moving unless someone asks them for something. Then they respond with a calculated expenditure of energy. They do not waste motions or words. They know all the items there and where they are if they exist in the store. Their minds quickly process any request and returns information about the item's existence in the store, its availability and its cost. Are we training students in school to operate in such a manner? Are these men true businessmen? Are they not highly organized? Maybe they are as they are because of their schooling or perhaps it a family influence. One of them wears glasses and is tall and thin. The other is of shorter stature and wears a thin mustache. Neither one of them ever rushes. They never do. They never talk unless spoken to, and they never smile. Nothing ever happens in the store. They are so precise in their behavior that they are unreal, unhuman. I don't think there are really any such men at all. They must be spirits of the dead. None of their body cells are ever excited or become restless. They are symbols of life after death in the cold.

How cold it can get in these highlands. How cold. I think about the day when we run out of wood, and there is no fire. I know around us are limited renewable resources. I regard them as important and I don't despoil them. I realize my personal impact on this fragile environment is a hard fact.

Ours is but a house on the road, a life of cold, the quiet sun, dust and stone. I wish life would provide more than it does so as to lessen the burdens my wife must bear. The walls of the house are made of stone and they never become warm. The air within remains chilly. Indeed, the icy air of the Kenyan highlands can overwhelm the body. Certainly it tests her strength. Nothing weakens her more than the cold, not even the loneliness and solitude. The cold is damnably real.

There is the rain. People walk helplessly in it. Small children walk along roads for miles to reach schoolhouses with small dark rooms and rusty leaking roofs. There is one thing beside the children and the cold that my wife remembers: the Kikuyu women. They walk for miles in unhurried barefoot ease with loads crushing their backs and deforming their bodies. There are old Kikuyu women seen along the roads. They cannot stand straight from years of torture to their bodies. In the rain these women work as usual, walk and struggle as they do on other days. They walk steadfastly as the rain beats them mercilessly. And though they endure and live on, hardly do they seem human.

Africa is a land of many stories. The other day in class we read a story from *Flame Trees of Thika*. This is a book written by Elspeth Huxley. She writes of her memories of an African childhood. Her family comes from England as settlers to Kenya at the beginning of the twentieth century. I go to the Nairobi Library and read this book and others she has written. She writes with an unpretentious and insightful view of African life. The story in class is one which a farmer's baby is lost. There is panic and a search. A python snake is found with a great bulge in its stomach. The snake is killed and the excitement of waiting to see what it has swallowed is described. It had been a baby goat that was swallowed. The farmer's baby is later found.

Africa is a land of endless drama. People are drawn to it for its mystery and wonder. Our family's life along the road is usually quiet, but things do happen. One night a carload of strange men stop outside. They say that their car has broken down. We give them water. We are probably as strange to them as they are to us. We never know what is going on with them but they vanish in the night.

One day when I am at work teaching, my wife discovers that our daughter is missing. She shouts for Mr. Mungai.

"Maleka is missing," she tells him. "She is not in the house anywhere. And I don't see her outside."

They both run out of the house in search of her. They have no idea where she has gone. They have no plan as they run in different directions. No one knows how long she has been missing. Mr. Mungai does not know where he should start. He begins to roam the fields. He finds her by the highway. She is standing there, looking at the cows. A ditch prevents her from reaching the road. She is one and a half years old at the time. Margaret, my wife, is seriously disturbed, imagining the things that could have happened to her. She is all right, and she never leaves home again. We always keep our gate closed after this incident.

I stand inside a classroom and outside the window grows Kenya. Green hills with rich growth surround the school. The earth I see outside is vast and magnificent. Its hills prosper with greenness. We are all quietly here in the great rift valley. There hardly seems any awareness of earlier inhabitants who have lived in this valley. Was it a million years ago or just yesterday that our predecessors roamed this same earth? It is due to the greatness of this valley that Africa makes the earth, as interesting as it is. Trees still grow here that have been here before the valley was formed. The rifting brought great force that pushed, pulled and brought violence and change to the previous earth state. The uplifting had come, formed this valley, and it had brought new life to our planet.

Our predecessors lived and learned in this valley that exists beyond our window. We now sit and pursue a studied view of life and nature. All of our knowledge is derivative. We obtain it from elsewhere and not through ourselves. The human purpose in creating schools is to give value to knowledge, but to learn we have to abandon the tradition of accumulated knowledge. Those who value learning sometimes abandon schools and the traditional world, because what is accumulated is continually being destroyed. Learning, then, is being created from the disintegration of knowledge and schools (the traditional world).

There seems little wonder that the Europeans love this land and long to possess it. It is said that no one fights and struggles for bad land. Land that is productive and offers human richness is what transforms some men into selfish beings who dominate others for its possession. And though Kenya is no longer a colony, there are still Europeans dwelling in these hills. They own vast tea estates and large herds of healthy cows, and they sometimes talk of Europe. When they do speak of Europe they refer to its advancements and greatness. But Europe seems more to them than it really is because it lies beyond the seas and is so far away. Deep down they know there is no great life there, there never was. They know as white men they receive great respect and numerous privileges in this country. They are unlikely to leave except with extreme reluctance because they realize their fortune is here, now.

The students here see the European and they respect his ways. Indeed, few of them complain of European intrusion and domination. One finds little strength in their bitterness. European living seems to overwhelm them like it does so many Africans. And it is easy for an African to imitate a European and for his own life to become a collection of imitations. It is true that the African from these parts lives close to the earth and feels a reverence toward it. It is his strength and comfort. The land is the one thing about which he will challenge the white man. His courage is with the earth. Fortunes are made and lives are lost in the pursuit of land possessions, just as in America, a century ago. There was not the treasure as there was in America, the Congo, or South Africa. An African student wishes to go overseas to better himself and says that he will return to this soil. But once there, Africa becomes thousands of miles away, and he forgets this soil. For the first time he has an access to personal success and security. That is why they come to this school.

It is a boy's school of traditional study. Some days I bring games that I obtain or bring with me from the United States. I have a puzzle ring that is given to me by a British student in Tigoni whom I tutor for his math examination. It is an absorbing puzzle. Another puzzle consists of four blocks (cubes) with faces colored in red, green, white, and blue. None of the blocks has the same arrangement of colored faces. The object is to stack them in such a way that all four colors show on each side of the stack. A single block can be placed in twenty four different positions, so a stack of four blocks can be placed in hundreds of thousands of arrangements. The students are overwhelmed at the endless patterns that do not work. It frustrates and mystifies them which challenges their thought and imagination. There is a solution using prime numbers that we use to solve the puzzle. As I inquire into the puzzle I later learn a way to solve this problem which is simple and direct and uses no mathematics. It makes such a seemingly complex problem easily solvable and the solution trivial.

When I study puzzles it tells me why schools still exist and sustain themselves. It is because the solutions, the intrigue, and the discoveries they bring about compel us to communicate our findings to others. In schools we are informed of earthly insights, mystery, and past celebrations. This becomes knowledge to be held on to by many in the schools which makes the schools places of insignificant purpose. They remain as such places because they do not re-invent themselves.

One day I share a picture of the earth, taken from space. It is significant to me what we see and discuss. I did not imagine it so alone, nor had I considered the actuality of it carrying life, wandering in space, and being so exposed in the universe. We know it has life. Who else knows this? It has profound beauty, loneliness, and impermanence.

Probably the most interesting experience I ever share with them was on the road near Mt Kilimanjaro during an encounter with the Masai. Most of the students seldom leave their villages and have never left Kenya or this highlands area. Other places and people always interest them.

The most unexpected event I witness in Kenya begins when I look out a school window. I awake and find the morning warm and pleasant. It is unusual because one becomes so accustomed to cold mornings. I feel fine. It is the last of May. Noon comes, and I notice the day is changing. Dark clouds come over the earth. In the early afternoon the rain comes, not hard but steady. After a while it falls with invariance. Because I am inside and protected I hardly realize that it continues to fall, but it does. Several hours later I look out the classroom window. It is almost dark and evening is arriving as the rain softens the earth. Quietly my eyes discover creatures in the outside air, which is saturated and swarming with life. There are flying white ants with fine thin wings everywhere I can see. There are hundreds of thousands of them, maybe millions, covering the earth. The rain has driven them from the ground. Like snow they fill the air. Their dead bodies stick to the car window as I drive through them. They surround me. I can hardly drive through them for as I move they are there, dying. At last I reach home, passing over fields of the slain. There is no song that comes from the earth. It is covered with their death.

Life in Kenya had been difficult to us as a family. After almost a year there, I tell Fr. Kelly, the headmaster, that we are leaving the school and returning to San Francisco. He, Mr. Mungai, the students and teachers at the school, friends in Tigoni, the nearby towns, and Nairobi are seeing us in our last days here. Fr. Kelly asks us if we will ever return. We do not know.

Our Indian friend drives us to the airport. As we are leaving, others are coming here for the first time. Before them is a unique time on earth. Greatness and wonder is just beyond this airport. The Africans themselves are as diverse as the land of which they are a part. They may belong to a small wandering band or to a highly organized group numbering a million. We had traveled to Lake Victoria, the Indian Ocean, the Mara River, Mt. Kilimanjaro, and the green and fertile earth that surrounded it. All such experiences lay behind us. It is a unique region of the earth here where wildlife exists as one can see nowhere else in the world. We came here thinking we may have stayed longer, hoping our daughter would live a life in a place of unique adventure and unknown wonder. It had not happened. We leave Africa and return to America and the schools there.

There is a new life before us. If we reach San Francisco, will it have changed? Deep down I have the feeling if we do get back there, and spend some time, it will be like we never left. It was like that when I went to sea and came back. I wonder if we'll ever come to Africa again. Years from now we'll wonder if we ever went. The world is only this world at this particular time. We are living now, it is what we all share. There had been hard times in Kenya and good days. There are few material things we are taking with us as we leave here. We appreciated our life while we were here. Just now it is a place we passed through. We came here following our hearts.

CHAPTER 7

East African Road

As a family we travel much on the African road. Probably no journey is more interesting than when we go to Tanzania and Mt. Kilimanjaro. All the days that I ever visit Kilimanjaro are filled with discovery and adventure. The days provide us as outside visitors with insight and vision into another country beyond Kenya. Our journey this time is an unexpected adventure.

We leave town on the main Kenyan road, which would have been but a quiet country road in America. It is a journey we have barely begun but it touches the soul and uplifts the spirit. Not far outside of Nairobi we encounter giraffes gracefully running free and curiously observing us as we enter their world. We have joy in our hearts for the wildlife that is around us. To see these animals so free are immense moments. My wife and I have seen animals locked away in zoos in California. There they are born in captivity. They live a limited existence where they will never be free. In this place we respect their feelings, their interests and their quest to live free. They are our fellow creatures, filled with an intelligence and a zest to live.

We enthusiastically travel among the wildlife and the land around us on the road to the Kenyan-Tanzanian border. We do take an occasional photograph with a camera we had bought from an Indian in Nairobi. He is a clever business man and in the end he sells us a camera and a telephoto lens for almost $200. I never really like taking pictures. I had lived for two years in Nigeria, and I never had a camera and had never even cared about taking photographs. But my wife says that she would like a record of our time in Africa, so we would take occasional pictures of our African life. Our daughter is a year old and does not grasp the significance of these moments. Not yet. Several times we see Masai tribesmen and their herd of cattle. We are forced to stop to allow them space for their herd to cross the road. The Masai are cattle keeping nomads who inhabit this area of Kenya down through northern Tanzania. They believe all cattle rightly belong to them. There is much conversation about them from our Kikuyu friends around Limuru where we stay. They live a more independent and defiant life than that of urban and rural Africans. They sometimes despise permanency and a peaceful life.

We reached the border and go through immigration with no problems. We have our passports and immunization records in order. Kilimanjaro is ten miles inside of the border because of the 1886 treaty between England and Germany. We see Masai nomads at the border and they reveal the absurdity of this imaginary line. It is a chance location held on to, fought for, and sustained by generations of persons. To the Masai tribesmen it is a meaningless and worthless boundary. They possess no documents and live in a world apart from all other travelers. They move from country to country without regard to any imaginary boundary that separates people and nations. But just as the Masai find this practice meaningless, others find some of the Masai practices absurd and unacceptable. One example is the living on blood from their cattle. And many travelers who come upon the Masai say that they smell and do not cleanse their bodies. The Masai say that the others (Europeans and other Africans) smell. They cannot understand the practice of using soap and perfume on one's skin. These odors alienate them.

We are in Tanzania moving in a world of vast, flat plains, then mountain towns and mountain roads. We are excited about being here and seeing the world of human origin. Though I am not moved by history and others' knowledge of the world, I do feel that where we are is a profound place. Everything matters! We see stalks of sisal and a baobab tree. Even though the animals here are multitudinous, I know that each one is also a unique, valuable creature.

We are excited about being here in places we have never been nor imagined. Skills that humankind once used to kill and to struggle for survival are now being used to preserve life and its variety and beauty. We are like many others who have traveled hundreds and thousands of miles who reach here.

We have yet to see Mount Kilimanjaro. Though the mountain is massive, the clouds make it lie in mystery and obscurity. We drive through this land where life seems to have wandered and roamed for millions of years, maybe forever. Up and down the roads people come and go. They climb the mountain, guide others, photograph the wildlife, camp along the rivers, and visit the marketplaces.

We travel on, knowing that the mountain surrounds our world as we travel to Moshi, Arusha, the game reserves, and other villages and places. We know that we can travel for days and years and that there will still be more to see. When I had first lived in Africa in Nigeria and had visited here for the first time, I had seen Kilimanjaro from deep within Kenya. It was spectacular, unexpected, mysterious. It held us. My wife is disappointed that the mountain is always hidden. We snap occasional photographs of ostriches, elephants, wildebeest, zebras, gazelles, and a Masai warrior whom we had given a shilling for a photograph. We drive into places we have never seen, imagined, or would likely ever see again.

On the road one afternoon the peak of Kilimanjaro appears. My wife discovers it. We get out of the car and see it for the fleeting moment it is there. We appreciate the moment of light from the mountain that is reflected to us. We move on, traveling on the road back to Kenya. The way of life of the Africans here is much like that of Africans elsewhere. They work on their farms, build houses, walk to towns, and attend ceremonies. I suppose in many ways the Masai are like nomads in other places. The Fulani in West Africa also live off of their livestock and move them from place to place. As we drive back to Kenya I decide to stop for a final photograph along the Tanzanian road. As I am about to leave, two young Masai children with their cattle pose for a picture. I am walking back to the car when they are joined by two other Masai. They are moran warriors with their spears and tribal dress. They seem disturbed. They do not want me to return to the car. At first I am confused but they indicate that they wanted their pictures taken. I agree. They are very cooperative and stand proudly along the road as I photograph them. When I take several pictures and am going back to the car, they prevent me from returning. They want to be paid. I had heard of problems with photographs in East Africa. I did not know how serious a problem it would be. Reluctantly I give them ten shillings. They want more. I think that perhaps they have been photographed before and they must have received considerably more for their photographs. I am unwilling to pay more. I refuse. They are annoyed and want to take the camera that is strapped around my neck. I resist and made it clear that I am not giving it up. They are just as determined as I am. They take the camera case and find a lens cover. I try to get it back but am unsuccessful. I really do not know how to deal with this situation. I know that I stand alone on the vastness of the Tanzanian plains. My wife and daughter are in the car. We are the only ones out here. I know in their minds that they feel that they are right in asking for what is a fair price to them. I do not agree, and I am not giving one shilling more. They continue to be physical. They try to look into the car, but my wife has closed the windows and locked the doors. It seems impossible for me to physically handle the situation. I do not know what I am to do. They are adamant that they will take the camera if they do not receive more money. It all hardly seems real to me. How had I gotten involved in such a dilemma? What would happen to my wife and daughter? I had heard and had read stories of the Masai and their bravery and courage. They are proud and self-reliant people who have little regard for outsiders. A warrior could show no fear of death. It is not uncommon for him to kill a lion with a spear in defense of the herd. I had read about a European who had a cow stolen by a Masai and had gone into the Masai herd to retrieve it. The youth and the European argued for some time, and the youth pleaded with him to take several other cows but to leave that one. The European took the cow anyway. The Masai youth speared him to death. It was said that they later hanged the Masai. The photograph is not as important to them as their cattle. It is that they have freely given a part of their soul and insist on collecting for it. I refuse to give in. In my mind stands the possible deadly force of the spear. God, what would happen to my wife and daughter! It seems like the hardest and worst time I have ever been in. How had I gotten us into this seemingly hopeless circumstance?

From nowhere a car drives up. It is so unbelievable, unanticipated. It is filled with Europeans. I do not know what they are asking, but they have gotten their attention. I manage to get back to the car. They no longer seem concerned about our dispute. The ordeal had seemed long and intense. I had lost the lens cover. I would never get it back. When I reach the car and drive off my wife and daughter never realized that there had been any problem or danger. She had closed the car window because she thought they were just being curious and inquisitive. We drove back to the border and then to Kenya and our home there.

This incident happened on a Kilimanjaro road. Unexpected encounters on the African roads are significant events in my life. From each incident I am able to make another journey. And just as I returned to Africa from the Nigerian road tragedy, I would one day also come back to Kilimanjaro.

San Francisco

CHAPTER 8

The Girl on the Road

What interests me about making the transition from Africa to urban America is the vitality of learning that is so absent with black students in San Francisco. At Mission High School occasionally there are black students who are inspired to learn. These few are fascinated with the possibilities that schooling experiences provide and they are sometimes extraordinary. I later learn from a high school study in San Francisco what different students expect from school. The black students' responses showed they expected the least. They were not highly interested in getting "A's" and "B's" in school. They were satisfied with a "C" and could live with a "D". This was what the San Francisco black students accepted for themselves. Many adults accepted the same system as the students did. A friend of mine from India who taught in both Kenya and San Francisco commented that the weakness of the American system was that a weak student got away with a weak teacher. They supported each other.

My wife was reared in Chillicothe, Ohio. When she attended school in the 1950's it was a segregated city and black students had few opportunities to be supported in receiving an education that most of the white students had available to them. She had to achieve the same education on her own for the most part. This is not the case in San Francisco for the black students I work with. They lack a mission to learn at a serious level. There is a need to transcend misinformation and inaccurate assumptions that continue to limit us. For most black students it is a case of moving through schools with the schools having no effect on them.

Some students in the school want A's and nothing less and they seek the best education the school can provide them. I have had such students over the years at Mission High School. My last year there I had my most interesting class of such students.

During this year at Mission High School, I have an advanced mathematics class with sixteen students. Fifteen are Chinese and one is Vietnamese. Several students can hardly speak English. From the first day of class I discover they have great energy and high enthusiasm for the study of mathematics. The responses to problems are varied and idiosyncratic, as the students are able to solve many problems in their own way. Few, though, are able to talk about and discuss why they pursue the paths they do. They present strange and new systems that work. I know we are immersed in new ideas, terms, and concepts. We learn new theorems, prove them, and discuss alternative approaches and solutions. The best student in the class is the Vietnamese student. He receives the highest grades on the examinations but never competes against the other students. He is so fascinated by the subject of mathematics that he wants to learn and to understand all problems in depth. He is also trilingual, speaking English, French, and Vietnamese. (His father had been a solider in the Vietnam war.) He is quiet and highly focused. Though there is great talent in the class no one ever receives higher scores than he does. Indeed most of the Chinese students have study groups and they work hard supporting each other, but the Vietnamese student is maybe the best mathematics student with whom I had ever worked.

The class is unusual. The students are rarely absent and everyone does his or her homework always. Out of my ten years at the school I never had a class that so transcended the school. The only other group of students who perform as profoundly as these students is the chess team. (I am the sponsor of the chess team and they excel as a team, and play as well as any school in the city. Students from all social and ethnic groups are on the team and their play is remarkable.)

There were similarities between the math class and the chess team. The students are personally competent and master the fundamentals of systems and of organizing. They are able to learn from others, and as important, they were able to teach themselves. They are challenged by difficult problems. They were capable of learning and performing as a team. Learning is more important than the school or the organization. No student in the mathematics class receives a score of less than 700 on the math section of the Scholastic Aptitude Test. The Vietnamese student receives a perfect score of 800 and is the first student in the school ever to do so.

What happens to them when they graduate and move on? I lose almost all contact because I too leave for another school assignment, and I only occasionally encounter them. The Vietnamese student, Bao Truong, does visit me the next year. He is studying at the University of California at Berkeley. In his visit to me, he tells me that he did not receive an "A" in his university calculus class but an "A+".

The students in the class are natural inquirers connecting and making sense of the things and ideas they question. These students, just like humankind from its beginning journey and exploration, use a fundamental approach to observe, investigate, and probe to understand the world. This has always been the primary way to learn.

*   *   *

Each morning I walk to school. I have walked five miles to school each day since we returned from Kenya. This is my final day of teaching at Mission High School. Most days are uneventful, but I remember this morning because as I walk along I see a girl in a car, who is trying to talk to me. I wonder what is it she is intent on saying. I see her stop. She wants to know how to reach Mountain View, a town south of San

Francisco. I know the place. I know it exactly. How does she get there from here, from this very place? I give her directions. She is patient, quiet, and grateful that I am helping her. I construct a path that seems clear. She expresses appreciation for my stopping to talk to her and help her find her way. We both move through the brief encounter. It is not until after she has gone that it occurs to me that I did not clearly understand the entire journey. It was a true path that did lead to the town but she will not be able to get there from my directions. She could reach the town from the path but she could not get on to the highway south from the way I just told her. I wanted to run and to tell her what happened. Where is she now? What is she thinking?

I reach the school. Many poor and oppressed students live in the community and attend the school. Each day I find there is learning, and there is darkness. The absence of learning causes darkness and conflict. Those of us who are not learning bring about disorder. There are good students here who are not learning. They memorize knowledge and hold onto rules and seemingly important ideas. There are teachers here who also add to the disorder because we are teaching and not learning. We use the knowledge we are comfortable with and we invent time to organize our monotonous thoughts into seemingly clear ways. We insist on teaching the way we wish to teach and don't concern ourselves with what one is learning. We expect specific outcomes but a serious teacher is creative and does not let curiosity and the spirit of learning die. I know that students should find and pursue the things that interest them, so ultimately they are their own teachers.

A student at this school who had taught himself a great deal about computers and how people learn, told me, "Don't give them the answers! Make them come to you. Let them generate their own interest in a problem."

I did. I tried what he told me. It has made me a better teacher.

To probe deeply into the world means leaving behind what we already know. Nothing is more important than what we discover for ourselves.

I am learning things from other teachers also. A friend shared a Nigerian proverb with me that states, **the person who is being carried does not realize how far the village is.** We learn on our own by questioning authority and doubting tradition.

A child in a classroom encounters conflicts and is not free when routine dictates his actions and imprisons his existence. But he wishes to be free. Are we attuned to each student in the classroom, the school, society, and the world at large, and do we expect the best from each person?

There is a black student who sits against the wall. He is both like and unlike other students. He is left-handed and he writes a lot when he wishes to work. He writes the things he gathers from the known world. He writes the facts he has already mastered and can remember. Sometimes he is unable to remember clearly, and I must attempt to clarify what his mind is grasping to materialize. He is a consistent student at doing the class work. In his day-to-day work he does not learn much new. He doesn't like being disturbed. He is protected by the familiar where security for his mind lies. He persists in holding on to a mental and social image of himself that can lead to a state of changelessness. I observe him and the others, but I make no attempt to give advice or pass judgment. Some days he brings a radio to class. Though I do not allow it to be used he yearns to play it softly. He seems conditioned to hear certain songs.

In a lot of ways students are the same. They lead uneventful lives at school and for many their whole lives revolve around being with their friends. This student is just like everybody else in many ways. Indeed, he tries to be like others. But his eyes are different. They have a yellow color. They had always seemed so ordinary until I am told by his counselor that he is sick with sickle cell anemia, and it has been diagnosed as incurable. Now I notice his eyes, and I see them seeing things. He never talks about them. He doesn't discuss himself in any of his conversations. He can die at any time, or he can live for many more years, I am told. I disallow a death dominated image of him to exist. What is important is how I see and understand him now in the absence of diagnosis, opinion, and history.

"Why aren't you working the problems?"

"They are too easy. I already know how to do them. I just don't know how to do them the way you are talking about."

"I am giving you something to think about so you can do these problems three or four ways. I'm talking about doing a problem more than once but in different ways." It is difficult for him to hear what I am saying because he is strongly interested in just getting problems correct, and I am talking to him about his thinking in more depth about them.

"I already know how to get the answer one way. Why should I learn something new just to get the same answer? I want to learn some other kinds of problems, not these. You are the teacher."

"But you know what you have to do to learn something new?"

"Yeah, you could tell me something new that I don't know. That's how."

"It's important for you to know that you can do these problems in other ways, new ways, on your own. And sometimes no one else is there to show you or lead you along."

"But you know I already know how to do these problems. You know that."

"Yes, but what you know are the rules that help you get the answers in just one way. If you really comprehend…"

"What does comprehend mean?"

"It means to completely understand the meaning of something. Sometimes its comes from making our own mistakes and sometimes making our own rules. It is a way to learn and understand things and to be our own teacher."

"You know I don't have time to do that. I want you to tell me the rules and I do the problems. I just like doing the problems, that's all."

He does like doing problems, sometimes never tiring. He learns things by rote, but often memory is not enough. He is energetic, and I know he is capable of moving to another state of thinking and understanding. He is not passive but unable to begin, to step into the problem. He never gets going. He does not accept viewing the same problem in a different way as new, or seeing it more critically, as important. I do not give him what he asks. But I know when I tell him and teach him certain things, that I am keeping him from inventing them himself. We both have our own view of the situation. He is asking from me that I allow him to learn something new and interesting. I see myself asking that there be an understanding of the world and not a fight for one's position.

"Let me do these tomorrow then," he says.

"Doing them tomorrow may be like doing them next year, or never. You are here now."

"What do you mean doing them tomorrow is like doing them next year?"

"You might not be here tomorrow."

"Oh, I'll be here tomorrow. You know I'll be here."

He probably would be. He likes being here with other students, but probably being here is not being here and besides, tomorrow has no existence outside of our mind. Tomorrow is a habit.

The bell rings and the students rise to leave.

"I'll see you tomorrow," he says.

I do not want to be dishonest with him. I cannot expect his learning to occur in any specific way. There are things about his life that fascinate me more than his acquisition of new material. It is important to me that he comprehends things and that he seeks a good education and a worthwhile life, rather than good test scores, a good report card, or a need to impress his friends. I am not here to give him knowledge, but to see him learn through serious ideas and questions and not living a trivial life. It is important to me that he makes his own meaning from the problems he works on and that he goes beyond the routine. I know he is capable of learning mathematics at a deeper level and is not yet able to observe that mathematical power is distinct from the power of authority or coercion. We do not learn through isolated skills and knowledge passed on by an outside agent (the teacher) to a passive and receiving mind but from our own inner quest. It is important for him to question his own understanding of what he is doing. Why? The sorrow and confusion that exists within us, and therefore in the world, must be dealt with through our own self-understanding.

One day someone broke a window in a door to the room. The space was first covered with paper and then later with wood. I never knew who broke it or why. After a while I no longer thought about it.

I am offered a position as an administrator at another high school. On this day I am leaving and the student with the sickle cell anemia quietly says, "You know the broken glass in the door? I broke it."

I don't comment. I want him to continue.

"I didn't mean to. It was an accident."

"But when I asked who did it you said you didn't know. You lied.

Why were you afraid? You seemed to be telling the truth. I believed everything you said."

"I didn't mean to break it. I just touched it, and it seemed to fall apart. I didn't know what to do. I just said what came to me."

I didn't say anything else about it. I believed him when he lied to me, and I believe him now when he says it was an accident. It was a mistake. I can understand a mistake. Just this morning I met a girl on the road and mistakenly told her something I didn't mean to. I wonder where she is. What is she thinking?

CHAPTER 9

Conversations

Numerous bodies are adrift in cold black space, reflecting light. There are beings who realize they exist and who wonder if they are inhabited. Were they worlds that were ever alive? What is their history? What is history? Is it anything at all? Is not space, matter, time, and thought but a single past event?

Today I have an unexpected conversation with my daughter as we walk along. She is in elementary school. I talk to her of the things that come to her mind and interest her.

Why do the leaves move?" she asks.

The question reminds me of something I have heard. It is that young children believe that the sun follows them as they walk, and that the wind and the sea are alive. Everything that moves is alive.

"The leaves move because of the wind."

"But where does the wind come from?"

"Do you remember seeing a river?" I ask.

She says she remembers.

"Well, where the river begins that's where the wind begins."

She does not inquire further. Perhaps that is just as well because a thing is not the words that explain it. Still I love for her to explore her curiosities. She must have a hundred thoughts. She must. A strange question occurs to me as I see the trees, the grass, other planetary organisms, the rocks and other substances. Are they there? I wonder. Are these existences fact? Everything that enters the mind lives in a slightly different world of time. It comes to me that I am only aware of that which has already happened. My mind is filled with images of a world that no longer exists and never was, except in a vanished past. What is the source of these images. Are they not like the wind?

"Where does God come from?" she asks.

"God is like the wind."

"Yeah, but who makes God?"

"Who makes anything? If something makes God then who makes that thing?"

She doesn't know, and realizes it.

"We create our own world by our thoughts," I tell her.

I look around and consider the cause of life, motion, order, and knowledge in the universe. The cause of these concerns the cause of causes. What is the cause of causes? What is the beginning of beginnings? Isn't it thought? Thought struggles to sustain itself. Where does thought come from? Another thought. Thought is always looking for reasons and these can be an illusion. The things that we ourselves observe that are outside of thought are the actual things in the world.

My daughter loves going to school. She loves learning, playing, and being with others. She accepts what she is told, and she accepts the school as it is and does not question it. What is a school? It is a cage that holds children. When they enter and study about nature and the trees and the wind, their freedom ceases. The freedom they study and think and talk and read about is only in symbols. Freedom becomes symbolic and no longer literal. A school is a copying machine. Why are we so conditioned about what we do in a school? Knowledge in a school is encoded in specialized and synthesized symbols. These are not interesting to all children. Why must we convince them of their importance? A school crowds time and closes in on the mind. A school has rules, depends on a system. It trivializes life. It wants to process and to control children. All of our invented rules are mechanical and are imposed from the outside. Being mechanical, they are dead. This machinery of society and government never brings freedom. It is not alive. It searches for pain.

My daughter wonders about the sun.

"Is the sun like the moon?" she asks.

I don't know what she means.

"The moon goes around us. Does the sun go around us also?

"The moon moves around our planet and our planet moves around the sun."

But who says this?

The sun and the moon are bodies spinning in space, communicating to us. We understand them because we observe them as they spin.

"But why is the sky blue?"

"It is because of how light is scattered."

"Where does light come from?"

"It comes from the sun and the stars."

"Does the sunlight make the ocean blue? Does it make colors in the rainbow?"

"Without sunlight there would be no blue sea, no rainbow."

"Is the color really in the light or is it in the water?" she asks.

"You know what I feel? I feel that the color is in us. We make the color in our mind," I tell her.

"What about smoke?" she asks. "What is it?"

"It is a gas," I say.

"Can you see a gas?"

"What you see are the particles in the gas, like the small raindrops in the air when you see a rainbow."

"But what are the particles in smoke?"

"Ashes and dust from the fire that is burning."

I am glad she asks me that. I realize one cannot see anything unless it is reflecting light. The ash and the dust of smoke are but particles reflecting light and communicating that things are there. I am also glad she asks me about the smoke because I know she is not asking just to ask. She longs to know things just as we long to know of shining bodies of reflected light that are adrift in cold black space. Objects in space exist to us because they reflect something. If a child or other individual is not held back by education, religion, or prejudice, he or she begins to inquire into the nature of reality and discovers a profound world.

CHAPTER 10

Conflict and Learning

After teaching mathematics, I become a high school principal. Several people think that I can provide leadership to others. I am both grateful for and excited by the opportunity to contribute in a new way to the struggles of youth. Every day when I return home my wife and daughter await the news of the day. They are always curious about the school and the things that go on there. I tell them stories of mystery, assault, struggle, injury, perseverance, joy, vandalism, and learning. Each day is created as I enter the school and face the new adventures. Its ever-changing events compel me to become absorbed in its life.

I had never thought about being a principal. I learn from others it can take years just to become aware of what it means to impact an entire organization. Sometimes we never learn. It can be a hard task learning as an organization. Though it is hard and complex and unpredictable, I accept it for what it is. I completely absorb myself in this new life. Nobody cares about the school more than I do. I understand that to impact upon an organization I must do so in a spirit of physical and mental balance. That is my mission. I know also that is as important for an organization to be in such a state as it is for an individual.

The first year brings challenge and misfortune. Though I have been a teacher for ten years, I learn much. The year starts with a teacher's strike. I am so determined that the school performs as an organization that I am untroubled by the strike. I am driven to have a school where we begin learning and keep it alive. I came having discovered the power of the computer and the technological revolution. There is a student who is profoundly creative and able with the computer and he helps us design, organize, and schedule programs that make the school a viable place. We are hardly concerned about the striking teachers. We are too absorbed in making the school work. The strike makes us rethink the school and modify the courses. It seems as though we can continue to discover new things, but the strike ends. The teachers return. I am not overly excited because some of the striking teachers have done some harsh things to other people. They slashed the tires of a parent who visited the school; they fought with the police, threatened and intimidated new teachers. The school survived and is now ready to move in a new direction.

The school year begins.

One day in January it rains. When the rain ends the entire school will be changed forever. I stand noticing the rain from the school window. From there one can see the hills, the sea, the gray sky, and the still, white fog. There are also the people, the cars, the buildings, and the freeways which compose the urban life of San Francisco. The city of Oakland is visible across the bay. I think that even in this human-made world there is beauty and stillness in the early morning. Technology has abundant significance as life renews itself. How quietly do all things exist in this rain. It seems unusual that it is raining this hard in San Francisco. It seems like West Africa. The weather report says that this is part of a storm that has just left Hawaii. It would likely be a quiet school day.

I enjoy the rain. It cleans the city, gives life to the earth. How quickly it falls and vanishes. By noon it is through. The earth is soft and wet. Shortly after noon I am summoned to the front of the school. An assistant principal comes and tells me that someone has been shot. I rush out and I find a student lying on the ground. He is still breathing. Blood is flowing from a wound on the side of his head. I do not recognize him. He is unconscious and is being given first aid.

Several students stand around the body. Nobody wants him to die. The ambulance comes and by now more people have gathered. More oxygen is given to the student. It does not take long for a television crew to arrive. Cameras are there. The police come.

The student is put into the ambulance and is taken to San Francisco General Hospital. He dies the next morning. An outsider came, shot him in the head, and is driven away in a car. It is as difficult a situation as I have ever had to deal with in my life. It is hard to believe that it is going on. The experience is one that shocks everyone in the school.

The shooting incident results during a fight in front of the school between Filipino and Latino students. Many people spoke of retaliation against those responsible. The victim is a Latino youth. The mother of the victim pleads that there be no revenge or retaliation for she does not wish any other mother to have to endure the same deep sorrow that she experienced. The victim's father, who exhibited calmness and strength, seeks justice and not revenge. Later a youth who did not attend any school confessed to the shooting. He had only recently arrived in the United States from the Philippines.

The death is a traumatizing and paralyzing fact and is difficult to accept. How hard it is to prevent the mind from wandering back in time, to consider how events could have been different. Indeed, the most difficult thing is to accept this situation as one that actually happened. Things are not different. I am not different. The nature of life reveals itself in a time such as this. I know what happened changed things forever. Still what is actually happening on earth now seems unclear and questionable to me.

Nothing comes more unexpectedly than a letter I receive from a teacher. It is short and clearly written, a resignation. I wait before responding to the letter to see if it is written with total commitment. It is. In the letter the teacher expresses that those in power to solve existing school problems always act after the fact. The feeling of the teacher is that a person is not a student unless he or she attends classes. The student who was killed was enrolled in a class of this teacher. He describes him as a typical and chronic cutter. From his experience at various schools he feels that large numbers of truants exist and violence and drugs have been, and still are, commonplace. He states his frustration and helplessness in contributing to a violent system that continues to deteriorate. He feels that the world changes when you yourself change; therefore he is leaving. The teacher is a genuine friend of mine. Suddenly, he decides to leave the school and quietly departs. Sadly, I respond to his letter.

It now seems to be a fact that you are leaving, Certainly I wish that good things come to you. I understand your deep concern for the tragedy of the student who was killed, as you perceived it. To me it has been a devastating and traumatizing occurrence. Because of it I know I shall never be the same.

Society and the world can change. They change when we change. (Unfortunately, most of our changes are limited and superficial.) The students themselves must also change. Learning and school have to be of meaning to them. When learning occurs there is no violence. We then have no images of ourselves and cannot be hurt. The school will miss you.

It is true that there are students who seldom attend class for much of their school life because school is not interesting to them, for them, the challenge is not in the classroom. What drives them? Is it fear of failure in class? Is it their self-image that must be maintained? Is it ignorance? Is it insight or intelligence? Is it known?

Certainly they are not born in the halls, in the parks, or on the streets. (Neither are they born in the classroom.) They remain outside the classroom because of an inability to change. In their own way they want to live interesting lives, but they are frozen in time. Their life is composed of habit and sameness. It is much like the habit of those who are obsessed with attending class or those who authoritatively present knowledge.

A school is a place that is largely maintained through conformity and darkness. Students are not free because they bring a heavy burden of the past with them. They seldom question their traditions and attitudes. They must make sense out of their own circumstances. Unexpected mistakes and failures that occur in their lives are only mistakes and failure at that time, that moment. But they live with these fears and past failures, expect failure, and when it happens it is seen as a lack of ability so they make no effort to persevere. They are not challenged to go on alone because they see no personal meaning in doing so and there is no person or reason to encourage them to explore other possibilities.

Unanticipated incidents continuously happen in the school. Two students are badly beaten and are sitting in the nurse's office. The nurse is absent. A teacher is treating the students. I ask them what happened. Their English is imperfect. They tell me what happened. They seem simple and accurate in their descriptions. I can follow their words. They were walking down the hall. Another student approached them. They do not know how upset he is. They do not understand English very well. The student who is talking to them is very angry and wants to know who they are and what they plan to do. He is certain that they were involved in an incident in the cafeteria. Even though they tell him they don't understand what he is talking about, he does not trust them. He is determined that they are looking for trouble. They are not. They are then beaten by this student.

One student's face is beaten without mercy. Blood has coagulated around his nose. His forehead is bruised and a laceration to the skin is inflicted. The other student is not so severely bruised. He sits on the bed. I leave them. I am told that an ambulance has been called.

I visit the student who inflicted the pain. He sits quietly. He is strong and solidly built. He tells me why he committed the devastating act I had just seen. He had suspected the two students were part of a fight that he had been involved with in the cafeteria. He had questioned them, and he didn't like their response. He felt that they were lying to him so he attacked them, viciously decimated one of their faces.

All is quiet now. He denies nothing and awaits any action he must face. He appears unafraid. A policeman comes, which does not seem to bother him at all. He is not bothered when told that he can no longer attend the school. He is uneasy though, when questioned about his parents and his past. He came from Southern California and suddenly he seems on his own and does not reveal his family situation. He admits he has been on the run from the police before coming to the school. He is told that the students he attacked were innocent and had nothing to do with the cafeteria. It is two other students who are presently sitting down the hall in another office. He felt no remorse. A policeman is going to carry him to juvenile hall, where waits a multitude of alienated youth. He leaves with no complaint, no resistance. He is too hardened to look back. His act shows the school that violence can occur anywhere to anyone. It demonstrates that school rules and policies do not protect students from being hurt and injured because of those who do not recognize this system. We learn things from harsh and, sometimes, painful lessons. Removing the student from the school does not make it less violent. Students daily enroll in the school and transfer out. What do they bring and take away? Conflict is within us. When an individual is in conflict it inevitably creates disorder and sometimes violence in the outside world.

Public schools are places that are supposed to exclude no student or set up barriers for any individual. In our schools we are unable to build fences and gates high enough to eliminate fear, but when students are learning there is no violence, no fear.

*   *   *

One day I receive a call from jail. It is from a member of the school staff (a security aide) who has been taken there because of an incident that occurred at the school. He asks me to hear his side of the story and wants me to bail him out of jail. This is not the first time he has been in trouble, but there will be no more chances for him in the school. People had taken chances on me before in situations just as I had with him, but this time he is going to lose his job. I would be willing to help him get out of jail though. I am serious about that because there are more than a million blacks in jail, and it is important I do what things I can to mitigate this fact.

On the previous day this person had broken up a fight between a group of students. He injured his arm in the incident and was sent to receive medical attention. He then returns with his wrist in a cast. It is broken. He comes to school to inform me that he will have to be out of school for a while. He leaves.

Early in the afternoon I am told that someone has a rifle out behind the school. I ask for specific details as to who saw the gun and who reported the incident, but do not receive any clear information. It is frequently this way in reports involving guns and firearms. Of all the reports on firearms that are supposedly seen, I have personally only observed one. I go to the back of the school. It seems quiet. The security aide is entering the building, and I approach him and ask if he knows anything about a rifle. He surprises me when he responds that there is no gun on him or inside his car, and I should check. I do check and find nothing. A witness comes forth and said that it is in the trunk of the car. The police had been called. They arrive to search the trunk of the car and find a gun. The security aide is taken away by the police, protesting that he had been unable to present his side of the story.

What occurred was that he drove to the back gate of the school, just off the campus, and observed a group of people who did not attend the school in a drug transaction. He asked them to leave. They argued. The security aide then went and got his gun and was threatening this group until another school staff member quieted him down and convinced him to leave and to drop the matter.

The security aide is usually a conscientious and hard working person, but the incident he was involved in with the gun could not be allowed to occur again and thus he was immediately suspended from the school and then dismissed. He was told that he would not be allowed to work around students in a school again. Even though the gun was broken and was not capable of being fired he lost his job. How quickly his life changed. How he swore and threatened what he would do if he lost his job, but he was gone. He had to go. Not long after he was dismissed, he was shot to death in a neighborhood fight one night on Third Street.

Violence and conflict remain in a school because they are carried with us from the past. Last year there was a teacher's strike and numerous violent acts were carried out by teachers. When teachers and school staff can be as violent as students how ordered is a school? Is society?

Certainly, violence is beyond the school. It is in the neighborhood where we live. It is usually a quiet street in San Francisco where my daughter, wife, and I live. The life of the fog and the nearby park dominate many of our days. At the corner stands a store, Roxies. An attempted robbery occurred one day in which a lady was held up at gun-point. The owner of the store realized her predicament, brought out a gun and forced the robber from the car until the nearby police came. How many crimes had the robber been in before? I had heard it was not his first. How many incidents had the student who had assaulted the two students, and who was dismissed from the school, already been involved in and how much of his past did he carry with him?

Though each conflict is new, many are resolved in a superficial way. Fear, intimidation, and violence are used to solve a problem between individuals or between groups or nations. Those who are acting to destroy and strike against others only see life in a superficial way. They are capable of understanding only what their minds seem to be seeing at the time. They do not see deeply. They therefore use violence as a permanent solution to a transitory problem.

Across the park from our house is a police station, which is on a quiet street where no one lives. I never think about the street or the station or the police who work there until one day in Roxies, the corner store, I hear a man talking about the street that goes through the park and how it got its name from a shooting that took place. It then becomes a fascinating place to me. I visit it, talk to the police there, and I read about the place. When I visit the station I find it smaller inside than I thought it would be. Inside is a bulletproof window, protecting all who work there, and three walls of brick. The street is named after a police sergeant who worked in this station. It all had happened one night.

Shots rang out from the building. The sergeant had been killed. Some people in the neighborhood still remember the night. The man who lives next door remembers hearing the shots. A prisoner is mysteriously killed in San Quentin, a nearby prison, which causes unrest and anger in the outside world. Death and violence occur and people come and bring devastation and destruction to this very street in the park. They come to this station.

A girl comes first. She is young, in her twenties. She files a false report. She comes to the station to study its details. She is casing the building. It is night and she comes in and says that her purse is stolen. She is wearing a wig and she gives two addresses, one in San Francisco and another in Sacramento, seventy miles away. The sergeant is standing in a cubicle beside the window. The woman's companion enters the building and shots are fired throughout the station. The sergeant is hit in the upper chest and his entire chest is blown out. Five or ten blasts are shot. His last words are "help me". Another policeman is injured as is a female clerk. She folds herself into a space beside a cabinet. With two bullets in her now broken arm she sends a message for help. The sergeant is the only one who dies. The killers enter the freeway behind the station and drive away. They have never been found. My next door neighbor says that they may be in jail or dead. They may have committed other crimes. Where are they and what are they doing?

The Takeover

It is about 11:00 am on Wednesday, May 15, 1996, when I go to our neighborhood bank to cancel the account of my lost bank book. I have been coming to this bank for almost twenty years, but it strikes me as unusual that no customer is in line to see a teller. I can hardly remember such a time. I go to one of the side desks. Three bank clerks are working. I go to the middle desk. I am welcomed and state my problem and the clerk, a young Filipina woman, is notably competent and pleasant. She tells me how simple and routine it is to cancel the old account and open a new one. The manager of the bank is at the next desk in the nearby corner. She gets up and says she is leaving the building, and it seems as though the woman working with me is now in charge. The manager leaves.

I am answering the questions that I am asked by the clerk until suddenly there is an interruption. I hear a loud noise and I look around. Three men in ski masks with guns storm into the bank. One man yells, "Get down, this is a robbery," while he brandishes a handgun. One man remains at the door and holds two customers at gunpoint while the other two vault over the counter and start emptying cashiers' drawers into a bag. The world stops for a moment. It is dead serious. There is a guy with a gun who sounds crazy. He tells us this is a robbery and to get down. He knocks several people down. An elderly white man in a seat behind me is knocked to the floor. I move without thought to the floor. I am unable to see the detail of what is happening but I know the other robbers have jumped over the counter and are busy taking as much money as they can from the clerks. The man at the door with the gun is shouting "Time, Time, Time...Every moment hangs in uncertainty. Would the police come? Would they be shot? Would we be killed? Would there be any hostages? Were they getting any money? Will they be annoyed if they are unable to get a large sum of money? A thousand questions pass through me. The man with the gun never rests and is never quiet. He seems capable of killing everyone in the bank. He is on that edge and impossible to predict. "Time, Time, Time...," his voice deliberately pounds out the pattern that keeps him wound up for death and destruction. Each tortured moment is a battle. They leave. It's over.

The Aftershock

The whole ordeal seems to last forty-five seconds to a minute. I cannot tell. They are quick and efficient. After they leave we all collectively breathe freely again. How relieved we are. It is a strange celebration, but we are quietly joyous because nobody is shot or killed. I get up and walk around the bank. An elderly Chinese woman lies on the floor, immobilized. I help her stand up. She had been knocked down by the frenzied robber. She walks around the bank in her own world still not recovered. The police shows up about two or three minutes after it is over.

My wife says they do this so that there will be no hostages. I do not know if it were so but it seems possible. The elderly white man who had been knocked from his seat is complaining. He says he was almost able to reach the robber and knock him down. He is angry. He says he wished he had brought his gun. We tell him that it is for the best because we did not want him injured. He says that he served in two world wars, and he seems undaunted by the robbery. The Filipino woman says this is the first takeover she had been involved in and she had worked for the bank for almost twenty years. She had been involved in a one-on-one robbery where a teller was forced to give a criminal money, but he was caught and arrested. She says that she was very nervous during this robbery that just happened because she had an alarm in her hand that she was activating as the gunman stood shouting. She was under such stress, because she did not know if the robber could read her actions, but she did signal the alarm and then fell to the floor. She had very nervously moved to the floor because she did not want to set off the gunman. Miraculously, he had not bothered her.

She finishes the transaction of canceling and opening a new account for me. I leave my name and telephone number for the police to contact me if they need information in their investigation and leave the bank. I have a meeting scheduled for 11:30. I call them and tell them that I will be late because of the robbery. When I get there everyone is curious about what had happened and what it was like. I did not realize until later that the after-effect of the incident may linger. Some persons who had been there may never enter this bank again in their life. It even affects my friends when I tell them about the ordeal. Some express how they dread such an encounter and question going into a bank themselves. Later that day I found the bank book that I had reported lost.

Carl Sagan, an American astronomer, said that we are a primitive space age planet. If we ever communicate with others who are more advanced than we are, he said that our first question should be how did you reach your level of advancement without destroying yourself? How do we live profound lives in our neighborhoods without destroying ourselves and leaving a planet of empty cities?

There is conflict between students, teachers, the police and all of us in society. We are our society, and it changes when we change. We are no different from society ourselves. We live in it. It is not an abstraction. We are the violence we observe.

In further exploring conflict, I realize that I must observe it without prejudice and prior views. I must see each situation as new for if I come into it with fixed views and ideas then I get caught in the same traps I have created. I understand that I create a world from my thinking. This world does not change without a change in my thinking.

It is a challenge of a society and a school to end conflict. A school is no different from an individual in its problems, feelings, and actions. Profound cooperation is needed for a school to transcend its problems and to create a meaningful learning environment. I have a deep feeling for those at the school who show compassion and understanding and who contribute to the life of the school.

There is significant energy in the school from those who deal with discipline, conflict, violence and anger, who are capable of working with the most difficult students and parents. It is in them to do so. It is not a matter of strength or intimidation, but they are fearless and dead serious about their work. Everyone knows they stand for something.

Whenever we separate ourselves from others by nationality, race, class, or whatever reason, there is conflict within us, our school, and society. We live with this conditioned way of life. One who explores and seeks to understand conflict knows that it must end. Such a person does not belong to any group or system and looks at it dispassionately without trying to manage or control it. Without inner peace how can there be peace in the world?

What contributes to meaningful learning occurring at a school? Learning occurs when meaningful dialogue exists. Things that seemed impossible are challenges to us. It is important to begin working to solve them. After solving a problem we move on.

One must also realize that success and failure come and go continuously. Indeed, success and failure monotonously live on because they generate contradiction. The energy from conflict, contradiction, friction, and resistance is superficial and insignificant. The quality of the life of a school is determined by how it collectively cooperates to understand itself as it continuously changes, and the realization that even though the future is unknown we must remain curious, continue to value learning and freedom, and explore those things that interest us. The world is continuously changing, and learning is more important than knowledge. Knowledge itself is endlessly created by humans to help explain the world. It can quickly become obsolete. Schools focus on what you know (knowledge) or what you are supposed to know and leave us unprepared to deal with what we don't know. Curiosity, exploration, and inquiry are fundamentally important to provide meaning in our lives. The exploration of space, time, the earth, or our minds communicates to us the endless depths of learning. There is no knowledge that exists in space, time, or our minds that is to be held onto. Everything is alive and changing, dying, being renewed.

What comes from learning? What do we learn from sports and other physical activities? During two years of play the school lost but one regular league basketball game, and that was by one point. The team participates in and wins numerous tournaments. Every game it plays it does new and different things. The coach and the team make appropriate changes as the game is played. How many of the games are won from coming from behind, by never giving up? and making things happen in pulling out games that were impossible? Persons who leave and graduate from the school return to join those still here in cheering and in witnessing innovative and intelligent play.

No matter how brilliant the playing though, you cannot win every game. Defeat has its place. It keeps us humble. The coach once stated after a season of exemplary performance that there would never again be anything like that season, that it was part of history and would not happen again. But every season young men continue to come and to play hard. Every season is a new season. The team brings great energy to the school. The men's basketball team reaches great heights.

In those years however the women's basketball team became just as great. From the very beginning of the year the coach and the team expressed that they wanted to achieve greatness. They studied hard. The coach learned with the players and assisted them in their studies. All school subjects were taken seriously. They never stopped studying and learning. They played basketball as well as they could, and the coach gave them all that she had to give them. They were special as a team. Their play was sometimes near perfect. It was rare that they ever lost. The team was special to us all. They defeated every team in the state. They lost the last game, the championship. It didn't matter. It was a great season and a hard season. They brought a time to the school which would not come again. They brought deep energy to the school.

Also in the school are students from all over the world. Some are newcomers from Asia, Mexico, and Central America. Many of them speak no English. A few have never even attended school before. Because they are enthusiastic about experiencing new things, their presence renews the school. They are dedicated to learning and are serious about attending school. They want to be here. Nothing else matters. It is an exciting time in their lives. Many have experienced hard lives in their countries and in coming to America. Seldom do they complain. Their enthusiasm pervades the school. Some have led lives that have been filled with death, escape, and wonder. They have haunting tales to share. They are lucky to be alive. Some are very serious about being here and exist next to persons who perceive life with a much more trivial attitude. One thing we learn from them is that with self-discipline and clear goals, learning cannot be stopped. They transcend their own mistakes and those of others. From these students we can see public schools as places where those in them have the energy to explore and to educate themselves and to renew and change lives. There is excitement in our lives when we experience things and ideas that fascinate us, which gives the enthusiasm to learn and to teach ourselves.

CHAPTER 11

The Immeasurable

We measure things because we see them as linear and capable of being represented by symbols. We do not measure the unknown. We are obsessed with the predictability and recursion of occurrences. We value a known world, but right now I am living in a world with new issues and situations each day.

One day I return to school, late, to find a security aide repairing a broken window in his van. The van had been bombarded by rocks and stones. Broken glass is evident everywhere as he works to secure the damaged window. He is not going to be able to afford to replace the window, but he says he knows who did it. He is pretty sure, anyway. This security aide is an interesting person. He is a concerned and conscientious member of the school staff. He had raised fourteen children and is a good listener and a hard worker. Sometimes he tells me about the days when he was in South Carolina working on a farm. He lives an unpretentious life. I have visited his house in the public housing projects. Very few things bother him or become barriers that he cannot handle for he loves life and doing new things every day.

Earlier that day he had asked several students to leave an assembly in the school auditorium because they were backstage unaccompanied by a teacher. They used abusive language toward him and also made threatening remarks as he directed them to leave the auditorium. He recognized all of the students involved in the incident. It was four of them. A counselor called the parents of all four students to a conference the next day. All the students, at first, deny any knowledge of the incident or any involvement in the destruction of the van window. They also deny making threats to the security aide. We are patient. The security aide never deviates from his comments on what happened.

The mother of one student, in a serious manner, tells her son, "You are lying. I know you are. I want to know what happened."

The student quietly confesses. Three people attacked the van and the fourth person watched. Three of the students confessed and removed the mystery and unknown facts they were struggling to hide. The lies are no longer important and the dispute seems settled. The security aide has no hard feelings toward them and all four parents agree to pay for the damages. However, the fourth student adamantly denies knowledge of, or involvement in, the incident.

The fourth student's position in this incident is a matter of special interest to me. His mother is a teacher, and he is considered a very bright student. He is articulate and has transferred from Lowell High School, which is considered one of the best public schools in America. It is not what we do in life but how well we do what we do that makes life interesting. His statements about not being involved were convincing, but inconsistent with those of the others besides him. Still he never admitted he was there or did any damage to the van. How consistent and believable he was. His statements had their own logical pattern. They were consistent unto themselves. However, others were there. They were outside of his realm and fundamentally challenged his whole system of argument. Lies, truth, prejudice, conjecture, and conclusion have interesting existences. They express human nature and the life of the school. Truth is outside of time and thought. A lie is a false statement of the truth. Prejudice, conjecture, and conclusion are barriers to the truth. Another day I encountered a student who had been such a skillful liar that he deeply challenged and intrigued me. This was so because I knew that a consistent liar was the same as someone telling the truth. I was unable to distinguish between them. How many students have I encountered who have been consistent liars that I thought to be telling me the truth? All of the inconsistent liars I know usually self-destruct within their own systems.

One day I was called to a classroom. I had been informed that a student there had three hundred-dollars worth of traveler's cheques in his possession and ostentatiously showed them off. He told others that he had broken into a house in Sacramento and had taken them from a guy there. When I entered the class, the student was pointed out to me. I asked him to come with me and he did. Outside the classroom I asked him about the traveler's cheques, and he denied any knowledge of them. He seemed shocked and surprised.

"I've been told that you have some traveler's cheques in your possession. Where are they?"

I observed his reaction to my accusation. I had already notified the police about the matter and when an officer arrived he, too, asked about the cheques. The student looked at us in disbelief. He told us he did not understand anything we were talking about. He wanted me to search him. I felt his pockets. Nothing.

"How long have you been in the classroom?" the police officer asked.

"Since the class started, sir." He was deliberately polite.

"You had time to do something with the cheques, then. Why don't you tell us where they are?"

He swore he was being accused of something he knew nothing about. The student was asked to come to my office. He was searched again by me and then by the officer and he emphatically decried that we were making a mistake.

"I have been told by several witnesses that you have the cheques. Where are they?" I asked him.

"I swear I don't have them. I am being accused of something I didn't do."

I had searched him twice. Nothing. I was certain they were not on him. The police officer did not seem as convinced. We were both unclear about what was going on. I left the student and the officer and returned to the classroom. I talked to the teacher and asked if he was certain about the cheques. He swore that the student had them and was bragging about how he got them. Several people had seen him. He had to have them. It was the truth.

I returned to my office and told the police officer that the teacher was sure he had seen the student with the cheques himself. (Last week there was a similar case in which a teacher reported seeing a student with a knife. The student told me and her parent that she did not have a knife and that the teacher was making a mistake. The teacher was called in. The teacher again stated that he saw the student with the knife and emphasized that he recognized a knife when he saw one. I knew the teacher had reported what he observed. It was the truth. The student was dismissed from the school. Her mother accepted the decision.)

All of these cases intrigue me. The student accused of having the cheques continued to deny any involvement whatsoever with which he was charged. It did not matter how many witnesses there were. I was seldom so bewildered.

I returned to the classroom. I told the class, "Three hundred dollars worth of traveler's cheques are in this room. No one is going to leave until they are found."

The class was ending, and it was time for the students to leave the room. Several students wanted to be searched so they could leave the room and not miss their next class.

"I want everyone to look around the room, and I want those cheques to be returned before anyone leaves." I went back to my office. The police officer had found the cheques. Where had they been? The student was stripped, and they had been tightly strapped in his socks. The student was taken to jail and booked.

The next day his mother called me and told me that he had found the cheques on a bus on his way to the school. I never learned where they came from or where he got them. Murders, thieves, and liars are caught because they make mistakes. Some are never discovered. He did have them. It was the truth. It was this fact that sent him to jail. Material things, such as money, become the most significant objects in the world in the inner city. There is a search for ways to prove that one's life is not worthless, to gain respect. A person's world can be so oppressed that there is little room for a serious or creative life.

A human being is inseparable, in the end, from humankind. There is no individual or separate freedom, nor is there a separate self. What is the self? It is an idea, a thought. With abandonment of the self, freedom exists, learning exists. Thought brings hope to a dark life. One's past thoughts are dangerous because one is caught in the prison of his or her own knowledge. Through thought one longs for freedom and a great future, but that freedom is itself within the system of one's own thought. Neither does one become free because of the words or ideas of someone else. Even though another person through words may express the truth and facts of freedom, it is useless unless one comprehends and internalizes those truths. Truth is not something we gain from knowledge. It exists. It comes to us when we are serious, when we are learning, when we are existing in present time and our lives and minds are quiet and alive.

One experiences learning when one finds one's own voice. One does not learn from things I say or others say. I talked to the fourth student in the incident with the van about the observation of others who were there. Somehow I knew all I was saying to him was just words. They were my words also. I had talked to him about being involved in violence, but it was useless as I needed to move beyond the inventions and tricks of the mind. Several weeks after the conversation with this student a policeman from a nearby town called about a person who had been identified in a robbery incident. The person carried a gun during the holdup and was

now wanted for strong armed robbery. In fact, it was a student at the
school. The police came and took him away in handcuffs. It was the
fourth student in the van incident. He was a student who struck back and
who was a time bomb who could explode any moment. The power and
lack of power of some urban youth bring anger and fearlessness. They
encounter a world of death, violence, crime and destruction.

He never changed his story, and I never saw him again. When he was
younger he had performed well in school and had always attended good
schools. Why are there good (elite) schools and bad (remainder)
schools or good and bad students? It is because society rewards certain
places, individuals, and achievements. This is based on our human prejudice and our conclusion and narrow view of other human beings. Our
society designs and invents rules for the race to success. In theory, in
public schools there are rules for each child to have an equal start so
that their lives reflect their varied talents and not the advantages or disadvantages of their social backgrounds. But what of those parents who
work hard and sacrifice for their children so they may have advantages?
Or those who provide material benefits, the best schools and good
neighborhoods? They wish to give their children a head start. In this
way environments of inequality are created. With the existence of elite
and remainder schools we engineer our own destruction.

Sometimes in school I encounter situations that do not involve students
or parents or any person.

One day I observe a bird in my office. It is frightened and lost. It is
early Saturday and I am the only one here. I try to set it free and have it
escape into the wind and rain. How complicated it is to be outside again.
It is not important how it has come to be here. I have seen birds in the
school before but never in this room. It never rests. There is no quietness
to its life. It crashes into the light and ceiling awkwardly flying about,
confused. It reaches a closed window. I approach it but it does not abandon the space it occupies. As I continue toward it, it struggles to fly
through the glass. The impenetrability of the material overwhelms it as

it struggles to survive. I open a nearby window, but it refuses to migrate from its existing domain. I am not forcing it into the world that I know and that I measure with my mind, I do not want to attempt to catch it and set it free. I do not want to break its wings. I leave it in the room alone. I know it is never going to be free, never rest. Unable to help it save itself, I abandon it.

I return. I have to. I open another window. A new door to freedom. How is the bird to discover it? I do not know. Finding it perched on the window ledge, I approach it, and open yet another window. It flies into the wind and rain. Suddenly, it is free. A boy walks about below the window, unmindful of the bird. I realize the encounter with the bird is from the wind and rain coming into the school, bringing new adventure.

What is measurement? It is a description of the universe in symbols. Time, words, and thought measure a world we seek to hold and capture and define. But life, learning, and freedom are endless rivers that never rest. They are new from moment to moment. The living state is endless, beyond measure. It is our own thoughts that struggle to freeze and isolate the world into a collection of symbols and theories. Seeing every moment in life as new does not allow the mind to get caught in the net of its own thinking. The world thought creates is meaningless, because one moment in time can confuse every thought one ever had. Everything is impermanent.

What is a school? What is to occur there? Many people blame schools for what they don't accomplish; some praise schools for contributing to society. All schools are made up of people, and people and schools are good at teaching and measuring what they know. A school, however, is no different from life. Meaningful experiences in a school occur not when one is gathering information and knowledge and being instructed on how to use them, but when one realizes the limit of knowledge. We should not be challenged by knowledge but by the mystery of living.

Recently in a classroom I hear a discussion about nuclear weapons and destruction and other possible human and planetary devastation. I have no dialogue with anyone about this matter, however, I see dark clouds arising from the bay and sense the beginning of the end of the world. I am aware that life is never more than a moment away from extinction.

We who inhabit the earth have images about space and our existence in it. Fascinating journeys to other places in space reveal newness and wonder. Satellites leave the earth and enter into space. They travel millions of miles a day and transmit information back to earth from the darkness of space. These are profound journeys that search for events elsewhere in space and time. The journey of humankind leaves the boundary of the planet to discover and explore things and places we never imagined existed. There is no place at which we arrive. When our total attention is in the journey, we do not look for places that are supposed to exist. We live in a universe where all objects and places are impermanent.

Conventional Objects

CHAPTER 12

Conventional Objects Prologue

After being a high school principal I become head of high schools and then later a consultant to the school district. In these times I see and work with many cases. My work in the school district is with students, parents, teachers, administrators, and others. I know about San Francisco youth who attend the more than one-hundred schools in the city, who excel academically and who are involved in unfortunate incidents. The students are the poor and the affluent and from many ethnic groups and nationalities. I learn and understand that the struggles of the underclass reveal the needs of the many.

What is meaning in our schools and societies? Young children are intrinsically moved to make sense and to learn as much as possible. In schools barriers are formed to discipline and control students as they are taught things for external rewards. The barriers and rewards become the coventional objects they encounter. I observe persons who derive the meaning of such objects as arising fundamentally from the way they are defined by others. Indeed, for many individuals it is not important what they do but what they think others think they are doing. Meaning is external and outside of them. What is the impact of this for students? Their goal is not a good education and a quality and worthwhile life but things such as a high test score, a good report card or an opportunity to impress others.

Today students are empowered when they have their own missions and learn in times of change in our impermanent world, but they are imprisoned by conventional objects which have unchanging meaning assigned through tradition, educational authority, and custom.

Some students experience themselves as objects and their condition as permanent. Some children of public housing and others experience life and school in ways that often haunt and dwell in them throughout their lives; few of them connect to the mainstream of the human journey and discover new worlds.

CHAPTER 13

Undaunted

One day a fifth grade student writes me about an incident in which he is involved. I am at his school, and I meet him briefly. He is encouraged by his principal and his teacher to write his story and send it to me. They know that he has something to say and something that I am interested in hearing. Of the thousands of San Francisco fifth graders, I cannot avoid seeing him and knowing him from among the crowd of other students.

He lives in the public housing projects across the street from his school where he resides in another world of reality. (In the public housing projects are the stories of killings, drugs, crime, violence, fearlessness, despair, hope, courage, love, and poverty.) He is a quiet and humble student. He is spirited and alert but does not speak much.

I first read about his story in the newspaper and I find it interesting. I do not think any more about it until the day that I happen to be at his school and am introduced to him by the principal.

The San Francisco Examiner headline reads **At 11, he got his chance to fight crime.** His picture is in the paper along with his name and the name of the housing project he lives in. The article details how he supplies the police with the make of a suspected kidnapper's truck and three numbers of the license plate. The sub-heading tells of how this fifth grade youngster who wants to be a policeman prevents a girl's kidnapping and aids in the arrest of the suspect. He says he thought he would freeze, "but I didn't". Police say that his quick thinking prevented a man from abducting a six-year-old girl who ran to him from the would be kidnapper. (He and the girl both attend the same school and live in the same housing project.) The girl was in a neighborhood park tying her shoe, and a man drives up in a pickup, gets out and starts to help her. She tells him she can do it herself, and the man tries to persuade her to get into the truck. She is afraid and starts running home but is followed by the man in the truck until she sees Michael and waves for him to come over.

Michael asks the man "Are you her father?"

The girl yells, "No."

The man offers Michael ten dollars to get her to enter the truck. He refuses. Michael and the girl run to a pay telephone to call 911. The police come. They later located the truck parked in the area and when the driver returns to it, both children identify him. The suspect is also wanted on a drug warrant in Texas.

This is the student's story. In his own words he tells about how he saves a girl from his school from being abducted by a stranger. He and a teacher sit at a computer and compose it and they then send me a copy.

I helped a girl named Helen. I helped her from getting kidnapped. I saw her coming towards me on the sidewalk and she asked me, "where is my brother?" I said, "I don't know where your brother is."? I saw this man pull up in a white car on Army Street and he waved his finger asking Helen to get inside the car. She said, "no". I asked him if that was his child and he said yes. I asked Helen if the man was her dad and she said no. I told her to come with me so we could call the police. She came, we called 911, and he drove around the block. He came back while I was making the call. Helen stood next to me while he tried to give me some money to get her inside the car. I said no and he did not know what I was doing because I just told him I needed to make a call. He told her to get inside the car and she said in my ear that, "that's not my father." I told her to talk to the police who were on the phone and she said "no" because she was scared. I got off the phone. I looked in the back of his truck, and got a stick out of it. I put Helen behind me and he told me to put her into the truck. I said, "no". The man got out of the car and I told Helen to run and she ran. I stood there and held the stick in case he tried to run after her. He got back inside the car and drove off. I looked at his license plate and memorized three numbers. Helen found someone that we both knew. Our friend drove us to the Precita Center and someone there called the police. The police came by and we went with them and found the empty car. The police waited for him to come out of a store, and when he came out the police asked us if that was him. We both said, "yes", and they arrested him and we went home.

Michael's mother is proud of her son. She knows how hard life is in their crime and poverty-filled dwelling. She had lived through her own battle with drinking and drugs, the paper said. But she would always talk to her children about staying in school and out of trouble and to kick and scream if anyone tried to kidnap them. The newspaper article said, "People here are telling him how brave he is," said his mother. "I just tell my children they have to strive. I can't do it for them."

I never met Michael's mother, but I do talk to her on the telephone. She is just getting ready to move back to Louisiana, where she was raised. She lives on a fixed income and is moving the family back. I wish her all the best and tell her that we are going to send Michael his own computer. We do. I also talk to her and Michael after they move to Louisiana.

The school principal, who is a young Latino male from this neighborhood, sees this as important an event as has occurred while he has been at the school. Shootings and deaths are common in the neighborhood and around the school, but this is an act of bravery that most of them would never again realize in their lifetime.

He talks about how it has transformed the entire school. Everybody knows about it and it affects all their lives. It has an effect on the system and gives them all something to reflect on and to discuss among themselves. It is an African American youth who has helped a Vietnamese girl who are both in the same school where everybody knows them. To help her had meant going beyond money and personal gain. It is a heroic story that touches all of them in the school. Sometimes organizations and individuals are changed and transformed because of the things that come into their lives, unplanned and unexpected. How an organization and an individual act without regard to personal interest can change and deepen lives.

It is natural for the school to recognize the students for the situation they endured. However, the recognition by the mayor, the state, and others is more of a societal convention. The most important thing is that a student shows he is able to stand alone, undaunted, in a crisis situation. He demonstrates an inner strength and does not have a need to be known or recognized for his action.

CHAPTER 14

The Money

Just as I learned an interesting story about a fifth grade student, a principal shares a unique school situation with me about a sixth grade student.

The student came to school one day with a lot of money. It was later in the day when the principal discovered that he had given other students hundreds of dollars. Word spread around the building that there was a student in the school giving away money. Certainly it was a way for a student to have friends.

When the principal found out about it, he called the student in and found out how much money he still had on him. The student had about twenty-seven-thousand dollars. How much had he started with and where had it come from? In talking to the student the principal learned that the student had brought the money from home. He knew where his mother put it, and he'd brought it to school to give to his friends. How much it was did not have a deep significance to him. His friends were surprised at having the money. One student, the principal said, had seven hundred dollars and was not sure what to do with it.

I sometimes walked around this school and found students mad at the principal because he took a bag of candy from them. They were mad because they said they had saved their money to get the candy. It was a school rule that they couldn't have candy in the building. Students found with it would have it taken from them and had to wait until school was out to have it returned. They would have spent two dollars on the candy and thought that was a lot of money. But no student would spend seven hundred dollars on candy. They probably did not buy their own clothes (though I did talk to a student in this school who was involved in drugs who said that he did buy his own jewelry). It took the rest of the afternoon to find all the people who had gotten money from the student and to get it back. Some students had returned the money on their own because they did not want to get into trouble. There was confusion, talk, misinformation, and uncertainty throughout the school. The principal had contacted the home and found that the student had brought more than thirty thousand dollars to the school. All of the money was eventually accounted for. Every dollar.

School life and large sums of money are abstract things to children. Just as large sums of knowledge can be. Few of them bring things which change the life of the school. More bring guns and weapons. They are more accessible. Rarely do they see such money in their world. Children experiment and explore new ways in which to have a voice in the world. What more conventional way to enter the world than with money? Its power is known and certain. It rules the world and can buy food, recognition, protection, drugs, and knowledge. For the student it also brought problems that were beyond his world. It momentarily changed his quiet life.

CHAPTER 15

San Francisco Bay

From my days in Nigeria the early morning has been the greatest time of the day. It's when the earth awakens and life is fresh. I love to be in the world at this time. It is a great time to reflect and run through the city and to see its life.

The principal from the school with the thirty thousand dollar student and I are running along the San Francisco Bay. We often do. It can be an exhilarating time to be out in the cool air, hearing the sounds of life in and around the sea. There is always activity at Fisherman's Wharf. It is too early for the tourists, and the fisherman are already at sea. There are many trucks loading up and warehouse workmen busily moving and piling goods on the trucks. The streets are often hardly passable because of the morning work that is going on getting ready for the day. It is an endless task, doing the busy morning work, preparing the city for its normal activities. Sometimes running through the city also seems routine, as one encounters numerous other persons running the streets and the hills and sometimes pushing themselves to their physical and mental limits and beyond. We pass the Dolphin Club, where individuals come out to swim in the San Francisco Bay and sometimes across it and sometimes from Alcatraz. They are rugged individuals to us, and we admire them and their ability to test and to survive the sea.

On this morning, just beyond the Dolphin Clubhouse is a white woman who is talking to herself and walking about in a crazed and tangled course. As we run past her she shouts something about, "niggers this and niggers that". I am disturbed at her language and gestures and wonder about her problem. I am surprised that she is talking about black people, when two black men are running by. She is not talking to us and not even looking at us, but she is certain that we do hear her. It is true that we do not know her and are forming conclusions about her. She could be a mentally ill person talking to herself, but it seems like she does not like black people or that she had a bad experience.

We keep running. It is usually a routine morning run and such an event is unusual. We run on to the Marina Green and past the many yachts that quietly sway in the restless bay. Foghorns penetrate the fog, never stopping. I have sailed from the St. Francis pier many times and have sailed to many places in the bay. My most recent trip was with a group of special education students from Galileo High School. I had written them and their teacher the following letter:

Dear Mr. Erickson,

Thank you for inviting me to join you and the class as we sailed in the San Francisco Bay last Tuesday. From the time we left the pier for the bay, a serious tone was set as Joel was eager to steer out to the open sea, while Kris and Steve assisted in handling the sails. Once out to sea I found it to be an interesting experience, observing what occurs in designating a captain and giving full responsibility to that individual. Carol's desire to change course from the Golden Gate Bridge and head toward Alcatraz was not well accepted by all crew members, but it did create interesting questions about leadership and cooperation from some members of the crew. For others it was not an issue as to our heading. As the boat sailed back to the pier I was glad to see Sophia assist in the necessary tasks. Each member of the crew was involved in the expedition and making it work.

I found the adventure to be interesting as the ocean drew our attention and became an innovative classroom setting. Compass reading, measuring the depth of the water (forty feet), observing the direction and the effect of the wind, studying the waves, and discussing the theory of sailing provided material and thought for a rich lesson. As a result of the information and thinking introduced and discussed, I am enthusiastic in learning further about the ideas that were provoked from our day on the sea. It was also good to see the expectation that each student had to remain until the entire sailing mission was completed, which included cleaning the boat down and anchoring it in the pier and leaving it just as we had entered it. In the end each student was given the opportunity to express the best and the worst things that had happened from his or her point of view. The seriousness given to the students' reflections showed the value and worth of the individual and the group.

I wish to commend you and the students for this outstanding program at Galileo high school. Keep up the adventure and enthusiasm as well as this serious and innovative approach to learning.

Traveling to sea is always a new learning experience for me. But it is not such a place of learning for some people. For many it is a tedious and uncomfortable place. Last year my wife and I went out with a friend on the bay. My wife was so seasick that she went down below and was miserable the entire time that we were out. One summer we sailed from Los Angeles to Santa Catalina Island and many of the passengers were seasick and throwing up all over the boat. My wife had become so ill that we had flown back from the island in a helicopter. Though she strongly did not like flying, she was relieved to be in the air and on a fast and smooth return to the mainland. But I love sailing on the sea. I always have. My daughter and I just recently sailed up the coast with others on a whale watching expedition.

We sail in the wind and the rain along the coast to Point Reyes. We seem like so many others who have gone to sea. You never know what you will encounter. When I was young and a seaman sailing from New York to Europe a school of dolphins from nowhere had appeared playing in the high seas. Nothing had seemed as great as life on the sea.

On the day my daughter and I sail we search for whales. There are people who have spent years of their lives studying gray whales. Of all the times I have been on the sea, I never realize the billions of years of existence that have elapsed through these very places where we move. The earth is said to be five billion years old. In its early existence the rocks and minerals are washed into the seas, which made them salty. The salt of our blood is that salt of the ancient seas from almost a half billion years ago. That is when our ancestors supposedly crawl from the sea and across the land, looking for water and other sea life. We are still bodies of sea water who live on oxygen and observe an immense universe. We are connected to the earth and all that it is and all that it expresses of itself. The world reveals itself through us.

For millions of years the gray whale has migrated within the seas. We stand at a point along a 5,000-mile journey from the Bering Sea feeding grounds around Alaska to Baja California. They are migrating south for warmth and shelter and to breed. In their journey humankind killed the gray whales for hundreds of years. It was not widespread until they were killed for profit. Their population diminished several times to near extinction. Laws were passed to prohibit the killing of gray whales, and in the last fifty years their population has grown from several thousand to more than twenty thousand. It is a great story that they are able to come back from near extinction. My daughter and I observe several of them in our trip to sea. We also see sea lions, a minke whale, harbor porpoises, and a colony of California elephant seals.

We return from eight hours on the sea and sail back to the Golden Gate Bridge and the Bay and Alcatraz and the Bay Bridge and all of the other structures and grand objects that stand. The activities are going on just as we left them, as though we have hardly even been away, as though we are fishermen coming back from the sea.

We sail under the Golden Gate Bridge which connects land and people. Thousands cross it each day. And more than a thousand confirmed suicides have occurred there. Hundreds more have killed themselves but their bodies were never recovered, never found. Still others have attempted the fatal jump but have survived. Interesting observations about suicide come from the individuals who survive and are not killed. Hundreds who make suicide attempts but are unsuccessful or are restrained or persuaded not to jump, who are able to last through their momentary deepest pain and disorder, usually do not ultimately die of suicide. They come back into life as though they have hardly even left. They show that those of us who reach rock bottom can climb back up.

We do not always come back. A year before Alcatraz is closed as a federal prison a famous escape is attempted. I learn of the escapes from Alcatraz and other things from a park ranger there. There were thirty-six inmates who tried to escape from Alcatraz in fourteen different attempts. One famous escape attempt involves three men who spent months making holes in the rear walls of their cells. They work at night in secrecy, concealing what they are doing with cardboard grates. The three men use dummy heads made from paper, wire, and hair as models of themselves to fool the guards during nightly head counts. They prepare tools and get-away equipment and on a June night they make it onto the roof and escape from the north end of the island in homemade flotation devices. They are never seen again. Could they have escaped the cold and strong currents of the bay? They likely never survived. I have worked with incarcerated youth and with imprisoned felons, and I know that if there was an escape they would likely have had to tell someone about it. It is our nature. We are social creatures. When I was a youth, a teacher once challenged each of us as an individual to do something good and not to tell anyone else about it. It is one of the few things in school that ever stirred and provoked me to reflect on my actions and those of others around me. I do not believe that the three men ever escaped the hell of prison; that they lived to tell the world what they had done.

*   *   *

My friend and I reach the half way point of the run. We turn around at the Marina and head back along the Bay. We reach Hyde Park again, and the white woman is still there. She continues to talk about niggers and complaining to herself. I run past her, but I come back and look her dead in the face and say, "If you keep talking and complaining about niggers, I'm going to throw you in the sea. I don't want to hear it anymore. I am tired of listening to you." I also tell her not to mess with me because I am dead serious.

I shock her more than anything else. She has no idea what I will do. She doesn't seem willing to take the chance. She cannot believe this black man is confronting her. She does not say anything and is initially silent. Then she gets mad but does not say anything else about niggers. My friend also says something to her which further shocks and annoys her. We run on into the haze and leave her to think about the encounter she has just endured.

I tell my friend that in school we often wonder about authentic experiences for students to live and to write about. This is a real experience that impacted upon our lives. It is a serious time that the three of us can communicate to others. The two of us can express our feelings about the matter, and she will never likely know about them. How did she perceive the incident? We'll probably never know. We still do run along the sea and through whatever unexpected meetings that wait along the road. Never again have we seen such a person or had such a confrontation. Life in the morning along the bay is so peaceful and seems to have been undisturbed for centuries. That is why our encounter is so unusual and unexpected. Our lives are built new each day, in the schools and in the world. Writing about events such as this is a convention that can enrich our lives and the world we encounter. The woman and the world she is in, as much as any other event, moves me to write this chapter. Knowing her point of view of the situation in which the three of us found ourselves would have made this a richer human adventure for me.

shortly knowing I must follow up on the call. It takes me twenty minutes
to get ready to leave the house. I tell my wife I am leaving. She understands. I leave the house and reach the school at 2:30 AM on Saturday
morning. When I arrive I see the principal who had been contacted by
the teacher. The building is a disaster. The principal's office has been
destroyed by fire. Smoke smells are thick and its residue is everywhere in
the vicinity of the principal's office and the main office. It is as though a
bomb has struck and left behind the shell of a structure.

It takes the principal several minutes to tell me all that she knows
about the case. I am impressed on how clear she is about the events that
seemed to have happened. Two students had broken into the school. It is
unusual because both of the students are female, and they are both
eleventh graders. It is the first incident involving two female students
breaking into a school in San Francisco that I have ever known about. The
principal is familiar with both of them as they are both outstanding students. One of the girls was absent from school that Friday. She had cut
school, and the school had notified her parents to come in for a conference on Monday morning. This is the second time this particular student
has been involved in a parent conference for cutting school. The previous
time she had been absent because she did not want to take a chemistry
examination, so she had cut school. When she had learned that the school
had scheduled a parent conference on Monday, she made up her mind to
do something drastic. The principal thinks she intended to break into the
school to destroy the school attendance records so that there would be no
record of her Friday absence from school. The principal later learns that
the girl tells the policeman, who had captured her, that she was mad at the
school and that she wanted to strike back in a destructive manner. She
was unhappy and spoke of crashing into the school with an airplane or
running a truck into it. The second girl had only come to assist the first.

Around midnight the two girls had brought two large kerosene cans
to the school. They walked to the window that led to the principal's
office. It was not known if they realized which office they were at from

the outside. It was the lowest entry point into the building. They forced an entry through the window into the principal's office. They did not realize at this point that they had already triggered an alarm. The police had been notified and were coming to the scene.

The girls had no idea of the school's alarm system and continued on with their plan of transporting the kerosene into the building. They poured kerosene on the floor in the principal's office. They each had wooden stick matches with them. The first girl took a piece of paper and twisted it into a roll. She struck a match to ignite the paper. It was too late! The vapors in the air were ignited and set off an explosion. Suddenly both of their lives had been changed forever. They are in a violent world that is burning and exploding around them, and they do not know if they will live or die.

They run out of the building. Both are on fire. The police arrives as they are fleeing the building. They are ordered to halt but both keep running. They have both been on fire but neither of the fires sustained themselves. The two police officers chase them as they climb fences to get away. The first girl is hiding in a nearby yard when she is captured. The second girl is caught from behind by the officer. They both have burns to their bodies and are arrested and taken to the hospital.

From a distance the world sometimes seems perfect. We assume that it is as we see it. We see the records of outstanding students and we assume certain things about them. We think they will have a great future, that they are happy with their lives and their performance, that they are respected for their achievements. None of these assumptions are true of these two students.

We once had a dog that my wife and daughter loved. Since he was a puppy he never stood erect. He was slightly misaligned, it seemed. It was noted but seldom considered. Before he died we had x-rays taken of his spinal column. Several vertebrae had thick calcium deposits and severe arthritis was dominating his movement and his life. All his life we had assumed his bone condition to be ordinary. It never had been. Therefore, I have learned I should question all of my assumptions.

The second student in this incident had only come as a friend. The first girl said that she had only met her by happenstance and that she had not been involved in her anger and actions toward the school. There had been a fire in the school several weeks earlier and no one was ever discovered but the principal suspected that the second girl may have been involved. The second girl pleaded that she was innocent of any arson attempt. In the end she was expelled from the district just as the first girl. It was noted that she did bring a large container of kerosene to the school and did assist in getting it into the school. Several days after the hearing, it was discovered that the second girl had been accused of two previous arson incidents when she was a student in Los Angeles. It was shocking to the many people who assumed that she was an ordinary student who had lived an ordinary life up until now.

It is just as interesting to hear from the other students and the school staff. Many are outraged that students would cause such destruction to their school, that the lives of firefighters and others are risked because of a foolish act of two students. There is no sympathy from those at the school. My attitude is different. For me it is also a question of how much do we condemn, punish, and destroy students' lives as opposed to understanding and supporting them through a crisis situation? I accept the decision from the hearing that they both be expelled. At the beginning of school on Friday both girls were honor students who were well thought of by many. By Saturday evening they had destroyed a school office and other places in the school. **They had used fire and violence as tools to challenge conventional authority.** Was the stress of school too great? Could we have done more for them, cared more about what burned inside of them? Was the burning of the building more important than their lives? They both faced ten years in jail on arson charges and their families were to pay damages of over one hundred thousand dollars. They faced devastating futures. I could only let them live their lives. Could they live beyond the horror they had escaped?

CHAPTER 17

Moment of Youth

I once met a student who was African American, attractive, articulate and bright. Her mother always seemed as though she was faced with conflicts involving her daughter. She wanted to be the one who supported her daughter and yet she also wanted to have expectations for her to live up to. When I first met the two of them the daughter had just finished the eight grade and had been accused of hitting a school staff member. As in every conflict there were several sides. In the end a decision was made that the daughter be put on probation and be allowed to attend a special academic high school. They were both grateful and great things were expected. The school year, however, was a disappointment for us all. The principal had several parent conferences with the student and her mother. I was present at the last conference. The student had been disruptive in class and had been involved in a fight with another student. It was not her first fight. The principal sought to recommend another school. There had been numerous conferences and the student's behavior was as bad as ever. Indeed it was often unexplainable. Her grades were bad. She passed her classes, but she had not performed well in several of them. I was always so impressed with how she spoke and carried herself. She was always a good listener and she was so open-minded in our conversations. She was an interesting and special person to me. I desperately wanted her to live a great life, to be a responsible individual. I did not want her to leave the school, but I could not save her. Just a year ago I had told her that she was being given a second chance. She would have new opportunities to prove herself as a student. I wanted her to live a worthwhile life and to have a good future. The school had worked hard and now it was time for her to leave. Her mother agreed. If she performed well at her new school then she would be allowed to return. She accepted the decision. She knew that she had let us down but was determined to do better. I was disappointed because I had believed so strongly in her as a person and I knew she could contribute to the world. She had a spirit that moved me.

The next year she went to her new school. I saw her there. I introduced her to the principal. She seemed happy being there. At the end of the school year I was told that she had died of drug overdose. I never knew she was a drug user, so I did not know how involved she had been with drugs and how they affected her in her daily life. A single dose of some drugs can produce seizures or heart and respiratory failure. The risk and the complications become greater as the amount and the frequency of drug use increases. What had been her involvement? She was dead. There were a hundred questions that died, and I never asked, never knew the answers.

Her family loved her. They share a poem which speaks to her life. The poem says that,

She wants so much
to have her own language…
to make her own dreams
as her life is taking its own course…

She wants so much
to make her own words…
to express the vastness…

to walk her own line

She wants so much
to see her own way

To have her own language

I did regret that I was not a greater factor in her life. I always knew her as youthful, enthusiastic, bright, understanding, and one who seemed so serious about being a better person. How silent and hidden any drug possibility had been to me. It did not seem as though she was known by or belonged to a drug world or society. In actuality all of our societies are artificial. They are contrived ways that divide humankind. The things that we share in the world are much more significant than the things which divide us. Because she had died suddenly and so young it was a stunning event in my life.

Her death was so unexpected and she was from a family with a parent who lived and struggled so hard for her to be a contributor to society, to be able to make her own way in the world and to master some of its social conventions.

CHAPTER 18

Family Incident

I view the world in my mind as varied and interesting. As I work in San Francisco schools over the years the variation in the cases I work with bears out that this is indeed how the world reveals itself. My work in the schools involves cases of suicide, rape, disabling accidents, child abuse, murder, teacher assault, high pursuit of personal goals, hard work, creativity and motivation, and perseverance. Some days I have an abundance of cases I study and pursue. I also know that San Francisco is like urban cities throughout America. I often think that there are just so many things happening along the educational streams. There are situations that can overwhelm us at times. I have lived for more than twenty years with those who struggle for understanding and a way out, those who are proud, humble, and grateful, and those who do not give up.

The other day a lady came into the office and she broke into tears. We know each other. She is a parent. The two of us have talked together on several occasions. She is Japanese American, the mother of Alex Tanabe. I have never encountered a more genuinely humble person in my years as a teacher or administrator. Her silence and seriousness make her a great individual. Her presence stirs my soul. And though she speaks with an accent, I understand every word. She is troubled and has a fragile life. It is a life that is so unusual that when she sees me it is always for the same reason and it is always hard for her not to cry. She cries from her soul. Inside, her heart may never rest. She is here to deal with a family tragedy that is deep within her. It is a special time to me whenever I see her. I never make personal exceptions for students or parents in gaining admission to the district's alternative schools. This is the one case that I had approved admissions without question. It was that unusual a situation. It involved a district transfer called an optional enrollment request (OER) which was approval to attend a school other than one's assigned neighborhood school. The OER became her mission.

Some days my work takes me to a juvenile facility, Youth Guidance Center, where students are locked up for their acts against society. (Some of the students who did well were sent to the Ranch School where I once worked.) The students at this juvenile center are sometimes connected to a violent past and often times a meaningless way of life. How do they overcome the obstacles before them? How many of them will ever become connected with a life that will challenge them to produce their own knowledge and understanding? How many will outlive their past and those things which imprison them?

Few individuals in society live in freedom. These youth find themselves in a physical and mental prison. There are 150 of them who live alone and are often forgotten. When I walk among them I do not know their stories and why they are locked up in this place. There is one student who attended this facility whom I never met, Alex Tanabe. It is his mother and younger brother whom I have met. The school director says he is a perfect student. He is quiet and receives good grades. One of his teachers, whom I know well, describes him as a student she had in B-5, the maximum security unit of juvenile hall. Alex, she describes, is courteous, disciplined, and intelligent in class. He reads advanced material with ease, and retains information effortlessly, and writes fluently. She describes Alex as tense and anxious in his speech and also in his writing, which is reflected by his ending all of his sentences with exclamation marks! He speaks and writes of physical and emotional pain, his relationship with his father, and how he worries about his little brother. He expresses the dilemma of a being a gang member among his peers and having their respect and support and the desire to live a straight and conventional life. He feels as though he has to change his name to change his past. He says that he wants to call himself William Kwan because all of his true friends are Chinese. He often signs himself with this name. He is also obsessed with the legal and ethical issues that confront his life. He is accepted and respected by both the students and the staff of the Youth Guidance Center.

I remember the first time I met Alex Tanabe's mother. He was already locked inside a juvenile cell. She brought a well-written and troubling story to me. A school administrator had called me on several occasions but until now I had not given the attention that this situation required.

She had come because of the promising future she was seeking for her younger son. Her older son's future was a disaster, and could become hopeless, and she did not want such misfortune for her younger son. Both she and the younger son had been deeply traumatized.

She seemed so happy to meet me. I was not accustomed to elder Asian women being so accepting and deeply genuine while meeting a black man. I reviewed the letter she had sent me. It had been diligently and patiently written by hand. There were no errors or illegible words. In the four hand-written pages she introduced herself as Alice Tanabe and stated that she was writing about her son William who would be attending high school next year. She was requesting that William be given special consideration for admissions into a small alternative high school. It was a request for an OER. She then stated her reason for this request.

In September her older son, Alex, attacked her and her husband with knives. (The knife marks are still there. She freely shows them on her face and her neck.) Her husband was killed in the attack. Alex's personality had begun to change when he started his high school career. He went to a large neighborhood high school and became involved in gang-related activities. Her younger son, William, she stated, had been having a difficult time dealing with the tragic death of his father and the violence of his brother. He was living under a great deal of stress and she wanted very much for him to experience as normal and stable a life as he could. She knew that facing high school would be a great change. She did not want him to attend the same high school as his brother, Alex. She was very clear that she did not wish to criticize any high school but wished to request another high school for William. She asked that I consider William's special circumstances before making a final decision. William, she wrote, had always been an excellent student and she did not want the family tragedy to get in the way of his future learning.

The mother was a special person in my life because in her own quiet way she showed me the depth of the human spirit. She lived through a catastrophe and was reconstructing her own life. She had struggled through the conventional barriers of our system to be heard.

CHAPTER 19

Threats

I received a message to call a parent. Some days there are so many people to talk to. It is sometimes a stacked array of telephone numbers and concerns to be processed. Some messages can be seriously important to the caller. They wait to hear from me.

I return the call as a school official. The caller is an Asian teacher in the district who is now teaching at an elementary school. The caller is also the parent of a high school student who has been threatened. I should not respond hastily. I realize that it is not unusual that individuals are threatened in a school. Had the parent talked to the child's principal? She had. I asked her to continue. I did not wish to prejudge her situation. This incident had occurred at school. Her son had been playing basketball on the school playground. When he decided to stop playing he went to get his jacket. Another student, whom he did not know, told him, "I want this jacket." The lady's son refused to give up his jacket. It was an expensive athletic jacket that was popular with many youth. It was perhaps why he was being challenged by this stranger. He did not know how serious the stranger really was, but he struggled to keep the jacket, and he walked away from the encounter. He did not think any more about the incident. When he got home he had forgotten about it and had not even discussed it with his family. As far as he knew there was nothing to discuss.

That evening he received a telephone call. It was from the stranger who had attempted to take the jacket. He told the stranger that it was his jacket and that he was not going to give it up. He did tell his parents about the incident and about the call. The student did not go to school the next day. The call from the stranger had disturbed him.

The stranger called again the next night. He repeated his demand. He told the student that he knew that he was not in school and that he would not be able to escape. The stranger wanted the jacket and insisted he was going to get it. It made the student think that the stranger had friends in the school with whom he communicated. It made him wonder who these other persons might be and whether they would bother him. The student had his parents talk to the stranger. The stranger was relentless in his demand. He told the student's father that he would burn down the house if he did not get the jacket. He warned them not to report this incident to the police. It was an Asian family and the stranger was Asian. The parents took the threats seriously. They contacted the school. The school principal told the family to make a police report. The mother had already done so. The principal then suggested that they change the telephone number. The mother refused.

When I talked to the principal, he said that the resources of the school were limited. The school's head counselor had been notified, and the principal had made arrangements for the student to be accompanied to the bus as he left the school to return home. The parents and the student felt no comfort or relief in this plan. They feared what might happen on the bus and on the journey home. It seemed too risky for them to subject the student to this uncertainty and personal danger. Therefore the parents picked up the student daily from the school. The student's performance in the school changed dramatically. He had been achieving A's and B's in his classes. Now he was receiving C's. His life was filled with stress. He did not like attending school anymore. The family was living a nightmare. To me it seemed hardly believable that this was happening to this family. To them it did not matter what the incident was that had precipitated this event. It remained a life and death matter to them. They had to take everything the stranger said seriously. He would not let them rest.

The stranger continued to call. The mother continued to discuss this ongoing situation with the police. She decided that she would not change the telephone number because she did not want to loose contact with the stranger. She had to take some risks in trying to catch the stranger. She was afraid for her son but determined to have the stranger captured. I talked to members of the Gang Task Force in the police department and they shared with me their involvement with the family and the student. The police tapped the family's telephone conversations and they traced the call to the stranger. All of the stranger's calls were made from his home. The police said that the stranger had a police record and they suspected he belonged to a gang and that it was part of some gang activity that he had to have this jacket.

The police went to the stranger's house, but he was never there. His father was the only person living there and he said he did not know where the boy was. He had not been home in a week. The student was still under great stress and his mother was considering changing his school. The stranger was arrested in Daly City and was taken to jail. His probationary officer said he was either going to remain in jail or be ordered to have no contact with the student or his family. I never heard of any further problems. This case was unique because of the mother's determination to have the stranger captured. Her courage and her will were greater than those of the stranger.

In San Francisco the number of cases of students having weapons and being recommended for expulsion from the school district is increasing. Weapons are pervasive throughout the urban areas in America. As rapid as the acceleration of weapons is the increased fear in parents and students. Some days I speak to mothers and fathers who hold such deep fear for their children's safety that they refuse to be denied a change of school for their child. They feel inside that there are certain schools at which their child is not safe or that the child is involved in a situation where his or her life may be in danger.

I attempt to face each situation with a clear mind. I am just as determined as they are to go beyond the emotion, intimidation, and fears that hold them. Parents are interested in revolutionary action. They are not interested in beauracratic obstacles.

Recently I participated in a Cherry Blossom Scholarship program to honor students from around the Bay Area. I was approached by a gentleman who spoke to me about a friend. I was not given many details except that the parent so feared for his daughter's life that he had missed a whole week of work and was considering moving his family from San Francisco. I told the gentleman to have the parent call me. When I reached home my wife told me I had a call from Mr. Higa. It was the concerned parent and he was anxious to speak to someone about his problem. He had made up his mind about what he was to do. This was the problem: his daughter was threatened by a group of Asian students while at school last week. The Asian students were picked up by the police. The victim, Mr. Higa's daughter, had told the police she knew of these students from during the summer when she worked at a shopping center. They wanted her to steal from the store where she was working. She refused. She told this to the police and the police told this to the arrested Asian youth. Mr. Higa's daughter had been accused of snitching on them and they were after her. Mr. Higa had visited schools in two cities outside of San Francisco. He visited schools that were integrated, he said, but with few Asian students. These students had threatened to take his daughter's life and he was not prepared to go to school and find his daughter dead. He was prepared to sell his house and move away. Also she was receiving poor grades and did not like going to school anymore. It was too much stress for her and the family to bear. He had not yet sold his house. I told him that he could not be sure that they would not follow her out of town. How did he know that her new school would not be discovered? He did not know, but he seemed willing to take that chance.

I told him that there were twenty high schools in San Francisco. There were small and well integrated schools that he should consider. He enrolled his daughter in another San Francisco school and I never heard from him again. Had his fears been real. Was death a possibility?

A person once told me about his life in prison. He said that it was so hard and dangerous that you had to take all threats seriously. If someone threatened you, you had to tell the person, "Don't threaten me, man, because I'll have to kill you." And you meant what you said.

I am absorbed in the life, survival, and deaths of urban youth. One day it was national news that two youths in New York City had been killed by another youth during school. I read magazine articles, newspaper stories, and talked to people who had been there. It was at a school where the principal was known as one who had fought hard for the soul of her school and who had been recognized as a hero in American education. Two weeks before the shooting she had suffered a heart attack. After the shooting, the newspapers descended on the stress-filled school and wrote stories, researched street life, and language, and interviewed numerous students. The media preyed on the school's misfortune. The incident had involved two students who had supposedly both been partners in a botched mugging incident that occurred some months earlier. They were both captured, and one served time and the other got probation. This precipitated a conflict that was never resolved. The student who got probation reportedly told the police that the other student had called him a rat, and he thought that he was going to kill him.

On the February morning of the killing it was stated that the two would-be victims had left their homes to attend school and to them and their families it seemed just another day. The assailant, it was reported, arrived late, which was not unusual. At the end of first period the assailant reportedly, from point blank range and with no words spoken, shot the student whom he had feared was going to kill him and also his inseparable friend. The assailant indicated to the police that it was kill or be killed. His mind was like the minds of others in the streets and in the prisons where the threat to kill was taken seriously.

Sometimes the talk or conversation is not threatening but disrespectful. In some students' minds they are determined that shame from an insult can only be undone through aggression. They rely on physical and mental aggression as ways of dealing with the emotional injuries they have suffered from someone else. Their image of themselves forces them to get even with the other person or they feel like they look like a sucker, a weakling, or a fool. If someone talks about me or my family, I must strike back. It makes me feel better. If someone disrespects me I have to fight them to get my image and my pride back. They do not accept the idea that a person who is strong inside can walk away from a fight.

Chapter 20

The Diploma

In a high school much attention is given to graduation requirements. A high school diploma is a predetermined path to a conventional life. As a student, the high school diploma was hardly significant to me. As a teacher and a school administrator it is no more significant, but I am more aware that it generates external meaning from society, teachers, counselors, students and parents. It is assumed to have significance and to be worth working toward. It is fundamentally accepted as a symbol of success which entire populations of students work to achieve. For many students it is a struggle to attain. For others it is a trivial path of conformity that rewards them for serving time and following the rules.

Some students work hard and never receive a diploma. Some are unable to qualify for the lack of a course or unable to pass an examination. Others are years behind in requirements and have little chance of changing their fate and graduating. Recently in San Francisco an administrator became so determined to help students attain a diploma that he gave five students an unauthorized chance to pass a graduation examination. They had shared answers among themselves. The students all passed the examination. This was their final requirement to attain their diploma. However, it was discovered that the examination was unauthorized, unofficial, and unsupervised when the students took it. The administrator was reprimanded. In his own way he had been an advocate for the students but the negative impact was so powerful he lost his job and was transferred to another school. The students then had to be retested. They all failed. They were devastated. Some of their parents were angry at the system and the ordeal with which their children had struggled. How close they were to attaining the diploma and how hard was their work to satisfy the requirement. How many more times would they have to take the examination? Some of them had worked hard and had struggled to be successful. The teacher went to another school and the students were all given another exam. They still struggle for the high school diploma. They are permitted to be retested until they meet this final condition of their graduation. Will they master societal expectations and live a conventional life?

There was not much sympathy for the administrator or the students. The proficiency test, a multiple choice test, was a high school graduation requirement, but it was really at an eighth grade level. Many students pass it as ninth graders and fulfill the requirement at that time. Some students would take it countless times and never pass.

One of the students who failed the test was an African American male. He had never complained about the testing process and immediately focused on studying for the test and taking it again. We worked together on preparing for the retest. He was enthusiastic and came to all of the practice sessions. He was late to one session and was very apologetic. He had come close to passing the test on his own but always missed by three points. I was able to tell him about several areas he misunderstood. There were problems on adding and subtracting fractions that he had been doing wrong for most of his school life. We had discovered several problems he had never understood. It was a special feeling to watch him discover new ways of learning. He was one of the most positive students with whom I have worked. Whether he passed or failed the test was never an issue. He seemed to want to work as hard as he could and felt that he was ready for the test when the time came. I told him that he was likely going to pass because he knew more than he ever had before. He knew that he knew more. There were problems he could solve that he had never solved before. The test came and he passed it. We both felt great. What was most important to me was that even if he had not passed the test it would not have devastated him. I do occasionally see him. What is good is his enthusiasm which transcends the earlier boundaries.

Four years later I met a young lady who lived in public housing. She had contacted me about taking the proficiency test in order to graduate. I learned that she had been one of the five students who was disqualified earlier. She had two children and she needed her diploma in order to get a job for which she was in line. I wanted to work with her, but our communication was not consistent, and I never heard from her until one day she showed up in my office. She was still serious about taking the test. We worked together and this time she passed and received her diploma. It meant so much to her. I still wonder about the other three students.

Multiple choice and standardized tests have devastating effects on many lives in our schools. Most of the tests are meaningless because they are constructed from idiosyncratic facts and problems which are insignificant to many minds. The answers to the pointless problems are as unimportant as the questions. This is complicated by the rule of only one correct answer. Many students accept this world. They live with the system. Once the student learns what is expected of him, he is willing to conform. He has a goal defined for him. That is the deep problem of education. It is brought about because the extrinsic objects of grades, diploma, report cards, and other rewards compel some students to believe and feel that they are better than others. They live in an unreal world in which temporarily-held facts they were forced to learn soon leave them. They have been motivated to exist in an artificial world of measurement, which has only an appearance of importance. It is not the actual world.

There are some high school students for whom learning comes with less effort. They do not work hard and receiving a high school diploma is not a challenge or an endeavor of special interest to them. Because they are not challenged, have no particular plan or purpose in life, and are not around others who do, they never know what they are capable of achieving. They live in conventional America with small effort.

Some students exceed the requirements of a high school diploma because their personal standards are higher than those of society and conventional America. Some have valued learning from an early age and have continued to live such a life. Some have worked hard to please their parents. Others have learned of learning from their parents, relatives or friends.

My wife is teaching a third grade class. The class has students who are African American, Argentine, Mexican, Chinese, Vietnamese, Nicaraguan, and Caucasian. She invites me to the class and I come and I try to work on interesting problems with them. Many of their minds have been conditioned for years to seek the correct answer. There is intellectual satisfaction in discovering paths that stop our wandering and time wasted searches to get to where we are going. We do not wish to be continuously frustrated or forever starting over. We wish to be mathematically powerful and to understand the world and our own thinking. We understand things when we do them in our own way and when we can do them in other ways.

They were good to work with because they all became so enthusiastic about solving problems. Initially not everyone was interested, but once we found questions that engaged us all then the whole class had a mission. As a group we were no longer struggling with distractions but performing at a high level. There was the interest and curiosity of seeing if their individual thinking and theory had found the answer for them. They were eager to find out and to keep trying as individuals and as a class.

Multiplication as Addition

I gave the class one problem in addition. I asked them to add the numbers one through one-hundred. I told them that I was told that this was the same problem that was given to a youth in school who later became a great mathematician. I told them that I was also told that the student always asked his teacher for interesting problems and one day was told to add numbers one through one hundred. To the surprise of the teacher the student found a path to the solution. He learned that 5050 was the sum. There are several thoughts to the student's approach. One of the possible paths taken was to realize that:

1+100=101
2+99=101
3+98=101

.

.

50+51=101

There were 50 sums of 101 and 50 times 101 equals 5050. That was a possible path. If this were so then he was able to penetrate the process of addition and to transform it into multiplication. This was relevant to his problem. It enabled him to discover what he was searching for. Multiplication had provided the mathematical power to reach the destination. This is a special mathematical example that I sometimes share with students and other persons.

In working with this problem with the class, we first looked at other problems and wrote their partial sums on the board. We solved the problem of adding numbers one through ten (1-10).

1=1
1+2=3
1+2+3=6

The partial sums were 1, 3, 6, 10, 15, 21, 28, 36, 45, and 55. I gave them the problem of adding numbers one through one hundred for homework. One student discovered the path they were all seeking. Many were in the neighborhood, but did not know whether they were there or not. They were unable to determine when they would arrive at the solution. It was an African American girl who discovered a path and knew she had reached the destination they all sought. This was the process she used. She used a calculator to determine each partial sum. Then her grandmother used her calculator to parallel the process. When the partial sums did not check they reworked the additions until they both checked. When they reached 5050 they had both verified each partial sum for the entire sequence and knew they were there. They had used the calculator to search for patterns and to provide the mathematical power to get them there. Each person's journey and understanding of math is unique and personal.

Is a diploma a challenging goal for all students to pursue? Schools no longer have the mission of educating students. Children are not to be taught, processed, or educated for a conventional life. Our mission is to live in a world where we are all free to learn, to explore, to observe, and where all of us have our own mission and a spirit within us that compels us to pursue a serious life.

CHAPTER 21

The School Society

I meet students for which schools have little or no effect or meaning. They do not respect or understand themselves or others or what is going on in the school or in the classroom. They are inconsistent in their school interaction. School is a bureaucracy in which anonymous beings live a chaotic and confused existence. Few persons ever change their worlds. The truth to them is simply what they choose to believe. Is there truth in a school? Is it understood?

I receive a telephone call informing me that there is a gun incident at a high school. I have no more details, and I am uncertain as to the seriousness of the situation. I decide to go to the school. I arrive to find a quiet and ordered environment. There are no students in the hall and there are no signs of any incident. I ask for the principal, and I am directed to where she is meeting. I walk into an office to find a police officer and several persons involved in separate conversations about the incident. In the room is the principal, her supervisor, the police officer, and three other school members. The principal's supervisor directs her to summarize to me what is known. A gun was brought on campus and several shots were fired is what I am told, in her report. The police officer and several staff members assist her in her statements. I find the report incomplete. It does not put me there in the situation. I ask some questions, What time did it occur? Where did it happen? Who was there? Was there a victim, an assailant? Were there witnesses? The supervisor told me what she knew.

It was a student at the school and an outsider who were in a fight outside room 239. It happened at 10:15 am. A school staff member moved to break up the fight. He felt a gun in the pocket of the outsider. He asked him to leave the building. The outsider cooperated. The student from the school followed him outside and the school staff member followed them both out of the building. Two shots were fired. Students ran for safety. Neither the staff member nor anyone else was able to identify who fired the shots. No one was injured. The gunshots were directed up into the air. The incident was still being investigated.

From this description I was able to assist the principal and the school staff to prepare a special school bulletin to inform the staff and students what had happened. Parents were also calling the school. They could be given the same special bulletin. Though the school was quiet there was uncertainty, misinformation, rumor, and confusion. No one knew exactly what had started the fight or what was the reason for the gun fire. It was known that individuals from rival gangs were involved. It had been going on all week in the community, a student reported. The actual person who brought the gun originally may have been a girl. The suspected student was part of the investigation that was going on. Nowadays there is a special gang task force that provides schools with resources to resolve conflicts between gangs and to help schools provide a safe environment for its students.

I received three telephone calls. All were from San Francisco newspapers. I told each of them the truth as I knew it. I read to them the bulletin that the staff, students, and parents would receive. One reporter had heard that the school was under siege and wondered who had been hurt and was the situation under control? I talked to all three reporters and two of them recorded the statements that I gave to them. I know because no one was hurt that it is less of a story than they may have anticipated. This was certainly true of the third reporter. I tell this reporter that the school is under control and that no one was injured. She is concerned about it being a racial incident. I tell her the fight was between two black male students and students from no other race had been involved. She seemed satisfied. She had heard that was a possibility and had to check it out.

She then wanted to know how chaotic things were and how afraid the people in the school were. There was no chaos, I told her. How could I be certain, she wondered. I told her that I was in the school and that I could see throughout the building and that it was as quiet as ever. I did not know how much fear there was. I would be surprised if there was not a great deal of fear amongst some persons. They knew there were gunshots and probably wondered what else had happened or what else was happening. They were in their rooms, cut off from communications and events occurring elsewhere in the school.

The school bulletin, however, informed each room about the truth of what happened. That would clear up much of the guesswork. Several parents had said that they might take their children out of the school. They were reacting to unconfirmed rumor. It was a fact that most of the parents in the schools did value the truth. They wanted to know what was happening.

A society needs rules that are sometimes meaningless to an individual. An individual walking through an empty school alone is different from a society of two thousand students walking through a school. Communicating with a single student in a classroom is different from communicating with a thousand students at an assembly. It is this fact that makes school interesting to me. When there is a realization in a school that it can live as a society with its own mission, it is then an empowered and self organizing world that can discover truth.

A school must create new life and discover truth as it is living and learn that it is not built up over time. Truth comes immediately and lies beyond all its remembered days. Each person in it has a unique and personal journey that is distinct but is not more important than any other person's or than a school's destination and mission.

In San Francisco there are no metal detectors in any schools, nor have they been considered. I can understand why there are places though that use detectors. It is in response to the empowerment of extreme individuals and preventing guns from entering the school. During the rapture of human discovery and innovation which leads to the invention of new ideas and devices, we do not realize that new and powerful technologies can take on lives of their own. Guns and other such devices make us a danger to ourselves and to others. (Several years ago a student at this same school was shot in the head from a gun accident. This is also the school where I was once principal and a student was killed by gun.) Recently I read a letter from a concerned citizen to high school students on the value of reading. He gives them a rough quote from a character in a book by Tom Robbins, *Even Cowgirls Get the Blues*, who says, "There are lots of things to live for, some things to die for, but there is nothing to kill for." I see this not as a statement of knowledge nor as one of any particular philosophy, but as a truth, an insight into our lives.

CHAPTER 22

Student Learning

Those who overcome poverty, hopelessness, and social disorganization are those who refuse to be bound or defined. They have their own creativity and determination, and others around them who support and understand them. They are able to take advantage of risks, opportunities, and ways out of poverty and hopelessness. They abandon victimization and are not limited by convention. They break the patterns and live with what life provides.

Forgotten souls dwell in a remainder society. African Americans and others who are there feel unfairly treated and dehumanized as individuals. Being black and poor and living in desperate conditions they are thought less of as people. Therefore they are forgotten and ignored. They remain unsupported in their struggle to change the conditions of their lives. Their conflict is from educational exclusion, poverty, drugs, discrimination, culture, class and lack of resources for their children and community. They are cut off from conventional life and isolated unto themselves.

For those who reside in a remainder society, what symbols and objects do they live with? What holds them in their state of exclusion and isolation? What frees them from living disconnected lives? A question I ask of students, teachers, and others is what is power? Money, title and position, violence and fear, are examples of power. Information is another example. One student tells me that love is an example of power. I do not provide much dialogue about his example, but the problem challenges my attention.

For students to do profound things they must know deep within them that there is something valuable and vital, which they learn can transform their lives. They are then able to take chances, live with uncertainty and push to their physical and mental limits. They discover there are things and people who come into their lives and who are there as they empower themselves.

I work with a group which looks for students who demonstrate extremely high academic performance in the face of extreme disadvantage. The mission of the group is to find such high school students in San Francisco and to present them with scholarships to study at the University of California at Berkeley. In the end twelve students are selected. I commend the selection committee whose members work hard in an in-depth effort to discover students who are able to transcend extreme obstacles such as family powerlessness, lack of financial resources, and language, cultural, and ethnic barriers to live profound and empowered lives.

I am impressed with the racial and ethnic diversity of the students identified. They are Asian, Latino, African American, and White. It is a representation of youth that is capable of arising from society and public education, that can contribute profoundly to society, but seldom does. Rather than the emergence of individuals with depth in their minds, hearts and souls, we produce individuals who conform to our predetermined standards. What motivates this diverse group of students to persevere through hardship and struggle? Do they have a mission in life? I read their thinking through their writing. Though there always seems to be students who transcend their circumstances, I am fascinated with what several students learn and observe about life and their existence in the world. They have all survived public education, they have acquired technical knowledge and skills. How does one receive additional technical knowledge? College. Work. Many wanted to learn more. They wanted to be contributors to society, to obtain challenging and satisfying jobs, to please their families, and to move beyond what their parents were able to achieve. They did the work to get to this point in their lives.

They all talk about and write about how they became the persons they are. Some individuals see things more deeply than others. When I was young and went to sea, crossing the Atlantic was a new life and a great adventure. I met a person who became a close friend throughout the voyage. I have never seen him since, though I have thought about him. He amazed me because no one loved the sea more.

His name was Luis, and he was Puerto Rican. Every moment on the sea to him was sacred. There were older seamen who had made numerous trips around the world and had been out on the sea much of their lives. They were accustomed to this life, to the harshness and the unknown days on the sea. Luis was unique. Even though this was only his second journey, this life was deep inside of him. When we drifted past the Azores, he admired the islands and their seamen and crafts. Europe and the Mediterranean had meant much to his life. He seemed blessed to live his life on the sea. He lived a deeper life on this journey than many of those who had sailed for countless years and who had even sailed around the world numerous times. As I read about the students who demonstrate exceptional performance in the face of extreme disadvantage it is evident there are those who see things deeper than others do.

One student is living alone in a foster home with no family. Since an early age she has never had a settled life. She moved around because of the military life they lived. The student lost contact with the father at eight years of age and lived with the mother. The mother recently remarried and now lives in North Carolina. The student sometimes lives with a relative in San Francisco. She is an "A" student. She has lived a life where everything is always changing but she manages to find the inner strength to be at this point in life. The mother's new husband has a chemical dependency and the student has a conflict with him. Both the mother and the new father are unemployed and provide no support to her. She works part time for the needed financial support. She finds that school and her friends provide a supportive environment. Studying with others and learning that being black in this society shows her how to understand the world and the role of education in it.

She participates in other school activities. In the cheer leading and Spirit Squad they are on their own for the most part. They practice two hours daily and they get from them what they put into them. The squad is held together by their common interests and their own dedication, which makes their effort and hard work worthwhile. She states that without any help they have survived many situations by working together and not giving up. Those who doubted their abilities gave them further incentive to accomplish the goals they had set. In the end her goal in life is to continue to be self-educated and independent as well to help educate others. She has learned much from personal goals and self-reliance which she hopes to give to others. She respects all others in society and appreciates and understands what life provides. For her life is a gift.

Another individual had a father who left home when the student was in nursery school. The student used a clover as a symbol of her life. It had a special meaning because the her name was Clover. Her mother was ill with a tumor and there were no relatives to look to in times of trouble. There was no help. Her mother was given up for adoption and had no relatives that she knew. She did not complain. Instead she stated that these circumstances had made for a stronger life and made deeper roots in life to withstand the wind. She stated that a plant or a life that was given everything did not use effort to grow on its own and lived in stagnation. Without luxuries one was given the opportunity to grow and to grow and to flourish. She was determined to become an engineer. She was good in math and science and had been exposed to successful experiences in these areas. She volunteered at local college science laboratories, but there was never a definite goal in mind. Something was missing. One summer she had the opportunity to visit the hills of Vermont. They were green with life. This had a deep meaning for the student. A four leaf clover is not ordinary and is often overlooked. Its special qualities lie hidden and dormant among so many others. She was a city plant and did not want to be a mountain jamboree dancer but met a researcher there who changed the direction of her life. Science suddenly came to life for her. She got a look at the depths and possibilities of work and life. It was an insight that came to her in a small Vermont town. She had gone there and found what was missing from life. Now her love for math and science had revealed itself in a way that had given her a mission to pursue and a fascination with life.

The stories of these two young women are examples of students who are examining what it is to live through unusual times. They are going beyond academic success because they question the world, and they work to further their capabilities in it.

One day I visited a school. It was late afternoon. School had been out for forty five-minutes and I walked down empty, quiet halls. I expected nothing, but I came upon a room and inside there were forty students absorbed in learning. A person stood before them, lecturing. This was a senior class and these students were almost all going to college. They were a motivated group. The person spoke of Africa and about things they had never heard of before. They were dead silent and listened intently. I was amazed to see so many black students who were so captured and intrigued in this human drama. Africa was their home they were told. For some these were just words and for a few it communicated a deeper truth. Africa deeply excited me also. I never read much about Africa as a youth but it was the place I began my life as a teacher. I lived and learned about adventure, hard work and struggle, independence, human determination, and freedom. I taught and learned with others who valued learning. For me it was a great life and a great place on the earth.

Africa is a land of youth, timelessness, discovery, and adventure. I am fascinated with the land and everything about it. I met and lived with great and spirited souls there. To the African students in the school, rich and powerful nations lie across the sea. They are curious about how the people in America live and its power in the world. (What is power?) In the village where I lived the children were loved and they were deeply dedicated to their families. The students in this San Francisco classroom have an energy to initiate change in their lives as they wonder about Africa. In them is a sense of human respect and the spirit of the people that was present in Africa. I loved life in Africa because of the human respect and the spirit of the people. I loved the African land. What is love? Is there love in the hearts of the students and is there curiosity in their minds about power?

Our existence can be a ceaseless demand for power, where our minds are filled with fears and attachments, and love is destroyed. Love is what we do without motive, certainty, or expectation. It is when the mind is unbiased and disinterested (having no stake in an issue or its outcome), and is not seeking to escape from danger and uncertainty by being efficient like an army, a government, or other such organization. These groups and organizations use their skillfulness and productivity to give them the power to fight danger and foreign and unknown things. Well organized societies are proficient and efficient but are not giving and generous from the heart and soul. Love is there when the mind is not bound by convention, ritual and conformity, or any condition that follows from inventions of the mind. It is new, unknown, revolutionary, and creative. It is the power within us that a student one day communicated to me.

School and Learning

Schools are traditional places. Societies build them for children to become participants, contributors, and leaders in the world. They are places which seldom achieve this promise because they transmit knowledge that adults think is important. Schools seldom liberate minds or produce independent thinking. They, the adults, are attached to a known world in which they have struggled and endured. Parents and teachers want their children to learn from these misfortunes and not repeat these lives, failures, and tragedy. They promise them to live and to experience something that is yet to be. Success is an illusion based on hope. But the student must live his own life, make his own mistakes, and find his own way. Schools cannot just provide answers and promises. Students must be compelled from within to be creative in areas that interest them. So they have to try things out, make discoveries, and suffer failure. Schools are dedicated to providing answers to questions students have not asked. They offer experiences that students have not encountered or lived.

The best teaching is teaching oneself. Sometimes students learn by having someone else around to listen to their thoughts, questions, and ideas. They do not often have the opportunity to try their ideas or thoughts on others around them. Teachers and others often do not give them the depth of attention to hear their voices. Often they are unable to hear students without passing judgment. But often students are ready to learn from their own ideas.

Students should not be given answers but challenged to a deeper understanding of their own knowledge. Their learning should not be based on having conventional objects to recognize. They should discover the answers even if everyone else around them already knows. They learn when they create their own knowledge, and the objects around them exist without history and prior meaning. Past knowledge and objects with predetermined meaning make them prisoners of time. They live here and now. Students do not learn when they are unable to break through tradition and convention and are unable to master classroom engagement. This prevents their fluency in achieving teacher goals, school system goals, and their own personal goals. Students are

Chapter 23

School Lives

Our minds are conditioned to romanticize previous struggles and achievements. A friend says that we cannot kill the ghost. We become attached to our worlds of walking miles to school each day and home again, of getting by with less and of not complaining of the trying circumstances and the hard life we or others once endured. Our minds and thought perpetuate these conditions and there is nothing to change the course.

Being educated to achieve distinction and to have importance over others leads to shallow, empty lives. It creates inequality in our society. Being educated to be a businessman or a scientist dedicated to accumulated knowledge contributes to the destruction and suffering of the world. Why build knowledge to dominate others, to destroy life, or to perpetuate fear and violence? We worship success and security. We escape to a life of minimum conflict where we are afraid to step out of our isolated place. This kills in us the spirit of adventure. We live apart from the weak and poor, above them.

Of the students who passed through the Ranch School while I was there, I did occasionally see several of them again later in their lives. One day I saw a student from the lowest reading group on the street in San Francisco. We immediately recognized each other even though it was twenty years later. He seemed an enterprising person, washing windows in small shops. In his own way he was a contributing member of society. He was proud of his work and what he was accomplishing. I began to see him all over town. He appeared to be successfully engaged.

One day I walked out of the building where I worked and he was sitting on the corner, homeless. I talked to him about his situation. His mind was confused and his conversation was not clear. He talked about a woman having a spell over him and how she would not allow him to succeed. He was convinced of her powers and that she had ruined his life. His success had been temporary. We cannot always count on being successful. I gave him a dollar. He thanked me as I walked away wondering what would become of him. I wondered about the same thing twenty years ago. He had no purpose in life. He was the first former student that I had encountered who was homeless, but eventually there were others.

What is the life of the homeless? Of those whom I encounter, I observe that they seldom examine their thoughts. Few have clear ideas. They are not grounded. They strive for and hope for a conventional life and its simple things. They grasp for a life of stability and changelessness, as they dream about a house, a friend, financial capability, eating a regular meal, and acceptance in ordinary places. They dwell at the bottom of society and seldom leave, seldom reach the conventional state. What holds them there? They lack the energy and personal power to cure themselves. In my personal observation of the homeless and those others who live outside of conventional society, I learn that mental illness is a one-way ticket to the bottom of society. San Francisco streets are an asylum for the insane. Some homeless are sane; some are intelligent. Many are unfortunate. There are many homeless people in San Francisco these days and some do find their way into the schools.

One day I received a message that someone would possibly be visiting. I did not know who the person was nor if the person would show up. It was after 6:00 in the evening, and I was leaving the building when I was approached by a stranger. No one else was in the building. He says that he had called earlier and left a message that he would be coming to see me. He wants to know if he can talk to me. I tell him that I can only give him fifteen minutes and he says that fifteen minutes is fine.

We walk up to my office on the second floor. His face is strange and ancient. His cheekbones seem prehistoric. The most striking thing about him is his hair. It is blond and orange yellow in its intensity. Several weeks ago I had been at an event hosted by ex-convicts and drug addicts. They had a strong social presence and understanding in their interactions with the individuals whom they encountered. It was difficult for me, however, to get accustomed to some of their eyes. They held a penetrating gaze that made me wonder about their lives. I had the same feeling about this fellow and his life. I wondered where he was from and what was on his mind. He carries a briefcase and the two of us do not speak as we walk up the stairs. We arrive in the office and we sit at the table. He takes out his briefcase and opens it. If he has a weapon in it I am uncertain as to what my next move will be. However, there are only papers. All papers and other objects inside were well organized. It made an interesting statement about him. I had seen the inside of several briefcases over the years, and they were usually disordered and chaotic. This was the most organized that I had observed. Why was this so and why was he here now? He had not made an appointment but had left a message that he would take a chance that I would be in and available when he came.

He tells me about his life. He is originally from Colorado. He has been a musician and done several different kinds of jobs. He was always fascinated by computers and wanted to learn to master them. It never worked. He started several times and had never been successful. I reminded him that I could give him just fifteen minutes. He said that he understood and that he would present what he needed to in that amount of time. He looked at the clock. He told me about the Business and Commerce school he was attending and the computer class in which he was enrolled. He was one of several adults in the class. The person who taught the course was an elderly gentleman who had never taught a computer course before.

The student commented that at first he had doubts about how the course would go with a teacher who was learning along with the students. It did work out though he said. The teacher prepared well for the classes and they were good. He liked the class and because the teacher's knowledge of the course was limited it provided a much freer atmosphere for learning. One could take more chances in working on a problem. Many of the assignments he found to be easy. He knew how to type and had made a living at typing before. So that helped him with the keyboard and he was an excellent speller. He searched through his papers to show me the A+ grades he had received. In fact, he told me about several papers on which he had not received an A. He went to the teacher and demonstrated that the question had been vague, and the teacher had agreed and decided to eliminate the questions. He had also then received A's on those papers. The student found some of the concepts to be difficult. The teacher was unable to answer his questions. He understood that the teacher could not help him so he went to two other teachers in the school. They were able to answer some of his questions. Still there were other questions. He was referred to other books. He was becoming fascinated with the subject, but he was also very frustrated because he was encountering obstacles along the way. He spent all of his afternoons at the public library studying. It was discouraging because hard work did not seem to matter. I wondered what kind of work he did that allowed him to spend all day in the library. He said that he did not work and was unemployed. He also told me that he was homeless and that he had no place to stay. This explained to me about his briefcase. It was where he housed his worldly objects and necessities. I also wondered if he was upset when he was unable to talk to me by telephone because I was possibly costing him money from a pay phone.

Although he had learned a great deal about this subject, he was again at an impasse. Was there some mental block that was not allowing him to master the subject? He had come so far in his knowledge but was unable to go beyond his own limited resources. One day a teacher gave him a version of a book that began to answer all of his questions. He was amazed at how everything was connected and began to make sense. It was as though I was listening to a seventeen-year-old mind in a thirty-year-old body. I knew about such students and their minds and their search for meaning in their learning. I have observed such focus and quest for understanding in students before. They have included youth in Africa, New York City, and San Francisco. The energy of learning exists throughout the world. It can bring freedom to our lives. I once worked in San Francisco with a sixty-five-year old gentleman with a seventeen-year-old mind. He was curious, enthusiastic, and excited about both learning and contributing to others.

I tell him that he has two minutes to finish up and to tell me why he is here. I still wonder what's on his mind. He continues. In the beginning I was enrolled in the morning session, he said, but some days I would be permitted to work in the afternoon class also. This term the teacher no longer permitted me to attend the afternoon class. In time I became quite advanced in the class. He went into his briefcase again. He found the paper he was searching for. He had entered a command into the computer which forced the other computer users to follow what he had programmed. I saw what he had done. (I once had a student who was obsessed with crashing the computer system, so I was not surprised at this fascination.) He has forty five seconds to tell me why he is here.

"I accepted the teacher's decision about not attending the afternoon class. I wondered about it, but I did not question it. I also understood the teacher being upset with my unauthorized use of the computer to communicate commands to the users."

"Is this why you have come?" I wondered. His time was up.

"Well, I guess why I'm here is that I want to protest about not being allowed to continue as a student in the school."

"I'll investigate your complaint. But how do I contact you? You have no home, no address. You have to contact me to find out about the investigation and any decision."

Weeks went by. I did not know if I would ever see him again. Then one day he left a message that he had called me. I wanted to set up a conference with him and the teacher. When would he call again? I talked to the principal and she submitted to me a written report. I awaited his call or visit. It never came. I reviewed the report of the principal and the teacher and decided that I would not have a teacher conference but I would meet with him again alone. Still he never called. I thought about him but communication was one-way and he had not made contact. One day I was driving down the street and I recognized him standing on a corner at the bus stop. I was not surprised because I expected to see him on the street if I ever saw him again. I stopped the car and told him that I wanted to meet with him to discuss his complaint.

"Call me tomorrow," I told him.

He said that he would. He did not call. He did call the following day and we arranged for a meeting. He came. The teacher was afraid of him. After he had dismissed him from the class, he started receiving telephone calls with no response from the caller. The teacher suspected him. The school also did not like the fact that he was using the school for his home. Apparently he shaved and cleaned up there. I told them that he had no place to live and that he had to overcome obstacles in his life. He was not to be blamed for the life he struggled to leave. Why do we continue to create inequality for any person in our schools.

I told him that I had investigated his case and found that the school had acted fairly. (The principal was one of the most competent people I ever met.) He had exceeded the number of days allowed for the course he was taking. He should move on to the community college. He had just finished a course there, he said. He accepted that, but he wondered,

"Could the teacher just dismiss me from the class with just ten days left? Can he do that?"

"Yes."

"But what I do not understand is what suddenly made him so upset to do this to a student. Why couldn't I have finished the ten days. Why was I so harshly treated?"

I read to him the teacher's account of what had happened. The teacher reported that the student had been unable to complete the semester course textbook in the prescribed time and had continued into the second semester. During the second semester the student had studied the Appendix of the book for three months. The teacher wrote that the exercise should have taken two weeks. The teacher reported that he copied a copyrighted document and submitted a fifty page long assignment. The student's statement was that it was his first book to write on a computer. It was a hassle getting him to leave the room each day. He always had one more file to print. The final act that upset the teacher was the message he had printed on the system network.

"The teacher said you accused him of being a "petty dictator" and said he wished to "control" people."

"I said that he was all right as an educator, but that he wanted more control over the class rather than to show concern for what the student was learning. A true teacher wants students to learn and grow. I was kicked out of that class because I made a mistake, which is a learning experience. The teacher was more concerned with mediocrity than with his students learning."

"The teacher made the evaluation of your performance as well as the performance of each other person in the class. You were like all the other students in the class. This is how you were treated." I told him that there may be a need to examine the system and do it differently as many of the things we do in school are trivial and bureaucratic.

He accepted the decision. His final question was whether the school could serve as a reference for his getting a job? Could he get a letter of recommendation?

The answer was no. The school could not recommend him because he had not worked for them. They did not know how he would perform on the job. They would send a copy of the course material he had completed.

He was serious about finding work. He had not had recent successes in his life. He was presently on jury duty, he said. I asked him how was he notified, and having no address he said he had a post office box. I wondered where was he living. He told me for right now he was living in a homeless shelter on Market Street. He could not receive telephone calls, so he was trying to get a job from the public telephone booth. I wished him luck. I never saw him again.

Children inherit the schools in which they are students. Many students do master their instruction and are skillful in its use and application. Most students do not question what they know and the derivatives of their acquired knowledge dominate their lives. Few of our students perform with insight, intelligence, creativity, reflection, or in-depth understanding. The few who do so are aware of their own education and that of humankind. They are aware of the source and the origin of knowledge. Students who understand mathematics do so because they are able to move outside the tradition of rules, proofs, and accepted school instruction. They are able to construct their own mathematical worlds, create their own learning, and use the collective genius of humankind to discover the beauty, consistency, and mathematical power that they seek.

I share with people a story I read about a child who became a serious mathematician in later life. As a child he counted four stones and then he counted them in reverse order and the number was four also. It was a startling discovery to him. It changed his world. He had discovered something profound even though many others in the world might have already known it.

I recently visited a classroom in which the teacher and the students had prepared for the day's lesson. I was there to observe them, not to evaluate, which could trivialize and artificialize my presence. They knew I was coming. I was impressed with the time I was with them and I wrote a letter of appreciation to the teacher for having me as their guest:

This letter is to share the joy and enthusiasm that I felt and experienced in being in your class. I was impressed with the preparation and the energy brought to the class for the lesson on **New Laws.**

The students were able to internalize the focus of the lesson which required a) creating three new laws for people's rights, education, and taxes and b) expressing their reasons for the laws. The lesson was organized so that students were aware of the technical and historical process in making new laws and, at the same time, were challenged to examine the present contemporary situation.

I must commend you and the class for an outstanding example of the use of cooperative learning to meaningfully involve the teacher and students in sharing and demonstrating a learning focus. I was also impressed with the reception I received as both an observer and a participant.

I had been impressed with the teacher because she had expressed an understanding and philosophy of teaching and learning. It is in her to be a teacher. She tells me that little learning takes place in many of our classrooms. The learning that does occur is most often done by the person who is doing the talking. This is most often the teacher. So most of the learning that is going on in a classroom is being done by the teacher. In cooperative learning groups each student is expected to speak and to contribute to the group and to the class. Each student does. Each student is able to teach what he or she has studied and knows. (I knew from my first job in Africa that you really learn something by teaching it.) All of the students in the class were involved in learning. All.

She is a serious teacher and does not rely on extrinsic motivation for students. Such teachers do not use artificial and conventional objects to compete with; or to influence, the attention of students. Teachers whose students learn for prizes, grades, rewards, and other material gain subvert learning because the student learns to see the prize, grade, or praise, rather than something interesting on its own. Extrinsic knowledge becomes an illusion to freedom when a student's goal or mission is to master the rules and to satisfy the teacher's expectations in the attainment of the contrived rewards. Students and teachers perpetuate this system because rather than explore and examine it, they conform to it. The minds of the students are not free and liberated because they do not have a mission to pursue.

When we are serious about learning the things we do, we seek a balance between certainty and uncertainty. The certainty is what we use for order and living disciplined lives. It is the technical knowledge that is collectively shared by humankind. There is also learning from the heart and soul which is uncertain and not cumulative, that which has no fear and knows no authority or boundaries and inspires us to be curious, to explore, and to live with intensity, to discover the beauty and the rigors of the world. With uncertainty in the world there is freshness, surprise.

The energy that the individuals and a school can sometimes reach at graduation is at times moving and special. I participated recently in a student graduation that stirred my soul and those of the others who were there, including the president of the board of education. The presence of the board president was significant because this was a continuation high school and not a regular comprehensive or special academic high school. The board president made it clear that every student's graduation was important. It was why he was there. I was always impressed with his support for poor students and schools. It was important to him. It was a graduation of twenty-six students who had been through some of the worst of times of their lives while in schools. The parents and family members presented the diplomas to the students and they each spoke of a time that they could hardly ever have imagined, which was this day when their son or daughter would graduate from high school. There was one white student who was from Seattle and had moved to Massachusetts to a private school and was now finally here in San Francisco and completing this hard journey. The father was in tears the whole time that he told the story. Others had come from the Philippines and Mexico. Most were black students from urban America who had struggled in an educational system and now were undaunted. They chose the theme **Against All Odds** for the graduation. This is my statement to them.

Against All Odds

I am glad to be here. I wish to acknowledge the principal and the staff for inviting me. I also wish to acknowledge the parents, family members, community, and the friends who have come to recognize this graduating class. I am grateful to be able to address you today. It was more than ten years ago that I attended the only other graduation of this school and it was then Alamo Park School. I have a strong recollection of the graduation and the speaker who was the leader of the American Indian Movement. As I recall he arrived late. What had been so remarkable about the graduation was that he had driven by road more than a thousand miles from South Dakota just to be there. Nothing could have stopped him. I come with the same enthusiasm for sharing this occasion with you. I had hoped to be here last year, but I was on a mountain climbing expedition which was an experience that affected and deepened my view of the world and of the others who were in it.

As you leave this school what life will you pursue? What challenges, barriers, obstacles and resources will others and the world present? Information and technology are new and different forms of power. Their nature is such that they can be shared by a multitude of people without diminishing their effects. We can all share the same information and it can empower us all. It is the most democratic form of power. We are in a world of technology. The computer is an empowering tool that is transforming our lives and our world. What is a computer? How would you define it? A computer is an instrument that breaks down barriers to communication. Last year during my mountain-climbing expedition I searched the world through the information highway to learn from others who had climbed the mountain. There were fascinating accounts of individual struggle and performance. This motivated me to write my own story about the climb which is now on the information highway and anyone in the world can read it.

How will you as individuals face this new world? How are you to empower yourselves **against all the odds** that await you? It will be important that you value learning more than knowledge. Learning takes place when there is good teaching. Good teaching is teaching ourselves. We must have rigorous expectations. It is important that you have deep goals. There are two teachers on the staff who have run numerous marathons. Indeed, on some occasions I have had the good fortune of running with them. (Another important aspect of learning is being around other motivated people and discovering what we can give to each other and learn from each other.) One teacher has run in the Boston Marathon. Few individuals from around the world even qualify for this event. Who knows how long a marathoner must run? It is twenty-six miles, three hundred eighty five yards. It takes personal focus, work, and self discipline. It is important that you discover your own interests and abilities and be willing to experiment and deepen your strengths in the areas in which you perform well. It is important that you find your own voice in the world. (It is significant to me that these individuals do run marathons because as teachers we sometimes confuse students by telling them that they can be great individuals and can reach great heights but as teachers we do not do these things ourselves.) In the movie, **Stand and Deliver**, the teacher Jaime Escalante, had students who achieved and learned Calculus where once students at Garfield High School had been satisfied to learn general math and other remedial subjects. He respected their minds and the students, through their own discipline and personal focus, worked against all the odds and performed at a high level. Doing Calculus problems, climbing mountains, running marathons, mastering technology, or excelling academically are just some of the ways to perform at a high level. Who's smarter; Einstein, Malcolm X, or Picasso? The answer is none of them. We all have different intelligences and strengths.

I want to speak to the question of empowering yourself against all odds. How do you live in human freedom? First, it takes energy to empower oneself, which gives us the courage to do and to learn new things. So we are empowered when we have the energy to both initiate and to sustain change and to perform at a high level. When we are performing at a high level we are not concerned about success or failure. Understanding is more important than our victory or our defeat or in becoming someone important. What does it mean to understand things? We understand something when we can do it more than one way.

My closing remarks are these. I hope that your lives are filled with worthwhile challenges and adventure. Although much is unknown—remain curious, value freedom and learning, and explore the things that interest you. The world is continuously changing so be willing to learn new things, and do not rely on past knowledge.

It is my deep hope that each of you lives a life that is full of meaning, where fresh ideas exist and are understood. I wish you each a good life and a great future.

Thank you.

Final Contributions

Schools are temporary places that are always changing. Many teachers have spent their entire adult lives in schools, but we all move on beyond the school. There are four friends who have given their lives to schools and to public education. I write statements about their services to students and to all of those they have worked with for sometimes almost forty tears. The four individuals are representative of the schools and city of San Francisco. Their ethnic groups are African American, Chinese, Caucasian, and Latino.

I reflect on what I say to each of them. They have given much, and it is important to me that I seriously express their contribution to public education and the youth whom they have worked with, struggled with, and whose lives they may have changed. The first statement is written to an African American woman who was a dedicated teacher and school administrator.

*   *   *

My purpose in writing this letter of recognition is to express my gratitude for your independent thought, human understanding, and special contribution in your twenty-five-year expedition through the San Francisco Unified School District. I commend you for your courage and endurance. You have acted profoundly to question a society that has given up on many of its youth, and where many youth have given up to live hopeless lives without personal goals in a world of violence, drugs, family destruction, poverty, and racism. In your journey you have persisted in your vision that all of our youth and students can live great lives both individually and collectively. You have demonstrated that it is crucial that they do. Indeed, it challenges the soul of our society to provide our youth with the opportunities to test themselves and to comprehend their deepest-held thinking and values. You have valued learning, and you have engaged your school community in a quest for mutual commitment for human respect, cooperation, and highest performance.

Your journey has had a special significance to us all and as you move on I wish you a great life.

*   *   *

There are good and bad times in our lives as educators. It is important to me that I recognize the significant contributions as I knew them
and observed them. The following statement is written for a Chinese
American teacher and administrator.

It is with great seriousness and appreciation that we recognize the
thirty-six-years that you have contributed to the youth and learning community of San Francisco. Your years as teacher and principal have made
your contribution unique. Throughout your career you have consistently
given attention to good and effective teaching methods, and you have
focused on current and cutting edge approaches to educational excellence. You are to be commended on your spoken and written usage of the
English language. Your writing has consistently exemplified perfection,
accuracy, and thoughtfulness. Your effort to encourage and to bring
about success in both academic and athletic performance expresses your
appreciation of the human spirit. In our complex world and the changing conditions of the American high school, you have demonstrated an
awareness and an appreciation for the multicultural, the multiethnic, and
the multilinguistic nature of our students.

*   *   *

The third statement is written to a White male educator with whom
I worked through the hardest of times and the best of times.

This letter is written in appreciation and in recognition of your
thirty-four-years of service to the students and all others who have
served with the San Francisco Unified School District. You served for
twenty years as a classroom teacher and later as a principal. As a school
educator you demonstrated innovative approaches to school problems
and how to resolve conflicts. You employed a variety of programs to
provide timely access to student information, and you stimulated and
encouraged your staff to become involved in current educational

issues. You acquired personal computer skills that empowered you as a manager. You demonstrated an energetic approach to solving the multitude of problems that came your way. You are to be commended on your positive attitude and willingness to deal with complex issues and problems. Your oral and written command of the English language contributed to stimulating and exciting exchanges of ideas with students, parents, and teachers. And in addition to each of the above areas, you were always a good listener.

Your hard work as a high school principal and all of your other service to the San Francisco Unified School District has been of special significance to us all.

*   *   *

The following was written for a Latino educator with whom I worked very closely throughout our careers.

We first met when he was entering the school as the new principal and I was leaving as a mathematics teacher to become an assistant principal. Since that meeting we have been involved in a multitude of activities that have involved us in talking, organizing, and discovering new things together, and we have held the highest friendship since that time.

It was great working with you and others in a dialogue to pursue the profound performance of the human spirit in our schools. You are to be commended on your written and spoken usage of the English and Spanish languages. Your language has consistently exemplified serious reflection, accuracy, clarity, and thoughtfulness. Your effort to provide and encourage students to pursue excellence in academic, vocational, and athletic performance, and in their other interests, expresses your understanding of the distinct and unique nature of students as contributors to society. You gave much in your work in the district and in addition to those contributions, you always listened and heard what others had to say.

As you face life's adventures, I hope they are profound, just as in the summer when you participated in the five-day rafting adventure down the Rogue River in Oregon. In such a life of living along the rivers, finding solitude, and repelling from great heights, we learn to cooperate, explore, discover, create and to organize our own lives. I hope that you continue to live with such adventure, open-mindedness, and free spirit.

*　　　　　*　　　　　*

They had spent most of their lives in the hardest schools in San Francisco, working with the poorest students. Much of it had been through periods of condemnation of public schools in the United States. Throughout America the question of a free and educated society has been seen as an extraordinary experiment. There has been much loss of hope from artificial social and intellectual differences amongst individuals in the cities across the nation. Public and mass education remains one of several paths to intelligent societies. For some it leads to opportunity. For others it is a place of failure and decay. Our collective vision for schools and society must be deeply examined so they are places where all students who are minority, immigrant, poor, affluent, homeless, motivated, desperate, fearful, undaunted, unbalanced, and adventurous, are respected and challenged as they move through the schools and cities to live profound lives in the struggle for a free society. Our minds, bodies, and spirits exist in complex states as we pass through life.

We pass through the schools and we never know where life will lead. We make what contributions we can. Schools are places where all who pass through them are expected to contribute. This expectation is not consistently communicated or carried out. Some contributions do not go unnoticed. Hundreds of teachers and thousands of students leave the schools each year. The schools have become a way of life for us. How they have changed over the last thirty years; how they have remained the same. There are educators in San Francisco who attended public schools here and say that the schools have not changed since they were in elementary school or middle school. Some schools have deteriorated, and new schools have been built and are still being built. In all cases the students have changed. Schools will not go on forever in San Francisco. The world is impermanent and changing. What meaningfully impacts upon underrepresented minority students meaningfully impacts upon all students. Life is a mystery that one has to discover for oneself and education should help us understand the totality of life. Education should also help us live freely, without fear, to create different societies and new worlds.

City Journey

CHAPTER 24

The Poor

The human race is not old in the universe. One wonders if we will destroy ourselves or further human exploration and go beyond earth's boundaries. The journey of humankind has brought us to a world of city dwellers and the urbanization of the planet. Our cities are islands of high income and modern areas coexisting with slums and ghettos. There is affluence and poverty. As I work in and for schools, I travel deep into places of those whose lives are at their worst.

*   *   *

When we leave schools and live in the actual world we observe that thought is theory. We often do not know this world from our lessons, books, and discussions. San Francisco teachers do not live in the communities in which their students live. Poor parents and students do not know and understand the lives and communities of most teachers. I work on projects for the schools with those excluded and dehumanized in isolated worlds.

The poor are the temporary faces that vanish into worlds, abandoned and forgotten. No one is poor or oppressed forever. Some things have to change. Revolutions, though, are never permanent. And there are those who work as hard as they can but do not escape poverty and suffering.

The poor watch the world in wonder and sadness. Those who live in hunger, who are homeless, who are in shelters or in subsidized housing, surrounded by condemned buildings and living on mean streets, lack ties to the larger society. They are accustomed to an underclass life which sometimes persists across generations. Life after life, poverty remains. It is not a question of being a victim or of there being a conspiracy to oppress them, but of opening a crack in a system that has operated forever in excluding them. To find our own voices and live our best lives rather than being forced to exist in a system at its worst, challenges humankind. Systems work at their best when we are all free and totally connected. We are like any other object such as a tree, an animal, another person, a mountain, a day or a century that is there without a reason. We are all transient beings. As long as there are the poor who are disconnected and isolated from others, our world is not free. When there is sickness in the world we are not healthy. As long as we are not all free we are not as we ought to be. When the oppressed (the poor) are liberated freedom then becomes real to the illusory free (the rich).

We are all vulnerable to addictions that are produced by a loss of balance in our lives. How do we abandon our previous temporary states? It is by wandering around, changing our minds, being invincible and unconquerable. I have discovered that those who are poor and oppressed are as intelligent, insightful, understanding, and as temporary as any other people in the world. It is an interesting phenomenon of human nature that we are capable of curing ourselves even when we hit rock bottom in our lives; that inside of us we can transcend external barriers and be free.

To impact the lives of the children who are from the poorest families in the worst and most impoverished neighborhoods in America is a challenge to schools. How are we to solve the problems of drugs, crime, and poverty and a continuing life in hell and awaken them to take back their lives?

CHAPTER 25

The Remainder Society

I lived in Nigeria, West Africa and in Kenya, East Africa. They were places of deep human journeys for me. Each time I found a collision of life practices when I arrived back in San Francisco. After the temporary shock of changing countries, I would readjust to the American way of life. After a while it soon seemed like I never even went to Africa. I first began in California after a teaching job in Nigeria. In the beginning I worked only in urban inner city schools. I was enthusiastic about working with poor black youth and all others who came to learn in the schools. The schools with children of poverty saw themselves as remainder schools because the more sophisticated and affluent families would choose to send their children to the more select schools in wealthier neighborhoods. It has always been of deepest importance to me that every member of our society, even the lowest of the poor, should have an opportunity to engage in, and prosper from, our world. Today we live in a technological age where information can move at the speed of light. It breaks down isolation and empowers the poor to be globally connected to the larger world.

We each learn freedom in our own way.

Life is a battlefield and a great gift! We understand life's journey in our expeditions through it.

If the lives of all children are valued and loved and their souls matter to us, then we will respect their minds and understand their lives. The children who are poor and in the minority are our greatest tragedy. In our schools the poor and the minority are the least loved and respected. Those of us whose lives are in the schools must help them liberate their voices and free their lives from oppression. All children have deeply felt passions. Let schools be places that they can be expressed.

The San Francisco society for poor people and black people seemed less organized than life and school in Africa had been.

When any individual remains oppressed in a society, it is not free. It is a limited society, a remainder society, a second class society. Life is a battle and a nightmare for those who exist in it. The remainder society is our own human invention and it is sustained by our actions. Some San Francisco schools define themselves as remainder schools. America is a country of possessions. No possession is more accepted than an individual's status or race. Those who are born affluent or white currently dominate American life and determine how others live and what possessions are left for them. Those who are born affluent or white cling to their possession of wealth or race hoping, they will never die. Our mission on this planet is human freedom. In our quest and our adventure here we encounter a life that is rich and great. Our past and our future lives imprison the human spirit. We all cling to past things that are no longer living and to ideas and dreams that are not occurring, and we hold to these things as though they will bring us the happiness that always escapes us. As we venture further into the unknown we learn of the depth of human endurance and performance, and our spirits soar. We are battling for our society's soul. As a black person in America I know that we must have the will and the determination to fight back from the brink of our own extinction. It is not what we possess but what is within us that will determine our destiny.

America is so advanced and so far ahead, yet still so backward and far behind. We are rich in technical knowledge but lack the heart and soul to make all of our people matter. We do not internalize the significance of each person's existence as sacred and important, nor do we understand that the changes in any life may effect the destiny of humankind. Who knew when Rosa Parks refused to give up her bus seat in Montgomery in 1955 that the incident would impact the consciousness of generations of black people, others in the United States, and the world? Or Nelson Mandela's imprisonment in South Africa would stir the world because of his invincibility and unconquerable spirit. I was amazed as a youth to see a single black family move into a white neighborhood and observe the changes this precipitated. White people could not live with the fact that a black neighbor could possess human worth or status equal to theirs. They protested in violence and abandoned their homes and towns. It happened in cities throughout America. The black families who came and who initiated this transformation are now forgotten.

San Francisco is a unique city surrounded by sand and sea and beautiful hills. It is also an urban wasteland. It is filled with wasted minds and oppressed lives. In its streets are desperate voices convinced that they have nothing to give to this world. They lack hope. They have weak memories, and they hardly remember yesterday or their past actions. They therefore risk everything everyday. Their minds lack a way out of poverty. They are in poverty because of the selfish use of resources by others (and by themselves). They exist on what others do not possess and what others do not exploit and consume. They exist as a remainder society. A remainder society is one in which none of us have immunity and one in which many of us die in. We exist in such a society because we are unable to focus our energy on transcending the world that is around us. A remainder society exists because those in it lack the energy to initiate and sustain change. Most black folks in San Francisco and in

America live in such a society. Also living in this society besides those of us who are poor and hungry and living in hopelessness are those who are addicted and living on the streets, who are imprisoned by public and private institutions and organizations and those who are imprisoned by their own lives. Those whom the world calls niggers live in this world also. The remainder society is really the niggers (devalued and unacknowledged persons) of the world. Such a society is dominated by others. It is sustained, barely, because the weak societies die and the strong ones live. Some of us begin to discover freedom and find a way out of this society when we see that we have more inner strength than some of those around us, when we understand that we must give more to this society than others, and that we must live with our hearts and our souls.

More than half the youth who are killed in our streets are black, and are killed by blacks. Society is conditioned to see the worst in black youth. There is a devalued status of the black race in America. And as blacks we do not often allow our performance to affect our view of ourselves. We let other people's opinions dominate our reality.

I am a black person from this society. I travel in it and work in San Francisco and in the surrounding cities. This allows me to observe learning and human behavior. For more than twenty five-years I have worked in schools in Nigeria, Kenya, and San Francisco. It has been a hard, long, joyous, and seriously challenging life. The black race in many places is living in a nightmare state in America and our children are being killed and destroyed and we live in grave danger as individuals and as a nation. Indeed who in America does not know of our situation?

The schools in America where I have worked most of my life are those which are attended by the oppressed and the disestablishmentarian (those who refuse to accept established order). The schools are forgotten places that exist in the poorest neighborhoods in urban America. They are attended by those who do not escape the violence, poverty or low expectations. Those who do not escape or who do not leave remain in these schools, which are forgotten and neglected by society. They become remainder and second class schools. They must save themselves in their own way, not in isolation, but in a life that connects them to other persons and worlds outside of themselves.

Is it knowledge, ability, resources, wealth, skills, education, or power that we lack? Or is it that we fail to see ourselves as we really are? How do we abandon poverty and hopelessness and discover the beginning of freedom? These questions awaken my soul.

I know that our mission as a people is freedom as it has been for hundreds of years. This has been so since before we left Africa. It is important to know that we are unique in our life as a people on this planet, but it is also a fact that we are like all other people who presently live here on earth. The underclass and the oppressed seldom fight for freedom. They internalize the hopelessness of their lives from childhood, and from an early age they live an imprisoned and an unexamined life. Some say that for black people this is a result of being taught to hate ourselves for the last four-hundred years.

In the battle and struggle of the wastelands of America more young black men in America will kill each other than will die from any other cause. Many black young men find themselves unemployed and unemployable. Many are unable to receive medical care in the richest country in the world. Drugs shock inner-city America every moment in the day. Inner-city America is on the brink of extinction because of disease, poverty, violence, and addiction. All people who live in the inner-cities are continuously vulnerable and dying.

Drugs have become a passion for living and they can take a family on a journey through hell. It does not matter why one is addicted. It is so or it is not. For too many addicts there is no way out of this timeless nightmare. Life is an endless agony. For the youth there are no more factories to work in, and for most of them they never existed. For them schools are the only factories they see, but the schools are not connected to their lives. For most youth the school is an artificial place of social and mental conformity. Teachers prepare them for a society that no longer exists. Many families are unable to help themselves, and they cannot help their children. No matter how deep is their hope and their love for their children. No matter how strong.

Though there are moments that are painless, it is an endless struggle to manage living through most days. Money, food, shelter, violence, intimidation, poverty, chaos, and struggle are constant realities in their crisis-filled lives. Their living places are hardly human. Their lives are often empty and unconnected. Few revolt against their oppression. Few have the power to find meaning in their lives and to triumph over their circumstances. Those who do live to reach and sustain freedom, achieve a glory that speaks of the greatness of the human spirit.

The earth itself and all of us who inhabit it are on an expedition in space and our compelling mission is human freedom for our societies and for us as individuals. Freedom is what deeply and endlessly motivates humankind. We are sometimes lost. This mission is forgotten when we break the links between ourselves and the earth, between our societies or between our individual selves. Our lives are destroyed and disorder dominates our world. How do we reconnect our societies? We must value all lives.

Those Without

It is so strange here sometimes. We dwell in this life wondering about our own mortality and our loneliness. Some days we never emerge from the dark side of our lives. We cannot escape a world of two cultures. We exist in a world of human societies and in them are those of us with power and those without, those of us with wealth and those without, those of us with knowledge and those without, those with tradition and those without, those with freedom and those without.

The sea crashes hard against the quiet and still San Francisco sand. Patterns form in the sand from the impact with the sea. A remainder society, group, individual, or idea is one that stands after a severe force has struck. New worlds appear. Though they seem permanent and inescapable to their inhabitants and to others, the remainder societies have a momentary existence, and then they vanish and new societies begin. Previous societies will not come again. Just as the sea washes away all previous patterns, all previous societies disappear and become places of the past. We live in the present. Our freedom begins in the new societies that arise.

The nature of our world is that our multitudinous human societies all connect. They do so in our minds and in the outside world we both struggle to escape and to perpetuate. Those who live in a free society break from past glory and personal achievement. They realize their illusion.

A society is not a discrete entity. It is a temporary collection of souls who characterize themselves in various ways. In a conventional society there are places, objects, and customs that individuals accept with high regard because they have been held on to and perpetuated for hundreds of years. The society's struggle is to sustain a successful and a changeless life. Its mission in life is to be permanent and lasting. In a conventional society, we hold on-to tradition and seek to perpetuate our existence. We hold a million memories of moments that are gone forever, of moments that never were, and that never come.

A remainder society is one in which the individuals and their hopes lack the energy to sustain themselves. It is a society in decline. It is weakly organized and easily dominated. Some societies refuse to have pollution and wastes deposited in them. No conventional society will accept them. Eventually these wastes end up in a remainder society. There are societies that refuse to have poor or minority people in them. In the end they will live in a remainder society. It is a society without a mission. Many of these communities in San Francisco, in America and elsewhere, are populated by black people, other minorities, the underclass, the uneducated, the unemployed and unemployable, the homeless, the addicts, and the unproductive. The earth will never be free as long as a single such society exists. It is in such societies that life is lived in its greatest despair, against all odds, where one is faced with giving up before one begins. In hard times we take from the weakest. Many black parents are filled with pain and sympathy for their children's plight and demand very little from them, as do the teachers and the schools. Their friends press them not to excel and many therefore never try, their lives never matter. It seems unfair that some of us start out with so many disadvantages, and meet injustice every step of the way, but this is life. Ever since we arrived here as Africans this has been our reality. It does not matter how we got to this state or condition. We must tear down the barriers before us. These devastated communities threaten us all. Those who do not reside in these communities avoid them and they feel a relief when they enter their homes in safety as though they have escaped something, and have perpetuated their own existence.

If we are to exist as free souls in our global neighborhood in space then there will be no second class societies. Our global mission stirs our cells and cries throughout our world.

A free society or a free world is one that moves further and further into the unknown. It does not struggle for permanence nor is it constantly deteriorating but is ever changing, emerging. A free society is not continuous but builds and rebuilds itself from moment to moment. It is always new and in a state of creation.

We now live in a world where we need a new vision and where the power of technology, communication, and information cannot be used for class warfare. It must find a new way for all persons living in the world, even the poorest among us, to be able to participate in, and prosper from, our globally connected life.

CHAPTER 26

Addiction

Death by drugs is common in San Francisco. I know of those who have lain unconscious on the floor from a drug overdose and who have escaped death. They know they are lucky because they have friends who have died from similar encounters.

Sometimes the fortunate ones seem to be those who are driven away by jail, crime, mental breakdown, and unknown disasters. John Doe dies of an overdose. He is listed as John Doe because no one knows who he is or where he came from. He was in the streets for five years and only had a nickname. Through death he has been released from the hell of drugs.

Last year a woman spoke to a group of youth who lived in public housing. She asked them why she was living a drug free life when all of those around her are addicts. She tells them that it is FOCUS, FOCUS, FOCUS. Those who are addicted are dominated by a world filled with and overwhelmed by poverty and illegal activity. There are rarely traditional, legitimate, and conventional activities to which they or those around them connect. It is not knowledge of the truth that stops them from being free. It is that they must discover the truth for themselves. Truth understood and expressed by others or forced on another person is meaningless. We must live our own lives and not ones in which our travels are on someone else's map. One must be an adventurer and understand personal challenge. Hard times change our lives and empower us to be free, to go beyond the world and society as others define them.

One can say that recovery and a drug free life are possible and be accomplished but those are words and statements that have meaning when one has the energy and focus to do what one says.

As a teacher I saw students who struggled in school. Many are still struggling. Life is now more severe. They are in and out of prison and constantly fighting drugs. What does this life offer them? They are lost in a heroine world. Last year there were eighty seven heroine deaths reported in San Francisco. A heroine user sometimes ties off the upper arms or the thighs with a strip of cloth, a shoestring, a stocking or whatever is available at the time. A small particle of heroin is dissolved into a few drops of water. It is then heated in a spoon, a cut off aluminum can, or a bottle cap. To fire it up, one often uses a cigarette lighter or a candle, and then the dissolved drug is drawn into a hypodermic syringe which is transformed into the instrument that will deliver chemical euphoria into the vein.

At times it is a battle and a struggle to reach a vein. It can become an endless search. Blood exudes from the body in one's hunt for euphoria. Sometimes there is failure and frustration. Abscesses form when the veins are missed. Track marks dominate certain areas of the body. A successful injection can take less than a minute to travel to the brain. One may feel the euphoria or one may collapse, stop breathing, and die. If the percentage of heroin in a particular batch is higher than the individual is aware of and used to, injecting it into the bloodstream can kill, at times almost instantaneously. No one knows when death will come and the next drug overdose will become a report in the San Francisco Medical Examiner's Office. Students I taught are on this desperate journey.

Still, it is not totally hopeless because everything changes, nothing stays the same. Indeed each life must be made each and every day. It is therefore also a struggle to sustain unbroken and continuous days of addiction, as one is in and out of addiction.

In cities like San Francisco one often finds an underclass without living wage jobs, that has lost the opportunity to live in affordable housing, and that lives with an epidemic of drug addiction. Changes from within us transform and cure us. It is an interesting phenomenon of human nature that we are capable of curing ourselves even when we hit rock bottom in our lives. Sometimes existing at the bottom of society is what awakens us.

There are drug addicts who hit rock bottom and begin their trip back to society. I read about a black woman who says that she was overwhelmed by the existence of a life dominated by uncontrolled drug dependency, prostitution, violence, rape, stealing and lying. She was overwhelmed by being carried to the hospital for drug overdose, of living on the street, of being arrested, and all of everything that made her life a nightmare. She said that she could have either entered a drug rehabilitation program or gone back out on the streets to die. She entered a rehabilitation program, filled with bitterness and anger. She went with the idea that she had been a victim of society. The life she had led was not her fault, she told others, and she told herself. She was asked who made her a victim. Who were the persons and what were the forces? Did someone make her rob and steal and hurt other people? It did not matter whether she meant to harm herself or other beings or not. The truth is those things did happen. In her recovery process she is reminded daily that she is responsible for the life she lives. She knows she hit rock bottom, but once she saw that recovery was possible she was able to take risks and start her life over again. She welcomed life and its struggles.

CHAPTER 27

The Street

The street lacks an understanding of itself. There is no one to organize its life. Urban dwellers whose transient lives are on the streets, ignore and violate the rules and laws created by others. Their talent and competence is seldom recognized, understood, or acknowledged. Their misery, mental instability, and poverty are sometimes assumed and sometimes challenged by the police and the law, and sometimes they are helped by others who are kind, generous, and compassionate. They struggle for freedom and order in their lives but often are too desperate trying to survive. Most have yet to figure out how to organize themselves and make sense of their world.

The other day my wife and I walked down Market Street in San Francisco. It is filled with filth, poverty, the mentally disturbed, the homeless, and musicians. My wife was shocked and discouraged. She saw San Francisco as an unhealthy place, dominated by the hopeless and the desperate. She wonders about living elsewhere. My wife loves the sea, the hills, the fog, the children, and the diversity of life which comprise the city, but not the countless beggars who confront us, who dominate our journey, and disturb her feelings for the city. The beggars fight for our attention as we move past them. They seemed to be the rulers who controlled this area of the city. The city leaders said they would deal with this problem, but after years the problem was worst than ever. How does one change society? It changes when the lives of the people in the society change. I sometimes speak to those who live in these streets about this dilemma and wonder if our world will ever change. Most of them are not concerned. A few do give attention to the question.

Some say, "I did not make the world the way it is."

I say to them, "We all make the world the way it is. The world will change when we change." Do we have the will and the determination to be free as individuals and to exist in a free society?

Twice I have encountered former students who were street persons. We recognized each other and I gave them money and wished them well. I never imagined that I would someday find or greet them in such worlds in which they travel, flee from, and thrive in. I listen to, read about, and live with their desperation, helplessness, and triumphs. The streets are filled with unrecorded events of hopelessness. There is no obsession with freedom. The streets cry and shout in their own misery and sadness. They are alive with crime and lawlessness. The youth are some of the street's victims. They are unable to hide and sometimes unable to escape. Some escape by leaving town, dying, going to jail, or killing themselves. I have been involved with students who have threatened suicide and who have committed suicide. Many youth who attempt suicide are seeking a friend, not death. They lack an immediate solution to their problem. By committing suicide they never live to find the friend. They do not live long enough to see that because one feels like killing herself or himself today does not mean he or she will feel the same way tomorrow. Most youth do not want to die, not at first, but when no one responds to their distress they convince themselves that death is the solution. The question of suicide is tormenting to the mind because part of the person wants to die and another part wants to live. The person does not want to permanently end his or her life. He or she wants to escape from suffering. Suicide is a permanent escape from a temporary conflict. This is not true for older persons who willfully seek death because their husband, wife, or close friend has died or because they have given up the battle and will no longer accept being terminally ill.

Many youth have prior criminal records that mark them and prevent an easy exit. One day I move alone through the streets in Hunter's Point, a poor black neighborhood. I am aware of those who constantly fill the street corners and who move through the streets. They want to sell me drugs, and I have no interest. I do not mean much to them as I am just another person passing through. Not far away is Double Rock which the police call the Kill Zone because of the recent number of murder and homicide cases. They say that every murder comes back to drugs whether it is a user, a seller, or an innocent person caught in the fire.

A former student, Duane Breaux, works with the youth there. He was a talented and spirited student who is still concerned with life and with others. He and the others working there say: "We got to work for ourselves and our kids, because nobody else thinks of us here. They stick us back here and maybe don't see us as very important people." It is a forgotten neighborhood, and those who remain dream of places beyond.

On my desk is a report that describes the sounds of street voices in a street corner incident: "I got work! I got work! I got what you need." A seller shouts to a buyer in a car. He waves and yells at the vehicle.

The focus is on buying drugs and on making money. The transaction is quick as pieces of white rock cocaine pass through another money exchange. The police officer, who is a plainclothesman, witnessed the drug deal. He arrested the buyer and charged him with possession. The seller is also arrested. They are both handcuffed and both refuse medical attention. The buyer was an employee in a school of the San Francisco Unified School District. He was later terminated. I met him when he complained of losing his job. I was unable to help him. His mother had accompanied him when we met and they pleaded for mercy and consideration in this case. Why could I not help this black young man? He was not the criminal type, the mother pleaded. Why were these charges just now being brought against him in April when the incident had been reported in December? I did not know. Besides he had been in a drug recovery program and only had a single meeting left to attend. Why was this happening to him now, they asked. The mother is a strong and concerned black woman who stands against city bureaucracies, schools, the police, and the courts in support of her son.

Their questions had forced me to learn more about the case. Why was he in a drug recovery program and why had the notification come to the school district, months after the incident had been reported and investigated? I learned that the employee pleaded no contest to the charges when they were filed at a hearing in December. He was then allowed to enroll in a drug recovery program and was not sent to jail. He did not miss any work. Three months later a police officer who knew the employee recognized his name on a report. He notified the captain of his station who notified the school district. If the policemen had not recognized the accused drug dealer as being a school employee there would not have been this reported incident. The drug marketplace is inside and outside of our schools. For many students it is all one single society. The school is not separate from the streets and the dealers and the sellers. But the schools fight to keep the streets out of the school. That is why he had lost his job. And though I had initially not agreed with his return, I later did. What was the goal, to keep as many black people in prison as we could or to help them help themselves? He is one less person who might be pushed back into the street. He and his mother had fought hard, and he deserved the opportunity of a new life. He was determined to change. Later he was allowed to come back to his job and he did well in his return. He was given another chance and he responded. He was grateful and fortunate. He is serious about his work. He is learning that the street cannot help him and understanding this gives him enormous energy to live in the world.

Chapter 28

Remainder School

Race has long been an issue in America. As a nation it says it condemns racial discrimination and the way of life of the black American underclass as a social disgrace. The government and others speak of integrating black people into the systems it has invented. America offers programs that it says respects and acknowledges the culture and identity of black people and that it does not intend to remake them—the black people—in the image of white people. They therefore are expected to express their way of life through their own music, dress and religion and to be acknowledged through the traditions they have perpetuated. However, in American academic standards and in conventional society, black people must conform to the white world and prove themselves as capable as whites. Some blacks prove that they are able to conform to this world and they are not violent or angry and they are responsible as individuals. This white world may accept a few such blacks who conform to its authority, standards and values. It is a world of power and privilege. It, in theory, respects the members of its civilized society and does not denigrate or humiliate them, but this is not so for those outside of their society. An individual or a society that is liberated and free does not disrespect or humiliate any person.

I recently saw a letter from residents of the Hunter's Point community in San Francisco requesting that the city assist it in creating a new school named Mt. Kilimanjaro. The request asked that it be formed and run by members of the neighborhood. I am moved that African life and places still dwell in their hearts, and am so surprised to find the Kilimanjaro world to be significant here so far away from its origin. I am surprised that its road reaches here.

Their vision is to establish an independent school in a predominately black area that is in one of the most economically depressed in the city. The school proposal has not yet been approved, but the vision and the possibility live. And though it may never come to be, I am struck by the feelings and fascination for Africa that dwell in the community and in the lives of the residents. When I returned from Nigeria many years ago and stopped in New York I was impressed and inspired by the interest and feeling for Africa that existed. I was surprised at the energy and motivation of the African people and way of life that existed in the city. It had enlarged their world and possibilities.

The community residents are not interested in socializing youth for traditional public school. They say that this system helped to destroy them as persons. They refuse to learn in a world where children were forced to meet the needs of a system that did not respect them as persons. Those in power determined their progress and success. What kind of freedom does one have when he or she can only participate in a world as defined by others? (I remind them that no one can stop them from learning.)

The force of tradition of the dominant society carries men, women, and children of the remainder society into the middle of a human's worst nightmare. Children from this society are usually assigned to the poorest schools. The power society or the dominant society as a whole does not care about their problems or their society's problems. It is content with broken families and with locking up those who live in this society. It does not seriously consider them because they are distant to them, because they exist in the other society, the other America, the other world.

There are those who say that if different races and cultures wish to express and maintain their distinct identity they should be allowed separate schools but with an equality of resources for all students. Such persons state that dominated minority groups have to suppress and abandon their cultural learning and identity for the appearance of equality and integration. It is argued that differences should not be destroyed or dismissed but recognized and valued.

In San Francisco remainder schools are those that possess an inequitable disproportion of youth who are not learning. There is an absence of teaching and an understanding that we are all here in the world to be free and to learn.

In several San Francisco schools, though, the students transcend the system. I once worked in a school that was filled with minority students of poverty. The teachers were enthusiastic and dedicated, and their spirit transcended the school. One year I worked with a school where the parents and the community were so creative and focused that nothing could stop them from being an effective school for all students. In such schools learning occurs all the time. These places are uplifting to the local and to the larger society.

Some San Francisco schools are remainder schools and are not working for black students and for other students who have lived desperate lives. They exist as they do because of the social and learning disorganization that destroys them. Too many students have already given up on school, and the school has given up on many of them. Students leave our remainder schools and are alone in a society inherited by the abandoned and forgotten. There were once jobs for those unskilled and uneducated. They have disappeared. A friend and a colleague stated the dominant society perpetuates remainder schools, which enables it to sustain its power. He states, "Powerful people cannot afford to educate the people whom they oppress, because once you are truly educated, you will not ask for power. You will take it."

This is an insightful observation that communicates to me both the truth and the human reality of our dilemma.

The truth is if anyone is oppressed then no one is free.

The human reality, and illusion, is that if others are oppressed then some are free.

The illusion is that we can be free through some system of inequality.

We start to change our lives when we no longer hide among our ideas, possessions and other objects in the world, when we are connected to learning and the human journey. Students can and want to learn and discover the beauty and the energy of the planet. My deepest concern is with those of the inner city living in concentrated poverty. If any school anywhere is isolated and segregated and those in it feel successful and satisfied, they have produced their own limited, confined and boxed-in world from which they do not escape and never leave.

Public schools become further condemned as they are more dominated by the working class, immigrants, and minorities because some students are educated to be in power and to be leaders, others to be at the bottom of society. Those who are treated inhumanely are devalued and ignored. Some take drugs, steal, and kill. They are misguided and self-destruct. Others live through the horror, come out whole, and continue to empower and teach themselves. Some of them make something of their lives. Others do not.

CHAPTER 29

Entrapment

In a San Francisco high school the principal, George Sloan, and I met with a group of students who were angry that two police women had been assigned to the school and had worked undercover in the arrest of several students. They were told to express their feelings in writing. They did.

As students of McAteer High School, we never felt a threat to our safety or well being on any real level. The fact that we, as students, as people, have been watched and video recorded over the last three months enrages us. We have also learned that school officials had no idea as to the "sting" going down at the school. Imagine…a principal unaware of hidden cameras videotaping his students' every move. We have been taught in our classes (yes, we do go to school), that the government and legal system has a responsibility to gain information in a reasonable, humane, and fair manner. This leads us to believe that we need to take a closer look at the way things are done in our city police force.

We have watched our peers go down in the last few days and have been witness to some of the deals that landed our peers in jail. We have seen the way the "new girls" badgered our peers relentlessly for the small amount of drugs they possessed. We have overheard our peers tell the officers dozens of times that they did not sell and had no intention to. Finally only after being pressured and harassed by these girls for three months did a few of our peers break down and do a deal with them as a favor for a "supposed friend". We understand that is not something they should have done. We are sure they do too. Another thing we are sure about is that it never would have happened if the officers hadn't ruthlessly badgered these young people. After three long months of listening to them beg and plead, you finally gain the mentality that if you get them what they want they will finally leave you alone. What we are trying to express is that these officers did not find drug dealers, they turned average kids into people willing to sell. We also witnessed them smoking marijuana and supplying minors with cigarettes on school campus.

What they did was a legal term called entrapment which basically means that the drug deals that happened would not have happened if the "new girls" had just left the students alone and not so fervently pushed them into a situation that they felt they had no way of avoiding. That is what happened here at this school. Probably a lot of other schools too. Our peers had no intention to sell to them in the beginning and were finally after months persuaded to do so. That is emotionally dishonest and a betrayal of young people.

We have also seen news broadcasts showing video footage of us and our peers, though we never gave permission to be on camera. Although our faces are still blocked out we are recognizable enough to go down with the students who were arrested and to be possibly fired from our jobs. This same news broadcast also gave false information stating that this particular group of students are tied to crack-cocaine and heroin use which is untrue.

If people are so worried about a teen population that uses and sells drugs, target the harder, larger criminals who are selling the drugs to these children. We personally know a number of the students who were arrested. Kids who are, or were, going to school every day. Kids who were on the honor roll. College bound kids who were entitled to their civil rights and the right not to be violated by secret hidden cameras recording everything they do.

We completely understand that the acts committed by our peers were wrong and they have to suffer the consequences but, at the same time we feel that our peers have a right to a fair investigation, not an investigation that is inhumane, unjust, and unfair. Not to mention the right NOT to be entrapped.

Concerned students from McAteer High School

McAteer High School at the time was a low performing school attended by many students of poverty.

CHAPTER 30

Public Housing Journey

Winds of hell and war blow through the San Francisco public housing projects. How much of the firestorm can the children and residents live through without refuge from the destruction of others and from a life of hopelessness waiting to explode? Few of them question the disastrous forces in their lives because they are struggling to exist. They seldom question the poverty and poor quality of life. A personal challenge for schools is to impact the lives of those who are from the poorest families in the worst and most impoverished neighborhoods in America.

At times I work closely with the Superintendent of Schools who understands inequality that has been created over the years through segregated housing, isolated communities of poverty, and failing schools. He is changing the schools in poor communities by eliminating the inequality of resources. In America, urban schools and societies deteriorate, but the vision in San Francisco is to renew and accelerate change and to further the learning of all students. A deepening of human horizons has begun and is sustaining a profound vitality.

All students long to be free, and the mission of all schools must be to liberate the minds and lives of all of its students. This is one reason that the San Francisco Unified School District collaborated with the San Francisco Housing Authority and the San Francisco Public Housing residents. Meetings and activities were established and organized for this collaboration with residents of public housing. The Superintendent initiated a summer meeting with the residents in July. I thought it was an important meeting. The residents attending made it clear that public schools had destroyed their lives and that it was with great reluctance that they had come to the meeting. They expressed a seriousness about their lives, about the failures they had encountered, and the devastation that public schools had caused them. The Superintendent responded that the schools could not take all the blame for their misfortune. They were articulate in their frustration and bitter in the defeat they had endured. Their mission was clear, a victory for their children. They did not want their children's spirits destroyed by individuals or a system that denigrated them or destroyed their hunger to learn. They do not want their children discouraged by school but encouraged to discover for themselves how far they could go. The Superintendent was as impassioned as they in his desire for the well being, the dignity, and the worth of all children. He was not dishonest with them in expressing that we need new ways to respond to the failure in public education to engage all students. The Superintendent was a determined person with a mission to significantly affect the lives and learning of all students. This meeting began the starting point of a journey to liberate the lives of all children.

The freedom of children stirs a society and impacts and awakens us everywhere life struggles to survive. This has been true since my first days of teaching. During the war in Nigeria everyone suffered and was diminished. There were those who escaped for the freedom and education of their children. Since I have worked in San Francisco schools, there has always been those who have reached America desperate for an education for their children. Many of these students fall through the cracks. The students who live in public housing have been as neglected as any group by the school and others.

Many of the public housing residents I encounter are the same students from the schools I have worked. We always seem to mysteriously connect and know that we have passed through a common place and time together. We unite again. For some it seems a miracle that we ever saw each other again. Some of them still know me by name. The others seem to remember things when I announce again who I am. Some of them have children who attend the same schools they did. In almost all cases they have good memories of our times in school. This is probably because it put them out of their current embattled lives to a seemingly simpler existence. Many have the same barriers to freedom as adults that they had as students. Living conditions in public housing is among the poorest in America. The residents suffer from disarray and breakdown from their own social disorganization which is everywhere one moves.

I was in a meeting recently and a public housing community organizer said that life in public housing is like that in prison. It promotes the same mentality along with the same violence, death, and fear. There is also a lack of human acknowledgment and acceptance from the outside world. Few from the outside visit or understand this existence. Within public housing developments life is one of human pain, desperation and tragedy. A question asked by a resident was why a different education or school program was needed for students living in public housing. The answer was that the children who reside in public housing in San Francisco are most often doomed to a permanent outcast system. Their needs are both like those of other students and also different. Poverty and racism diminishes the educational attainment of public housing students. They live different lives from other students.

One resident stated that his community was damaged by illegal drug activity, vicious dogs, uncontrollable graffiti, vandalism of vacant units, gang activity, drive-by shootings, child abandonment, poverty, neglect, and numerous survival difficulties. The youth and others stand around, waiting for something to happen or to do. They get involved in conflicts that destroy the human spirit as well as the community. It is a spectacular and a sad world that they stand watching in wonder and grief. In the end many youthful lives are filled with fear. Power is too often viewed through violence and material possession. We feel power over others and things and we become fearful because we feel a need to protect this power. If we have no need for power outside of ourselves then we have no fear. When we are learning there is no fear, no violence. This is true for all students. All students, regardless of their race and social class are born curious. They are driven to discover and to understand the universe and to be free.

"Use what is dominant in a society to change it quickly," was something that I read as my wife and I walked down Forty Second Street one day in New York City. The Superintendent asked me to coordinate a collaboration with public housing and the school district, and I became deeply involved in programs that impact the lives of children and the others living in these developments. How do we work to liberate and transform the forces in the lives of children and those around them? I know that we change quickly when ordinary things in our lives are altered. To change the way we live we are compelled to examine our own thinking, learning, and actions.

The district works with the residents to focus on student learning and empowerment and also on jobs for youth and residents and to bring computers and other technology to their residence.

From the first meeting with the superintendent it was clear on what was needed to initiate a meaningful relationship. It was jobs! I was assigned by the superintendent to work with the residents to get jobs for students in the Potrero Hill and Hunter's Point areas. It was June. When I spoke with the summer job's coordinator he said that it was impossible for several reasons. It was June and the summer jobs program ended in July. It was too late to start a new program. The current program had begun in January which was six months earlier. Also, he said the district already hired many public housing students in its present summer jobs program. My response to him was that was fine for a normal or conventional community and program. I though was working with people who had already viewed public education as destroying them as persons and discounting them as students. I would not further denigrate them. We had to have the jobs. We got them.

The residents themselves said that there was no possibility in our working together if there were no jobs for the youth. If those didn't exist nothing else was possible. A resident expressed that the parents and students of public housing must take charge and create a new way of learning for themselves. And that this goal must be achieved through partnerships between them and those outside of public housing. She reminds us that the ultimate goal is a life and a world where their children matter.

Exciting things happen. Ten students were selected by the residents for a summer job program to work for the school district. Nine students were eventually employed to work in the schools. It is an interesting first project for me. I expected the youth to appear at an orientation for their jobs, but none of the students knew how to get there. In the end I brought the five of them and a mother to the job orientation center. The mother came because she said that the students did not know the way back home. (I knew their lives were very isolated. When we drove by other public housing developments on our way, some were coming upon new worlds they had not seen before.) The other group of five students still had not arrived when we reached the center. After another hour, I called the resident (Theresa) who had fought so hard for them to have these jobs. She had dedicated herself to giving something special to the youth in her development. I called her home. I told her that she was several hours late and that we were waiting for her and the students she was bringing. She had been so enthusiastic about their all being there and ready to work.

"What happened?"

"My ride didn't show up," she said. She was calm and seemed undisturbed.

The students had no way to get there. There was nothing she could do. She was overwhelmed, a single parent with fifteen people living in the same house. I then picked them up and brought them to the center. We got through the first day. Three of the students from the first group did not have bus fare so we paid their way back.

One student who was eager to work told me that he had to see his probation officer and would not be able to report for work the next day. I never saw him again. No one knows what happened. One student who was pregnant was sent home on the first day because she was sick and throwing up. I was contacted and told she should not return. At first this seemed reasonable and in the interest of the student. I spoke to the housing resident Theresa again and, she was determined that the student would not be abandoned. She said that I had to find a place for the pregnant girl. She was very serious. There had to be a job somewhere in the system. I called the district information and publication office. They hired her. She did an outstanding job. Theresa had pushed me to get the pregnant student a job which pushed the program to reach a higher level. It takes me the first day to learn who we are as a group. And from then on the group performs strongly as individuals and as a team. In the end it is exemplary. It brought new energy to the school district and to the workplaces. The number of students increased from ten the first year to more than two hundred the next year. What is important is that it was an idea and a demand from the public housing residents. They had placed this as their highest goal. Years later I learned that it was as significant as any activity we ever did with public housing residents because we worked together to complete a task. There was much national research that said summer job programs were too costly and showed no lasting benefits. This was not our issue, however. We were working with youth from socially disorganized communities who were now connected to a larger society and had to organize and manage their own lives and affairs (sometimes for the first time ever). Some of them had become participants and contributors in new and demanding situations. Some did not make it the first year but did the next year. Though the program was temporary for most of the youth, it gave them new life.

Other serious changes come from the presence of technology. In my work I have connected with Ray Porter, who also works for the school district. He is responsible for students and community publications which transform thinking and learning. Books are being published and disseminated, and the schools and community centers are seeing technology as an empowering tool. Students write books that are being used in their classrooms, in other schools, and in the libraries. It is a transformative endeavor. Community residents are learning new technologies and are establishing publication centers, making their own jobs, and collaborating with the schools. Museums and others collaborate with the schools and produce publications by public housing residents that impact upon the schools and the community.

Of all the schools that I have worked in, and of all the cities and countries I have lived and worked for almost twenty five years, this is as serious a journey into learning as any I have encountered. When I taught in Nigeria I was always enthusiastic about persons living in third world countries emerging from an agricultural existence and going beyond the industrial age school system the Europeans had brought with them. It never happened. I looked to the day that their lives would be impacted by electrical messages moving at the speed of light, reaching the villages rather than the cause-and-effect fragmented view from an industrial age. In inner-city classrooms one always hopes for breakthrough experiences that would impact all students (especially the poor and unmotivated) to go beyond the bureaucracy of schools and find their own way to truth, learning, and reality. I am now immersed in a journey to an unknown place that has started from scratch and we are traveling light and unburdened. We find ourselves going to places that compel us to express new direction. In our own dialogue one morning Ray Porter and I agreed to these learning and community goals:

• Using technology and information to empower people
• Enabling people to solve their own problems

- Replicating technological power by bringing access and availability to the community
- Sharing information locally and with other people in the world
- Expecting excellence
- Being actively involved in one's own learning
- Using what one has available to change one's community
- Accomplishing what you want by doing what is needed to accomplish it
- Utilizing what the community has to say in our actions
- Performing in a world where no one knows whether we are sending or receiving information from the Sunnydale Housing Development (the inner-city) or Pacific Heights (a high wealth district) or whether we are seven, seventeen, or eighty-seven-years of age
- Providing means for true expression for all students
- Continuously seeking other technology centers to make contact with
- Performing our activities with a minimum of bureaucracy and outside dependency
- Providing pathways for community people to become leaders and allowing them to express their own capabilities and find their own voices
- Implementing activities which have the interest and approval of persons living in the community
- Documenting the life of the community before it disappears
- Realizing the older people are leaving and there is serious work to do
- Defining work as making one's own job and not being put into a position or given a title
- Expecting all individuals to be contributors to innovation
- Enabling the community to drive schools with appropriate and relevant uses of technology
- Providing students from the community with new power by their bringing in products and ideas which will impact and transform the schools

- Using tools which accelerate learning and production and transform individuals and the community
- Keeping excellence in our community and our schools while providing opportunities for all to get there

We worked on exciting things with interesting people. One unusual person was Mark Reed, a worker hired by the city, who was from Stanford University. He was white, young, enthusiastic, open-minded, intelligent, competent, and inspired to work there. He loved the children and was an important person in their lives as he deeply understood the conditions in which they existed. He seemed born to be there. I knew he was from Seattle but little else about his earlier life. I did observe how he dedicated himself to the urban world in which he existed. He tutored students, visited their schools and homes, took them on trips, and struggled to bring technology into their lives. We worked together to build a telescope for the students. Though we never completed it, we later connected to the information highway and searched for sites to further the possibilities for students connecting to the universe.

In time this housing project was closed and everyone had to leave. They lost the struggle to sustain the community. I never saw him again. But other people came, such as David Lanham who also worked hard and with a mission in other housing projects.

Everything in our life ends. All we do here will one day disappear. From our own work we struggle to make a serious impact so that when this present time and journey vanishes there will be the energy to sustain serious life and keep this human spirit alive.

Breakthroughs

Three middle school girls who lived in public housing and knew of a plan to allow students to take computers home went to the principal and said that they had a writing assignment and were asking to take a computer. The principal was surprised and excited. He instructed them in the technical use of the computers, and their parents came and helped them bring the computers home. One girl came the next day with her assignment written on the computer. This is the first breakthrough. She discovered the computer as an empowering tool and her learning had an impact on those around her. Each day she completed new work. She could observe her own capabilities. She had set out with another's vision and somewhere along the way had created her own. This is also a breakthrough because, as a friend once told me, teachers lie to their students. My friend says that a teacher will tell a student that he or she can be an artist or a scientist when the teacher has never struggled to be an artist and is unaware of what it takes to make it in that career. So my friend says that teachers lie. They speculate on things they have never experienced or on a world that is yet to happen. I have been asked, "But aren't they just trying to instill hope?" My view of the matter is that with good teaching students can do significant things in their lives. I have expressed this to students who would be teachers: Know your subject well. If you know and love your subject, and deeply believe that all students can learn and that you are responsible for their learning, the chances that you will be a good teacher are great and enormous.

Few students from this middle school ever experience the lives that school promises. Most teachers are born into safe and conventional learning places with healthy and supportive families in protected neighborhoods. They attend decent schools. They are treated when they are sick. They have found favorable employment and some have had numerous chances to reach goals in their lives. The youth in the schools in these neighborhoods and in our society are denied the opportunities that these teachers have known. The youth live in threatening places. Few become productive citizens because the obstacles for most are too great. The computer, though, has allowed this one student to do things that people around her only dream about. She was learning to educate herself.

One afternoon Ray Porter and I went to Geneva Towers, a public housing development, to work on a publication project. We were not sure what we would do until we got there. An African American student, John, who lived in a public housing development in Hunters Point, had been working at the elementary school at which we were meeting, so we invited him to come along with us.

He was given a digital camera which he had learned to use and he was enthusiastic about taking on an assignment. On the way he talked about himself. He said that he was out of school and was anxious to be enrolled again. He had been in special education and he had also been in a psychiatric hospital for children. Twice. On this day he seemed normal, grounded, and sane. I asked him what he thought his problem was, and he said that he had a temper.

He wanted to talk about his brother. It was important to him. He had been murdered on the street and it never made it into the newspaper. It seemed as though the inattention to it diminished its significance in the world. It really bothered him that those in power were ignorant about life in the streets on this side of town. He had always assumed that they knew.

We reached Geneva Towers. He took pictures. We returned and he made a calendar of the persons whom he had photographed. While he worked he said that this work was good for him because it stimulated his mind. He finished his work and took a copy back to the residents of Geneva Towers. They were surprised and impressed by the work. He had done a great job in only one day. We saw that there may be other projects and other things for him to work on. He is interested in doing other work.

Right now we just want him to have some good days in life. Sometimes we go through periods of struggle where there are no good days. He is keeping a journal and he writes about life in the streets. He writes about the cold streets and those murdered and those who are rushed to San Francisco General Hospital with bullets in their backs and chest, sometimes dying, and sometimes surviving. He also writes about the community centers that serve the youth.

John was out of school because he reported that he was threatened by gunpoint by a student at his school. He was transferred for his own safety to another school. At the other school he got into a fight and the principal and the assistant principal were injured while breaking up the incident. Though John is being productive right now we know that at any moment he can be unpredictable and suddenly explode. We are therefore very serious about our work with him. Every day is a new day for us.

To me John is like so many youth from public housing. A number of young people have been killed and almost every one knows someone who has died or has a close friend or a relative who has. A lady at a community center keeps the pictures on a wall of those who have died. She is unusual because she has a mission to work with the youth and to give to the community. John's life is unique and like no one else's in the community because of his brother's death and his particular experiences in school, but he is like others in the community in the human dilemma he faces. He, like the others, searches for a way out.

The Other Side of the Battlefield

The neighborhood of a San Francisco public housing development is one of concentrated poverty and one of deep social disorganization. It is racially segregated and socially and economically isolated. Even so I tell a resident that no one can stop her from learning. She tells me in a penetrating way that I underestimate the powerlessness that people feel when children are raped, starved, kept out of school, violently beaten. They learn to hate themselves and are incapable of learning.

She may be right and it might be the way that she sees life. I am not here to judge her view of the world. And I know that it is so that few here ever follow a dream or a vision. But I tell her this. The other day I visited a public housing development and police cars filled the street. There had been a shooting and young children were being directed away from the violence and to their homes. I went inside a community center to talk to someone about the writing project that we had begun working on. No one ever got involved with the project because there had been a breakdown in leadership and management at the center. No one was motivated to begin the work. There was no discipline, no use of resources, strategies, or vision. The program director had gotten into a fistfight with a staff member and was unavailable for work. It was why there were no activities and why there was not hope of change and cooperation at the center.

Down the street at another center where residents lived with the same degree of poverty there was strong life in the writing project. Several persons enthusiastically shared their work with me. One person's written text showed me that hours of discipline had driven him toward excellence. Another person shared a fifteen-page book he had begun on his life in public housing. The book when completed would have one hundred fifty pages, I was told. I was inspired by the energy, creativity, discipline, and vision displayed by these people. I was amazed and struck by the variation in individuals and communities hardly across the street from each other. I tell the resident that even though some members of the same family are devastated, other are changing their lives and contributing to the world.

The Vision

I recently heard a friend say that all students can learn and want to learn. He said that he first discovered this in Africa, first in Nigeria and then later in Tanzania. In his work as a teacher in these places it was assumed that all students could and would learn. He then came to America and taught on Indian reservations in Arizona and New Mexico. For the first time he heard people speak of why students would not and could not learn; poverty, isolation, disinterest and other factors. He then came to San Francisco and heard the same things. He found that Black, Latino and many other students were seen as at risk and were isolated, segregated, tracked into a lower caste system and given up on. The secondary schools would say that the elementary schools had failed the students or the colleges would say that the high schools had not taught students the basic skills for research and independent thought. Everyone blamed someone else. My friend said that we do not take personal responsibility, and we point fingers at everyone else. What we envision never happens as we continue to live in the world as we always have. One group waits for another to do what it is not doing. The schools become worse and students do not learn nor teachers nor society nor our planet.

Can adult actions renew student learning? They can. I saw students from public housing at Malcolm X, Carver, and Drew Elementary Schools in Hunters Point who were from the poorest community and from the poorest families in the city, and their math performance was exemplary in district and national results. They were excellent thinkers and students. Their talent often went unnoticed by the outside world. The teachers at the schools took responsibility for student performance. They did not blame students but examined what they themselves did. Students became literate in the language of testing. They and their teachers learned, explored, observed, and solved unconventional problems. Sometimes much of our teaching is inappropriate to the way students learn because each student's understanding of the world is uniquely personal.

As a teacher in Nigeria I worked in a village school in a town with no running water or electricity. The crude buildings seemed as though they would be barriers to serious learning. They were not. Students and teachers found learning itself to be a compelling activity. While learning, the world itself is not set into boundaries and divisions. Learning is outside of excuses, blame, caste systems, corporate society, alma maters, tribal hostility, or places of exclusivity. When the students in public housing and urban America exist in worlds where there are unchanging barriers, real or otherwise, there is no learning. The traditional school and conventional education then just deals with these barriers as fixed objects and extrinsic obstructions and invent rewards that are irrelevant and unattainable.

A friend who is a teacher and an American Indian, told me about a school on an Indian reservation. A medicine man was brought in to work with students who were truant, dropouts, involved in delinquent and criminal activities, and who had been school failures. He discussed with them Indian medicine, Indian chants, sacred objects, healing powers, dancing, singing and story telling. Students became fascinated and serious about what he had to offer, and the class became the most interesting place in the district. He spoke with depth and moved those who came. Students who were not learning and unmotivated to continue in school were now deeply absorbed in new worlds. All students are curious, can learn and want to learn.

It is a fact that poor children on Indian reservations and in San Francisco can learn and do learn. The dominant society is not interested in this fact. To them education and knowledge are achievements, and possessions they want to hold onto. They hope these possessions will not vanish.

Those who live in affluence judge those whom they have segregated, isolated, and abandoned. Through their own possessions they entered a life that flows against them. They work to sustain it through the patterns they favor and incorporate. They have never discovered the will and capability to break them.

In working with public housing youth and residents, much of their lives are disappearing and they are leaving the community. Their homes are being boarded up, and their energy is in the detail of their departure.

There are few places in San Francisco for them to relocate while their housing project, targeted for demolition, is rebuilt.

The street crime will stop when the corporate crime stops and our human greed ends.

No voice cries for them as they leave. The impact of the exodus of hundreds of poor and black people from San Francisco is hardly felt. They leave in stunning silence. They are forced to journey toward uncertainty. Few if any are likely to return. For most the same poverty of other generations continues through them.

The Adventure

Chapter 31

Adventure Prologue

All people can learn, want to learn, and do learn (no one can stop us). We satisfy ourselves by living a conventional life, but we hunger for new things. Adventure is a road through our hearts and souls.

The energy inside of us sets us free for the personal journeys that create new lives for us. Running along roads, in streets and up and down hills, climbing mountains, and writing ideas and reflections, I discover new worlds and fresh insights. I observe how the mind, the body, and the universe work. Through travel and exploration our lives connect us to the mainstream of a human journey that liberates us and sets us free.

The traditional American urban high school does not reach all students. Most schools do not. Time has passed them by. At one time instruction and forced discipline were used to direct followers. Human minds learn without forced knowledge and coercion, but independently and cooperatively. Collaboration empowers students but instruction makes them dependent. Education is hard, discouraging, and demeaning when it does not make sense to students and is fragmented in a decontextualized way that fits into someone else's system—the school's or the teacher's.

I discover there are many ways to learn and to teach; on the sea, in the city, and in the wilderness. One day I personally learn some new things about life in a wilderness and adventure school.

Those with whom I learn and work are not extraordinary, but enthusiastic and driven to contribute to each other and to strive toward challenging goals. As individuals we do not reach all goals, but we are empowered to construct our own paths in a strenuous world. The adventure program allows us to step out of the system of traditional school instruction and to learn in other ways.

I begin climbing mountains when I am invited to join an Outward Bound wilderness school in the Sierra mountains of California. I am forty-seven years old. There are eight of us, the youngest student is a seventeen year old from Seattle and the oldest is a fifty-six year old librarian from Concord, California. It is as physically strenuous and mentally rigorous as any school I have been in. We all want to be there and we all work hard together and learn from each other.

There are two instructors who are competent and enthusiastic and have a passion for their work and for the wilderness. They seem born to do this work. The only thing in our world that matters is whether the group makes its destination that day. We are driven. Nothing else matters to us. There is no individual achievement greater than the group. Our understanding of ourselves as a team transforms us as individuals and empowers us to question ourselves and to change as an organization. We are also a family of distinct individuals and personalities who all resemble each other in our shared vision and mission.

CHAPTER 32

Adventure School

It is a surprise that I am here. This is the first of my fourteen days at a wilderness school. My purpose for being here is to see what a school such as this can contribute to the lives of inner city youth. I was supposed to have participated in a Rogue River expedition in Oregon in May, but I had been unable to attend. I now find myself in California in the southern Sierra mountains with nine other people. I do not know what I'll be doing, but I do expect an intense challenge.

My preparation for these two weeks seems inadequate. One day I walk around Lake Merced in San Francisco for five miles carrying a twenty-five pound backpack filled with books, accompanied by my wife. We also have the family dog with us. I try to break in a new pair of boots that we bought in Berkeley. I learn that another student has practiced by carrying around bags of sand as well as by climbing Mt. Diablo near San Francisco. He is from Concord, which is on the other side of the bay from San Francisco. He is the only person here who is older than I am. In addition to him there is a fellow from South America, who was born in Canada and who has come 7,000 miles for this expedition. There are five younger women from Georgia, New York, California, Washington, and Michigan. There are two instructors, both men. One is from Oregon and the other is from California. Today is Friday. On

Tuesday I ran for fourteen miles through Golden Gate Park in San Francisco to prepare for this time. I hope that it pays off.

Running through San Francisco in the light, the sun, the rain, the fog, and the darkness makes me a more serious person and teacher. In school each day is new, and running through the city gives a focus to life as I find myself going into school with the energy for creation and change like during my first days in Africa. To run long, hard, along the ocean, in the cold mornings, and alone, makes me greater than my thoughts. It renews the days. It is unimportant why I, and the multitude of others, are driven to discover our own running rhythms and find ourselves on earthly ventures. I have run for years usually alone. I have run in numerous events and races mostly in San Francisco.

I now learn that all of my years of running has significance as the instructor tells me that those who run do well in this wilderness school. That makes me feel somewhat better and makes me see that all the years of running are important in the grand scheme of life.

We meet at the airport in Fresno and are driven to a location 6800 feet above sea level. Immediately upon disembarking from the van, we get acquainted through activities that help us to become more familiar with each other and we participate in exercises where we collaborate to free ourselves of knotted rope entanglements. We then go through the articles of clothing needed for our journey, as well as the food and other gear that we will use for the fourteen day expedition. Our backpacks weigh fifty to sixty pounds each and represent an ordeal for all of us. The first day we travel for one and a half miles and camp for the night. We learn about digging latrines, using compasses and maps, firing up camp stoves, and sharing the responsibilities of leadership. There are daily duties of cooking, setting bear traps, and obtaining fresh water. The instructor tells us that everything has weight. After fourteen days, we will find that nothing we carry is insignificant.

There are mysteries in the mountains that we do not know. In the days I am a seaman, I see towns from the sea. They seem mysterious and inviting. They are distant and unknown until we dock and disembark, ride the buses, walk the streets, and get lost. Then the towns become real. So it is with the mountains. At first we only know them abstractly and remotely from a distance. During the fourteen days we are together we all enter the life of the mountain.

Our instructor, Phil, says that we shall use the wilderness, specifically, its challenging situations, to deepen our own self-discovery.

We live together in an adventure that reconnects us to the human journey, the Rift Valley and to Kilimanjaro, to the beginnings of wonder, exploration, struggle, uncertainty, and new life. The spirit of discovering a new earth lives in us.

Who are we?

Alice

Alice is black and from New York city. She works for a national television network and recently returned from Korea. She is twenty-nine years old. She says that she had heard of this wilderness school for many years, and that she now feels prepared and able to survive its challenges. Alice is tall and thin and she slowly glides up and down the rocks. She is very skillful in using her height, arms and legs to an advantage in her climbing. In hiking along the roads and through the mountains she moves more awkwardly because her knees are not strong. Sometimes she is the last member of the team on our journeys. She has many interesting things to talk about. She works with the number one television show in the country and recently returned from working on the Olympic games in Korea. She is an articulate and genuine team member who works well with all the other members of the team. She is always concerned about me and she always assists me whenever she can.

The hardest time for her comes on the fifth day. We start early with a morning map reading session and then rock climbing practice. We are preparing for the peak climb up Bear Creek Spire, which is to be attempted on day six. After rock climbing and lunch we hike for 7.5 hours from Lower Mills Creek to Abbot Pass. We ascend 1,440 feet in our course and we descend to our base camp to make the peak climb.

That evening everyone is exhausted from the day's struggle and we discuss who will attempt the peak climb. Laura, Gwen, Alice, and I say we will. The instructor, Phil, refuses to allow Alice to be on the team. She will hold us back and jeopardize the expedition, he says. She cries and pleads for the opportunity to ascend the 13,713 foot mountain. It seems the most important thing in life for her to have this opportunity. Why has she come 3,000 miles? She will never be as close as now. This is why she is here. Making this peak climb means everything to her. She is refused the opportunity. Alice breaks down and cries. A chance of a lifetime is lost.

Several people dislike how harsh Phil is in his decision. He is the instructor, and it is final. Later that evening people come to me and discuss what to do. It was hard, but I say we are going to live with the decision. Alice later comes to me and says she is very upset but that she has come to accept the fact that she is not going on the climb and that maybe it is selfish for her to want to go if she will be a hindrance to the team. She only asks one thing of me, that I bring her a gift from the mountain. I tell her that I will. I bring several small rocks, and I bring her back a wild mountain flower. It is difficult picking the flower because we as a group live a life of minimum impact on the environment. We are aware of all of our acts that contribute to the contamination of the wilderness. I quietly take the flower from where it grows and bring it back to her. I never tell a soul.

Brian

Brian is originally from Canada. He has worked and traveled in Europe and is now living in South America. He is the chief executive officer of an international manufacturing company in Columbia. He is forty five years old. He has come 7,000 miles to this school. He is not an outdoors man, but he is very competent in dealing with new situations. No problem seems too daunting for him to confront. He is a positive force on the team and a natural leader. He was never absent when someone on the team needed someone to turn to. The two of us decide that we will make a journal of the expedition and mail it to the others when we complete our time here. Thinking of the journal and composing as we go along makes it a special expedition for us. On the tenth day of the expedition I am weak from fasting during a three day solo experience. Brian helps me with my load as I am so weak and have lost considerable weight. He is aware of the condition of others and their readiness to perform. Some of us encounter more frustration and devastation than others during the expedition. He is good at helping keep us focused on our destination. This life is hard on all of us at times.

Gwen

Gwen is the youngest member of the team. She is eighteen years old and has just graduated from high school in a town near Seattle, Washington. She is usually quiet and seems comfortable in conversing with Phil and Laura. On day three we all become aware of how determined she is. She and Cynthia are the first to attempt climbing the rocks. We all work hard on the climbing drills. They attack the rocks aggressively, always looking for footholds and handholds. Cynthia is the group leader this day. She is also the most athletic amongst us. Cynthia is impressive in finding a path to the top of the rock. We all cheer her accomplishment. Gwen is struggling to make it. There seems nothing more important to her than to prove she can climb this rock. Cynthia struggles for thirty minutes before reaching the top, and now Gwen is as determined as ever to reach the top of the rock she is climbing. We all cheer Gwen on. Everyone from the ground is trying to invent paths for her to pursue. Nothing works. She is strong and persistent. Even if it takes all day it seems she is going to struggle to reach the top. If there exists any possible way for her for her to make it, it seems she will find it. After thirty minutes or so, she gives up. She can go no higher. She is deeply disappointed, but the group respects her will to go to her limit and beyond. It turns out that none of us are able to climb the rock, except for Vern, an instructor. Vern's climb to the top is swift and flowing. He pauses and reflects as he climbs and composes his way up. He is one with the rock, living silently and deeply in the moment.

On day six, Gwen, Laura, and I are the three students who attempt the peak climb. We all make it to the top. It makes us special friends. On day nine, day ten, and day eleven we each are on a solo experience alone in the wilderness. Before we depart we each select the name of a person we are to give a gift to when we return on day eleven. The person's name I select is Gwen. I write a letter to her about her on day ten when I was on the solo.

The peak climb

Dear Gwen,

It is the sixth day of the journey, and we arise at 4:00 AM to ascend Bear Creek Spire. At 6:00 AM when we prepare to depart from base camp it begins to hail ice upon the earth. It is accepted as strange and unusual as we move through it. We proceed on because every peak climb must begin. You travel on because you are able to go beyond your past and your present limitations. A point of turning back never exists. There is no prior experience to cling to, to follow, or to learn from. We live on the edge, push ourselves to our physical and mental limits. We learn that power and courage come from letting go of the familiar. You gather the energy to perform at your highest level. You overcome all the obstacles before you and the technical climb which you struggle through to reach the peak. You realize the final state the three of us reach. It is a special place but we do not rest there long. We then descend from 13,713 feet above sea level. It is a spectacular feeling hanging in space as we repel down 120 feet of rope. We all know that life is profound.

Cynthia

Cynthia comes from Atlanta, Georgia and has just graduated from the University of Texas. She is going to be a teacher next year in Georgia. She is twenty one years old. She is the most athletic person in the group. She is a strong climber, a marathon runner, and an excellent swimmer. She is excited about being a teacher. I tell her that the wilderness school experiences will make her a more serious teacher. She will have many personal discoveries to share with her students. The hardest time for Cynthia comes on day three. She is the group leader and performs well in getting us to our destination from Cold Creek to Fish Camp. We travel hard for four miles and reach our destination at 7:30 PM.

When we reach the camp site, we are not well-organized and do not focus on getting the camp settled and our various tasks completed. We do not perform to the satisfaction of the chief instructor. We have a discussion that evening. Cynthia is given feedback on her performance as leader. She does well all the way to the end and then things break down. It is unclear who is doing what. As a result of the situation we become more systematic in the assignment of chores and duties.

Several people tell Cynthia that this has been one of our more chaotic experiences. She takes the comments badly. She is a strong person, but still she cries. She is deeply upset. She says that she has not come several thousand miles to be told she is a failure. She is a strong student in school with an A average. She loves her studies. She has run a marathon, and she has accomplished many things in her life. She admits that she is not an accomplished wilderness leader and that she has much to learn. I am personally pleased with her performance as the team leader. I state such. We work hard on climbing the rocks, and we are productive. We reach our destination after a hard day. She has done well. Leadership has to do with finding our own way. Cynthia, like the rest of us, does not become a wilderness leader in a day. We are all still learning about living out here. This is a crisis evening for Cynthia. She cries all night and is unable to sleep. She becomes a stronger person by living through this human storm. She is devastated and almost surrenders, but she gets through the night. Like all of us she becomes tougher as we move deeper in to the expedition. She is as good as any of us in reading maps, following trails, and cooperating with other members. After this night we never openly criticize each other. It is not necessary or welcomed. On day thirteen we have a ten mile run at 7,600 feet above sea level and Cynthia runs the strongest race from beginning to end. Only the assistant instructor, Vern, finishes ahead of her.

Laura

Laura has just graduated from college in Massachusetts. She is from Michigan. She is twenty one years old. She is very serious about this expedition. This is the second wilderness school that she is attending. Last year she was on a seven-day expedition. She tells us how serious she is on the fourth night when we are discussing how we feel about our own lives. Laura breaks into tears as she fights to tell us what is in her that needs to be expressed. She is deeply bothered. Several of the members of the team (she does not mention names) are spending too much time bitching and complaining and are carried away with superficial expectations. Laura is tall and strong and is the fittest person among us. She has no problem in carrying a sixty pound back pack, without complaint. Whenever we stop to rest, she is always the first person up and ready to move on. She is very disturbed by anyone who she thinks is not focused on giving his or her best efforts, each moment of the way. She states that this is a great time in her life. It is a much more rich and rigorous experience than her previous expedition. She is realizing her fullest and highest capabilities. She feels herself daily becoming more competent. She feels power that she has not felt before. In every climb and on every hike, she pushes to her limit, and beyond. She is driven to learn and to give back all that is in her capability.

We make the peak climb together. Reaching the peak requires technical skills that are a serious test for the three of us. Laura is the first to attempt the final climb to the peak. She struggles and struggles, and in the end she makes it to the top. Once she has conquered the peak, it shows that Gwen and I can get there. Still it is not easy for Gwen who goes next. Then I go. We all have a hunger in us to reach the summit. It is a great day for us all. What does the climb and descent mean to Laura? She describes the descent from the 13,713 feet as **wicked awesome**. They are her favorite and strongest words.

Several times on the way down from the peak climb we lose and find our way back toward the base camp. I drift away from the group, thinking I am on the right course. I lose my way, and I lose my contact with Laura and Gwen. Laura catches up with me and guides me back to the trail. Eventually we get back to the base camp. She is living a great life in the wilderness.

Sylvia

Of all of us on this expedition, Sylvia is one of the few that I observe who never struggles from any personal devastation. She is quiet and the most fragile member of the team. She has just finished college in Santa Barbara and she is twenty two years old. She possesses the greatest inner strength of any of us in the group and we all respect her composed manner. She understands the complex world we all exist in and is very knowledgeable about herself. She, most among us, symbolizes the strength and the mission of the wilderness school. On the hikes and the climbs we make, she often trails behind, struggling to keep pace. She does not complain and she endures all obstacles. She recently had surgery on her right knee, and she has been given a medical clearance to participate in this expedition. Sylvia so strongly wants to be here that she is absorbed in all aspects of the school and its activities. She has planned for years to be in this wilderness school and is delighted that she is now doing the things that she had always dreamed of doing. She is driven to be here. She has been in other schools but none as demanding as this. Not all that she is doing here is new; she has experienced such challenges before. She is here and performing at her highest capability. We probably all are, but it is most evident in her.

Jonathan

Jonathan is the most organized team member and is the person who has done more prior planning than any other. He is from Concord, a town across the bay from San Francisco, and he is fifty seven years old. He is a school librarian, a quiet and serious man. He has tirelessly climbed Mt. Diablo near his home, before coming. He carries bags of sand with him. He has also lived in the wilderness before and says that he has prepared for this wilderness school in southern California before coming. This life is not new to him.

It is not until day four that we learn of his deep understanding of the wilderness. He is an expert at crossing streams and rivers and teaching us what he knows. All such crossings provide risks to the group. We all have to get across with our heavy loads without anybody falling in or getting wet. During our first crossing several people get wet. We all stop, change clothes, and discuss hypothermia and staying alive in the cold. Our instructors, Phil and Vern, get us through the ordeal of the first crossing. Later on we become more independent as a group. It is in these times that Jonathan provides strength, and expertise in helping us deal with obstacles that bring danger. Jonathan is very knowledgeable about many books and programs that deal with the wilderness. He accomplishes so many things without ostentation and overstatement. He understands this life. He has planned for years to be part of such an expedition. He is here now, and he is performing at his highest level.

What makes this expedition so penetrating and significant to me is the individual resilience which occurs. This maximizes our performance as a team.

Day 1   Friday   July 7th

Leader: Alice

	From	To
Campsite:	Vermillion	Edison lake
Camp altitude:	7,600 feet	7760 feet
Activity:	AM-travel to camp PM-gear inventory; loaded backpacks (50-60 lbs) of food, equipment, and clothing.	
Time traveled	4:00 PM	5:30 PM
Miles traveled:		1.5 miles
Cumulative miles:		1.5 miles

Journal entry:[*]
For whatever reason the eight of us have decided to make this journey. We have chosen to take a chance and find out what we really can do. For whatever reason we have decided to live on gorp, to sleep on the ground, and to be eaten by bugs for the next fourteen days. I wish us all the best! The coyotes are on their way.

---

[*] Each journal entry is written by that day's leader.

Day 2   Saturday   July 8, 1989

Leader: Brian

	From	To
Campsite:	Edison lake	Cold creek
Camp altitude:	7,7600 feet	8,019 feet
Activity:	Am-travel PM-practiced ropes and rock climbing on flats	
Time traveled	9:00 AM	3:00 PM
Miles traveled:		5 miles
Cumulative miles:		6.5 miles

Journal entry:

This morning, our first one together, went very well. We got up at 5:15 AM. Everyone was in good spirits. We served breakfast and did our chores without any hassle. The major hurdle of the morning was overcoming the fear of the "shovel patrol" (the outdoor latrine). However, the challenge was properly addressed as everyone "pinched a loaf" (used the latrine). At approximately 9 AM we started the journey toward Cold Creek (4-6 miles). Six hours later we arrived. After a short rest, Vern taught us some knots and the techniques of rock climbing. On the flats everyone looked great. Although we heard thunder, Phil assured us that it would not rain, since "it does not rain in California in the summer." The highlight of the afternoon was finding the "local hotel" which very willingly let us use their outdoor swimming pool, fully equipped with cool running spring water. Some of the participants, including this writer, took advantage of the offer. It was refreshing to say the least. Since everyone was exhausted, lights were out by 9 PM. And so ended the second day.

Day 3   Sunday   July 9, 1989

Leader: Cynthia

	From	**To**
Campsite:	Cold Creek	Fish Camp
Camp altitude:	8,019	8,560
Activity:	Am-rock climbing exercises	
	PM-hiking	
Time traveled	2:30 PM	7:30 PM
Miles traveled:		4 miles
Cumulative miles:		10.5 miles

Journal entry:

We woke up bright and early to the sound of the bugle at 5:15 AM. We were all excited and nervous to go on our first rock climbing expedition. We all attacked the rocks with immense strength and courage. Then we took a break for a picnic lunch. The rock climb represented our ups and downs of the day. A bit sore and a lot scraped up, we packed our gear and marched out singing for a very hard hike. At last, after our first day of learning exactly what a contour line meant, we reached camp, ate dinner, and went to sleep.

Day 4   Monday   July 10, 1989

Leader: Gwen

	From	**To**
Campsite:	Fish Camp	Lower Mills Creek
Camp altitude:	8,560 feet	10,800 feet

Activity:	Am-river crossing/ hypothermia lesson PM-hiking	
Time traveled	7:30 AM	4:00 PM
Miles traveled:		4 miles
Cumulative miles:		14.5 miles

Journal entry:
Aside from a few cuts and scrapes, the day before held a distant memory of accomplishments and moments of defeat. As a group we are growing closer each day. We rejoice over each individual's personal strides and find humor in our moments of stress.

Day 5   Tuesday   July 11, 1989

Leader: Hoover

	From	To
Campsite:	Lower Mills Creek	Gabb/Abbot Pass
Camp altitude:	10,800 feet	11,840 feet
Activity:	Am-map lesson/rock climbing PM-hiking	
Time traveled	2:30 PM	7:33 PM
Miles traveled:		3 miles
Cumulative miles:		17.5 miles

Journal entry:
Life is a tale told by an idiot, full of sound and fury, signifying nothing.
William Shakespeare

Life is an introspective adventure and we must each make meaning out of our own lives. We arise at 5:15 AM; study maps and compass readings at 7:00 AM, and then practice rock climbing skills in order to prepare us for Bear Creek Spire (13,713 feet) on day six. On this day we traveled to an altitude of 12,240 feet. It was a hard journey as we encountered a change of weather and unexpected trails through packed snow. It took strong endurance and unyielding attitudes to get us through the day. The changing weather conditions forced us to stop, change clothing and to protect ourselves from hypothermia. Having reached our destination altitude of 12,240 feet, we then descended to our campsite which was at 11,840 feet elevation. I was proud of each member of our eight person team. Arriving there deepened our belief in ourselves.

Day 6   Wednesday   July 12, 1989

Leader: Jonathan

	From	To
Campsite:	Gabb/Abbot Pass	Bear Creek Spire
Camp altitude:	11,840 feet	
Activity:	Am-peak climb of	
	Bear Creek Spire(13,713 ft)	
	PM-return to camp	
Time traveled	6:00 AM4:00 PM	
Miles traveled:		3 miles
Cumulative miles:		20.5 miles

Journal entry:

The day of the peak climb started unnaturally early: 4:00 am. Three intrepid explorers-Gwen, Hoover, and Laura-were courageous enough to tackle Bear Creek Spire-13,713 feet up in the sky (actually several feet taller since reported that they stood on each others' shoulders). The five lazybones stayed behind at the camp, ostensibly to guard our worldly possessions from ravaging marmots, but actually to pick up, clean up, throw down, and rest, rest, rest. The peak climbers reported a peak experience: gorgeous views, terrifying rope work, and a very challenging climb. Their hike was worth the effort. Those who stayed behind had a ball: sleeping late, greeting two hikers from a distance, joking, socializing, and alternately building tans and, when the sun disappeared, looking for warm clothes. The menu for supper was marmot stew.

Day 7   Thursday   July 13, 1989

Leader: Laura

	From	**To**
Campsite:	Gabb/Abbot Pass	Lou Beverly Lake
Camp altitude:	11,840 feet	11,140
Activity:	Am-hiking	
	(1.5 hr stream crossing)	
	PM-hiking	
Time traveled	7:00 AM	7:00 PM
Miles traveled:		9 miles
Cumulative miles:		29.5 miles

Journal entry:

As I am reconstructing this day from memory, with the help of my personal journal, the details may get a little fuzzy. I remember waking up very tired at the usual 5:15 AM morning call, then eating a quick cup of oatmeal (prepared by our in-house gourmet chefs of the day, Sylvia and Laura) before setting out on our ten-mile journey. I have worked hard at blocking out what happened next out of my memory, so suffice it to say that the day was long, hot, slow, and exhausting. After almost fourteen hours of walking, climbing, falling (some of us more than others), weeping, path finding (or losing as the case may be), river crossing (1.5 hours of river crossing, actually), and chatting with strangers on the trail (which we later learned was against Outward Bound etiquette, as others are almost guaranteed to be more lost than you are) we made it nine miles to Lou Beverly Lake. There, we were given the option of completing the ten miles or continuing on to Medley Lake. The group consensus was to rest where we were for the night and to continue on to Medley tomorrow. We had a supper of brown rice and green pea soup, which was undercooked but surprisingly yummy (at least I, the chef, thought so) and crashed for the night.

Day 8   Friday   July 14, 1989

Leader: Sylvia

	From	To
Campsite:	Lou Beverly Lake	Medley Lakes
Camp altitude:	11,140 feet	10, 640 feet
Activity:	AM-hiking	
	PM-rescue/peak climb	
	to 11,516 ft. of an unnamed MT.	
	Start of solo-6:30 PM	
Time traveled	7:00 AM	4:00 PM
Miles traveled:		3 miles
Cumulative miles:		32.5 miles

Journal entry:

Having decided to stay at Lou Beverly Lake the night before, our day began by finishing the last mile of day seven's hike. This brought us to the Medley Lake area where we took up our day packs and set out to fulfill the Outward Bound commitment to service by looking for a lost sixteen year old red-headed boy in the area of Three Island Lake. Additionally, we decided to climb an un-named peak of 11,500 feet. Along the way we saw another Outward Bound group (a twenty two day trip) and met one of their instructors (Eric). In the evening we each set out for our three-day solos. Eager for rest and apprehensive about nearly seventy two hours alone, we ended our day (without dinner) together with a group coyote hug.

Day 9   Saturday   July 15, 1989

Leader: Solo

	From	To
Campsite:	Medley Lakes	Solo
Camp altitude:	10,640 feet	
Activity:	Solo	
Time traveled		
Miles traveled:		
Cumulative miles:		32.5 miles

Journal entry:

New wonders

How does being alone amongst these mountains, lakes, streams, fallen trees, fragrant plants, insects, birds, and mammals connect to the living of my life until this moment? The significance of the moment here is knowing that I am living a new life and everything else has disappeared. It is quiet and still here. As a youth I sailed the seas in wondrous ships, and the sound of the water was soporific, and the power of the sea was endless and immense. Again the sound of water is all around me as these flowing streams rush over the earth, displacing the solitude. It is as though the earth that I lie on is the ship that is moving me to new wonders.

Observing the soul

The soul of humankind, the mountains, the rushing rivers, the sea, and the wind are beyond our thoughts and expressions. Our powers lie in observing what is. For the first time in these mountains I am aware of a hummingbird, of its lightness and swiftness. Its flight is a perpetual and endless renewal of life. The moments that I share with it touch my soul.

Day 10   Sunday   July 16, 1989

Leader: Solo

	From	To
Campsite:	Medley Lakes	Solo
Camp altitude:	10,640 feet	
Activity:	Solo	
Time traveled		
Miles traveled:		
Cumulative miles:		32.5 miles

Journal entry:

Knowledge and freedom

When I was a youth living in Manhattan in New York City, I once got lost downtown. I knew in my search to overcome my lost state that Manhattan was an island only two miles wide. I proceeded to walk due west on the island to the Hudson river, and then I worked my way north until I reached home. My knowledge about the island got me home. Our knowledge allows us to reach the moon, to probe into deep space and to receive transmitted information. Knowledge allows humans to climb the highest mountains, to save lives, to write books, to destroy the earth and ourselves, and to relentlessly and unthinkingly cling to, and fight for, the accumulated knowledge, traditions, and customs of mankind. Our collected human knowledge brings us our own invented happiness and solutions to human problems. It does not bring us freedom. Freedom runs deep, silent, and fresh. It lives in each soul. It lives around us and within us. It flows as a river and is as still, as silent. The stream beside me only runs three miles an hour to an external observer. The stream itself is free and uncertain of its life. It is always moving on.

Day 11   Monday   July 17, 1989

Leader: Solo/Alice

	From	To
Campsite:	Medley Lake	Marie Lake
Camp altitude:	11,640 feet	10,576 feet
Activity:	Am-solo	
	PM-debriefing (solo gifts)/hiking	
Time traveled	3:00 PM	5:00 PM
Miles traveled:		1.5 miles
Cumulative miles:		34 miles

Journal entry:

   We returned from solo very well-rested and so happy to see one another. We exchanged gifts with each other. In some ways the gift exchange was a very touching experience. Given a bit of land and a little time, people can find lovely gifts. We all shared bits of our solo experience, and then hiked about 1.5 miles. We reached our camp at sundown-feeling good. Then we learned of the next day's challenging journey. Marie Lake mosquitoes were a special problem.

Day 12   Tuesday   July 18, 1989

Leader: Brian

	From	**To**
Campsite:	Marie Lake	Vermillion
Camp altitude:	10,576 feet	7,600 feet
Activity:	Hiking	
Time traveled	6:00 AM	7:25 PM
Miles traveled:		20 miles
Cumulative miles:		54 miles

Journal entry:
We started the final expedition at 6 AM. From Marie Lake, and within a mile of our beginning, we joined the Pacific Crest Trail and remained on it until we reached Quail Meadow approximately ten miles away. The journey was very demanding and rigorous. We climbed nine hundred feet in 1.5 hours and then we descended 1,250 feet to Lake Edison. On several occasions we ran out of water, however, our will prevailed and we arrived in camp at 7:35 PM, thirteen hours later.

Leadership
A leader is best when people barely know he exists,
Not so good when people obey and acclaim him
Worse when they despise him.
Fail to honor people,
They fail to honor you.

But of a good leader who talks little,
When his work is done, his aim fulfilled,
The people will say, "we did this ourselves."

Lao tzu

Day 13   Wednesday   July 19, 1989

Leader: Phil and Vern

	From	**To**
Campsite:	Vermillion	Vermillion
Camp altitude:	7,600 feet	
Activity:	Am-10 mile run	
	PM-return of equipment	
	and Recreation and Relaxation	
	-Individual discussions with team	
	leaders, Phil and Vern	
Time traveled	7:00 AM	10:00 AM
Miles traveled:		10 miles
Cumulative miles:		64 miles

Journal entry:

Day 14   Thursday   July 20, 1989

Leader: Phil and Vern

	From	**To**
Campsite:	Vermillion	Vermillion
Camp altitude:	7,600 feet	
Activity:	AM-pack and exit camp to Fresno, Ca	

Group assignments

Leaders

Day 1 Fir 6/7	Day 2 Sat 6/8	Day 3 Sun 6/9	Day 4 Mon 6/10	Day 5 Tues 6/11	Day 6 Wed 6/12	Day 7 Thur 6/13
Alice	Brian	Cynthia	Gwen	Hoover	Jonathan	Laura

Day 8 Fri 6/14	Day 9 Sat 6/15	Day 10 Sun 6/16	Day 11 Mon 6/17	Day 12 Tue 6/18	Day 13 Wed 6/19	Day 14 Thur 6/20
—solo	Solo	Solo	Solo— Alice	Brian	Phil Vern	Phil Vern

Daily duties

	Day 4	Day 5	Day 6	Day 7	Day 8	Day 9	Day 10	Day 11	Day 12
Alice	1	4	3	2	1	4	3	2	1
Brian	1	4	3	2	1	4	3	2	1
Cynthia	2	1	4	3	2	1	4	3	2
Gwen	2	1	4	3	2	1	4	3	2
Hoover	3	2	1	4	3	2	1	4	3
Jonathan	3	2	1	4	3	2	1	4	3
Laura	4	3	2	1	4	3	2	1	4
Sylvia	4	3	2	1	4	3	2	1	4

1—cooking 2—cleaning
3—water/tarps 4—sump/latrines/bear traps

Group inventory

Alice	Shovel	Rope
Brian	Climb equip	Repair bag
Cynthia	Extra ropes	Water bags
Gwen	Tarp	
Hoover	Stove	Rope
Jonathan	Kitchen equip	Bear hang
Laura	First aid kit	Tarp
Sylvia	Stove	

I lived in San Francisco for twenty years, and I had never climbed a mountain. I had once come close to climbing Mount Shasta in California and Mount Kilimanjaro in Tanzania, but I never did. I am asked what is significant about being in a wilderness school or climbing a mountain. For me personally it was never important that I climb, or don't climb, a mountain. However, for whatever reason, I found myself in a wilderness school, and I was presented with the challenge of making a peak climb. I was deeply motivated to go where this life took me, into the depths of nature and human experience.

We impacted the environment to the least extent possible. When the school ended after fourteen days, no one knew where we had passed. We were that anonymous. We saw great beauty in our world. There were lonely mountain flowers, vast mountains, and quiet glaciers that communicated with our deepest feelings. Many of us cried in frustration, disappointment, and wonder. When we made our peak climb, it was to the summit of a mountain that was just another peak among many. When we struggle in life to ascend the face of a rock and to reach mountain peaks, we are absorbed in life. We are inside of adventure, surrounded by it. We cannot observe it from outside or manipulate it by rules or logic. There is no outside to our lives. Being free in these mountains is unlike being in all other worlds that might have been. Reaching the mountain peak brought an awesome moment that was joyous and profound. As we climbed we lived with the feeling that death could totally destroy us at any moment. And though it was a great achievement for us the fulfillment did not last. It had no permanence. We never stay in such states. Freedom surrounds us and is in us. We never capture it. It never dies.

In the wilderness school we all knew we were living as profound a life as we were capable of. Each day we lived extemporaneously and free. We were seriously challenged. Many times we lived a bold and daring life. We were fortunate. It was as interesting a life of learning and schooling as I had ever experienced. Just as Africa was interesting to me when I lived there, life in these mountains is as profound.

Maybe as important as anything in my case is that the school sparked in me other possibilities in life and provided ways to connect me and my family to travel, to discover interesting places and have immeasurable adventure.

CHAPTER 33

Philadelphia Family

We sit on the train; passing through towns and cities which are urban wastelands. Our motion is hardly broken as we move through the dust and destruction. There are days in life where we rush to get places. This train is driven by a hidden electrical force that propels us on from place to place. We exist in a uniform state of motion on the train that takes us to New York. I am going there with my wife and daughter to run in the New York Marathon. We just rode out of Philadelphia, and the hours we were there seem like a brief, unreal moment.

We had come to town to visit friends. We arrive at night after a long drive from visiting our daughter on the Virginia coast and then to seeing friends in Washington DC. On a Philadelphia road we made a wrong turn and lost the way to our friends' house. It seemed as though we could retrace our path and correct our course. My wife is very uncomfortable as we drive around in a neighborhood that is strange and sometimes frightening. This place to her is foreign, unsafe, dangerous, and unknown. Our daughter is quiet and makes few comments. She does not seem concerned. We are not able to travel back to where we started, and we have become so lost and confused that we call our friends to tell us how to find our way out of the desperate problem. We have come in the night, and we are scheduled to leave early the next morning.

We follow the directions and see large apartment buildings that stand on the street along the way to our friends' house. My wife studies the houses wherever we go. She always wonders about the unusual stories of the numerous places that we pass through in our travel. What are the people in them doing? There is something noteworthy about these large, old brick structures. Do they have stories? In the night they seem quiet and silent but curious. They are strange places to my wife. We hurry past them. Our friends are glad to see us again. We talked about Philadelphia, San Francisco, our families, and other things, well into the night. After several hours of sleep we awoke, and before we headed for the train station to leave for New York, I looked through the Philadelphia newspaper at our friends' house.

Last night we had been curious about the streets, the residents, the river, the automobiles, the crowds, and the houses we had discovered during our wrong turns. Among the places we had passed was a house we had wondered about. I came across a story in the morning newspaper. It surprised us to be reading something that we had encountered from our brief stay in the city but confirmed my wife's doubts about the places that we were driving through and the people who were moving about in the night. She had wondered about, and had feared, an unpredictable occurrence.

The story is about a mother and her children. They lived in one of the houses we had driven by. They were residents in the same area that we were lost in. This is what makes the story interesting and amazing to us. Was the mother like other people we passed in the night? Was she a unique person? I do not ride with this thought long because although she is a distinct individual, I know that her story is our story. She loved her children. She is overwhelmed by life.

She had left her two sons downstairs in their apartment. She ran upstairs and talked to two maintenance workers. She had stabbed her two sons in the neck and in the head and had left them there bleeding. She had stabbed herself in the neck and the chest. She had asked the maintenance workers to kill her. She told them not to call any emergency service for help because they would take her children if they came. She left, bleeding, and she then took a taxi. She was driven to a bridge over the Schuylkill River and she jumped into the water. Her body was found because others had observed her jump. My wife could not understand why anyone had driven her to the bridge in her condition. It was one thing we would never know.

The relatives of the woman who spoke of her said that she was an exceptional mother. She cared deeply for her children. They were both in the hospital, and one was in critical condition. The mother was overwhelmed with life. She thought that her former husband was going to have her children taken from her. However, it was never shown that anyone planned to take her children, though she was convinced that the Department of Social Services was going to take them away. They stated that they had no such plans, however, and had no knowledge of her case. But she had acted under the stress of her own reality. Also her grandmother who had reared her had just died, so there was also deep grief in her life. She had faced the hard world she lived in and had acted. She attempted to kill her children, and she had killed herself. She was unable to live through the moments that tormented her.

My wife could not get over the incident. How short a time we had spent passing through Philadelphia, how serious a tragedy had occurred, and how close we had been in passing among those who had suffered and who died. It deeply touched my wife's life and dominated her thoughts of Philadelphia. We rode on to New York.

CHAPTER 34

New York City Marathon

The train from Philadelphia arrived in New York City. We had not been here in ten years. At that time my daughter, wife, and I journeyed here and spent several hot July days in Manhattan and on Long Island. My daughter was ten-years-old then and we climbed to the top of the Statue of Liberty and traveled by subway. Each subway ride was a deep disappointment during which we were immersed in a graffiti-filled world, traveling from station to station through hell. The subway demonstrated how the city was devastated. I observed the nightmare caused by those in the city who killed sanity, who destroyed order and who lived in destructive chaos. Each subway ride was an intrusion into the human spirit.

The three of us are excited to have returned. We find ourselves living a miracle as we ride the subways where graffiti no longer exists. It is an impressive human accomplishment. I am deeply moved at humankind's attainment of a vision and its self deliverance from hell and destruction. In my first visit to New York as a youth this had been a place of vitality, wonder, endless energy, diversity, extreme poverty, reckless opulence, and greatness. For my daughter it does not seem to offer such possibilities because many of the things and events that I lived through were of another time. Much of the city is old and its possessions, ideas, and tradition prevent it from fully entering into the information and communication age that the earth is immersed in. The days I lived here are gone forever. They never were just as the subway graffiti never was. But from Midtown Manhattan to Brooklyn to Wall Street to Harlem, still New York is a new and interesting place to my daughter. For my wife it is filled with fascinating places and people. She genuinely loves her visits there. I also still see the richness of a diverse and varied urban world that is filled with life.

New York probably has the best of schools and the worst of schools, like San Francisco and elsewhere in America. There were few subway miracles in our schools. The schools need to meet goals that sometimes seem to be impossible. The schools, like the city, must absorb ideas, observe existing patterns, and solve unconventional problems. In the industrial age humankind labored for a living; in the information and communication age we are challenged to think and to connect for a living. If more is expected, more is achieved. Content, textbooks, examinations, and teaching habits are of the mass production and industrial age, but the students are not. They are of this age and of this time. They are living now-in real time. Their quest is for exploration and adventure. They wish to discover in school an opportunity for self-transformation.

New York City Marathon

It is my ninth marathon and my first marathon outside of California. I awoke at five in the morning to travel down Sixth Avenue to Forty Second Street and to the New York City Public Library to board a bus to Staten Island. As I ran down Sixth Avenue I was approached by a young, black male who was crossing the street to talk to me. He seemed suspect. Why was he out here at five in the morning, and why was he coming to talk to me? I decided not to invest the energy in an encounter. I kept running as he crossed the street. He did not have the energy to keep the pace. It was another early morning incident that I had run through just as I had in the California mountains. I never knew what the individual's thoughts were and did not linger on them. I ran on to the library and took the bus to Staten Island.

It was cold and quiet on Staten Island. There were tents and food and outdoor toilets, people reading newspapers and continuous talk and movement. We had four hours before the race began. People from all over the world slowly gathered. Announcements in numerous languages were continuously being made over the loudspeaker. Though the staging area seemed saturated with pastries, coffee, and water, all the runners were frequently reminded not to experiment on eating food before the marathon. If one's body was not capable of fully digesting it before the race then it would likely be thrown up in crossing the Veranzano Bridge to Brooklyn. This instruction was repeated over and over in several languages. We were also told that coffee was a diuretic and resulted in excess water loss, and that anyone drinking it should compensate by taking extra water. So much food and drink had been brought out here, and at the same time we were told of the penalties of consuming it. It seemed an amusing morning contradiction.

We were also told the temperature would be in the fifties and there would be the need for everyone to hydrate (take extra water) to compensate for dehydration from the sun. After four hours the area was filled with bodies preparing for the twenty-six mile and three hundred eighty five yard journey that would end in Central Park. Of the twenty five thousand runners, fifteen thousand had run marathons before. Ninety-five percent of the runners would finish the race. I followed the green line to the start with a friend who was a teacher from a high school in San Francisco. By chance we had met minutes before the race was to begin. We started together, and I soon lost track of him before we crossed the bridge. It was a great feeling to finally be on the road amidst the mass of others who had also prepared for this event and, particularly, for this moment. It was a slow first mile as we ran for open space and fought for an uninterrupted pace.

We crossed the bridge and into Brooklyn where the noise, excite-ment, and the multitude of cheering, curious, and supportive people provided the energy that was going to last until the finish. When I had run marathons in Napa Valley there were probably a few hundred people out cheering us on; in the San Francisco marathons there were several thousand people. In the New York City Marathon, I was told, there would be two million people cheering the runners on. I was not very knowledgeable about the race course. I could have studied it more but I did not. I knew hardly anything about Brooklyn and did not know that its people would provide the most encouraging and inspirational miles of the marathon. The run down Fourth Avenue seemed endless. We ran through neighborhood after neighborhood. Each was distinct but each was strongly unified in encouraging the runners to reach Central Park. All of New York seemed organized and united for this special event, living beyond its conflicts, poverty and opulence. But no one seemed more alive and enthusiastic than those in Brooklyn.

We are an unbelievable mass of runners passing through unbe-lievable crowds that observe us as we observe them. There are so many young children putting their hands into the flow, curiously making brief contact with the passing runners. We inundate their streets as we pass neighborhoods of Whites, Blacks, Puerto Ricans, Hasidic Jews, West Indians, Chinese, Finnish, Ukrainian, Russian, and Polish New Yorkers all linked and connected by a marathon of world runners moving through this city of islands and bridges. They waved, cheered, offered food, played music, and personally inspired us. A black brother looked me dead in the eyes and said, "You are a winner. You can do it!"

The only problem with running through Brooklyn was the sun and the strength it extracted from you. By the time we reached the Pulaski Bridge to enter Queens I was noticeably weakened. We were welcomed to Queens by an enthusiastic young lady. We continued on quickly through Queens, across the Queensboro Bridge and past cheering crowds at Fifty Ninth Street and First Avenue. We had come about twelve miles. I wondered if my wife and daughter would be there. Thousands of people crowded against the road, but I was unable to see or to hear them calling out my name. I continued on. It was weary, working the miles up First Avenue. Each numbered street seemed a challenge to reach. Sixty First, Sixty Second, Sixty Third...It was a known world that barely seemed attainable. I did not know if its existence was actual for me. I ran without thought. A girl ran in front of me. The back of her T-shirt read:

Conceive it
Believe it
Achieve it

I ran on. At One Hundred Tenth Street we reached Harlem and followed this Puerto Rican neighborhood to One Hundred Thirty Eight Street. At last we had exhausted all of the streets in Manhattan and we crossed the Willis Avenue bridge into the Bronx. We had come twenty miles. It was here that I was reunited with my friend from San Francisco. We left the Bronx and crossed the Madison Avenue Bridge into Harlem. There would be miles of black people until we reached One Hundred Tenth Street and Central Park. In Harlem an older black man told me, "I can see it in your eyes; you're going to burn it up."

He was dead right. Nothing was going to stop me from finishing the race. I was dead tired, but I knew I had it in me to finish. Still, I had not seen my wife and daughter. How dedicated the volunteers had been all along the course. Some seemed to have a cause greater than the runners themselves. We reached Central Park and the last three miles of the race reached its most challenging dimension. The energy that was once so freely available to me in Brooklyn was not there. I had not expected the numerous hills and turns. It was a hard price to pay to reach the end. It seemed beyond the limit of mind and body but those who lined the road were noticeably supportive. They pushed us on, believed in us, and expressed the deepest hope for us to make it. Their presence was real and spirited. At last I reached Fifty Ninth Street and there were my wife and a friend from Baltimore to greet me and encourage me. I struggled on to the end. It was a hard four hours and fifteen minutes. To the people of New York it did not matter who you were or where you were from. They cheered for you.

It was good to run in New York and leave the California schools and its life. I step out of its system but come back again to start over. Running and completing one's own race makes the world richer and clearer. I come back to San Francisco with new depth and intensity.

*　　　　　　*　　　　　　*

Running Hard, Running Wild

It is important to state that I do not run to become a better teacher or better person. I run as hard as I can and as far as I can to see where running takes me. It is the adventure.

When I started teaching in San Francisco I worked with students who were so energetic and restless that they amazed me. Their lives were out of control, and they refused to allow themselves to be students. In a lot of ways they seemed as troubled as the woman in the Philadelphia family. They were busy doing everything except what a serious student should do. I had been asked to teach a course in African Studies where there were many such students. This was in the early 1970's when I had recently returned to the United States from Nigeria and African village life. I agreed to teach the class because I was so eager to share Nigerian and African life with black students and others who were interested. I had read many books on Africa and I had traveled across the continent.

The Nigerian students had been so eager to learn even in the harshest of conditions. They studied until deep into the night and into morning. Most of the students were poor but to them learning was a privilege. It was probably the most important thing in their lives. They were eager to learn about America and how the minority populations were segregated and discriminated against and the great resources and wealth of the nation.

I enthusiastically entered the class on my first day in Nigeria and there was total silence. There were forty-two students. I was new to them but also they had come there to learn. I talked a little about myself but I talked most of the time about mathematics. We were totally engaged in mathematics for the two years I was there.

We worked laboriously with a common focus. In the end all of the students at the school passed their examinations in mathematics. It was a great adventure that held and sustained our collective effort and brought individual and school achievement. It became a great journey for us all.

I had gone to Africa as a teacher with enthusiasm and excitement. I was just as eager when I entered the African Studies class at Mission High School. There were thirty students. It was not quiet, and I struggled to be heard. I had just returned from Africa, and I had been there during the Nigerian civil war. I had traveled throughout the country of Nigeria, survived accidents and illness. I had visited farms and homes and had learned much about the Yorubas, other Nigerians and Africans, and their lives. The students displayed little interest in African life. I brought books, African clothing, games, stories, proverbs, and other African objects and materials. This was a tough class. It was not my first class with black students in San Francisco. My first job had been at a school with juvenile delinquents who were locked up. The classes were smaller and the students had to be there. They lived with few alternatives. They were excited about Africa, though, and were reflective about how Africans lived. I was disappointed in the African Studies class at Mission High School and what I was able to share and discuss with them. They were as capable of learning as anyone. It did take great energy, though, for them to discover that they could learn at a serious level.

For many of the students the important thing was what they wore and how they looked, or how they thought they looked. Many of them wore expensive leather jackets. I would ask them, "Why are you giving the white man all your money for those leather jackets?" They told me that they had to have the leather jackets. But it was not important who they bought them from. They said that they would gladly buy them from me. That I was a black person teaching mainly black students had some significance but it did not deal with the fundamental issue of students not learning.

These African American students run hard with the energy of youth. They are not serious students or contributing deeply to society. They are distracted by their contradictory mission to defy authority and also to conform to the limited world of those around them. They run hard, but because of this contradiction in their effort, their lives in the school are filled with disorder. They run wild. I was running hard also but I had a serious interest in Africa which I enthusiastically pursued and worked to know about on a deeper level.

They run hard, but do not know what distance they can reach. They are not yet examining their goals and interests and they pursue no mission of their own. They never get started. For some individuals completing five miles gives them a new world. They leave behind their former lives. Completing a distance run for them gives them the feeling that they can accomplish anything. They run through heat, rain, and cold. Running a marathon is not only showing up for the race but all the training that leads up to it. Training to run twenty miles seems long at first but you struggle through it and you learn more about yourself. And sometimes, though you have trained well, you fall apart during the race and don't recover. You leave that experience behind you and you start to work for the next race. You begin another adventure.

It is difficult for the students to leave their way of life for an inward journey. How can they stop the hard and wild running to experience solitude in their lives and get in touch with themselves?

Education cannot be forced but is a matter of pushing from within. What impresses me about the running of a marathon is the depth of the human spirit which allows us to move through this strenuous event. It shows what level humankind is capable of moving to. In a marathon we all come there to run. It is why we are there. It takes us further into life.

The black students in the African Studies class run hard but do not come to learn. It is not until many years later that I teach a math class to students living the same lives in San Francisco who do seriously learn.

CHAPTER 35

A Mathematical Expedition

We struggle for high school students to learn algebra when elementary school students are capable of learning calculus. Why is it not our mission that the most highly skilled and understanding teaching force be available in the classroom?

I sometimes find life in elementary school classrooms profoundly interesting. My wife is teaching summer school again, and I am the math teacher. Several years ago I visited a public housing resident (Theresa Coleman) and I found a fascinating book in her overcrowded dwelling. It is about teaching calculus to kindergartners. How surprised I was that it was there. I ask to borrow the book and reluctantly she agrees. I give her my word that I shall return it in a week.

The concept is powerful and engaging. I am glad to read and to study it. When my wife invites me to teach the math class, the idea is still in me about teaching calculus to young children. I search the information highway and I find material on teaching calculus to the young. I communicate with Don Cohen who wrote the material for *Calculus By and For Young People* and had been using it for seventeen years. He talks with me, and I am impressed with his materials and his ideas on learning. I start with a lesson on the sum and convergence of an infinite sequence on the first day. It is a fascinating adventure that involves all of us. The class each day is intense and demanding. The students work hard. They learn to use calculators and computers in new ways and to diligently study the partial sums as they endlessly merge, crowding toward a point.

One day in class a black girl who is struggling with infinite repeating decimals asks why we are doing this college work in elementary school. She is the only one who voices such a concern. The others work on. What I tell the class is that we are working problems that are sometimes difficult to grasp and understand. It is important to know that playing, studying, laughing, being good, and doing difficult things are all a part of life. If we do not work on hard things, read books, or see the beauty in a leaf, we are not really living. I tell them to take school and education seriously and to learn, new, difficult, and demanding things as they go through life. It is important that they do.

The students are nine and ten-years-old and will be going into the fourth and fifth grades next school year. The class is mostly Black and Chinese. There are two White students and one Latino. I think it is quite possible for four or five students to master such concepts of calculus. The deep goal is to have all of the students in the class participating and learning. There are thirty students in the class, and my mission is to have every soul here moving deeper into mathematics than they ever thought possible.

One student is from China and cannot speak English. She grasps the math with much more certainty than the English. She does all the work that everyone else does and does it as well. Others help her with her English, which is significantly improving, sometimes daily. She is a new immigrant with a deep personal mission. There are two special education students who started slowly but stay with the problems and learning process and gain strength in the subject and in this world we all form. One student, Lawrence, can see deeper than others into problems and can comprehend abstract and novel situations. It is good that he is here because there seem to be no ideas beyond his understanding. It is often his insight and understanding that ignites the class and excites their thinking. Some things make us question our capabilities. Other things deeply transform and move us. There are also many students who struggle with multiplication, subtraction, and division. The division algorithm is too complicated for many to master so we view division in other ways such as subtracting quantities that are contained within other quantities and sometimes discover new ways to understand our results. Fractions, decimals, addition, and division are not isolated exercises but are used in determining the limit of an infinite set of partial sums. It is important that we learn what we can now, no matter how we got to where we are.

Calculus is a collection of thoughts, objects, and symbols closed in a system of descriptions. New methods and streams of descriptions come into our consciousness, bringing a hint of the real world, revealing it through symbolic form. One day I would like for us to drop and propel objects and to understand their displacement in space. This can show us that this mathematics does work in the real world.

Some students do not become deeply involved in learning because of social and academic inequality from tracking, segregation, a diminished curriculum, and negative categorizing. This mathematics class where we all worked hard, profoundly challenged and changed us all. We find learning, discovery, and understanding, which connects each of us to a larger world. We all live diminished lives when the environments that we exist in do not challenge and deepen our capabilities.

CHAPTER 36

Stranger

It is five thirty in the morning and I am out along a California road, running in the dawn. I am a black person in a vanishing darkness who wonders if he can be seen by the occasional passing motorist. My mind is immersed in the mountain wilderness that surrounds me. My mind is often empty but it becomes alert to any moving object that awakens its consciousness. My goal is to run to the town center; which is two and a half miles away, and back again to a Sierra Club lodge. Sometimes I awaken to the uncertainty of events that a black man on a road can encounter. I am a stranger and an outsider here. My wife and I came here two days ago with friends, the Risks. Nobody knows us. To some who speed by me I provide a brief passing encounter while the beauty of the wilderness surrounding us is momentarily forgotten. Others do not notice me. Every soul that passes me vanishes into the past and this road becomes just another stretch of earth to travel. I run with a strange feeling that on this day something unusual may happen. It is why every car that passes me is on my mind. The morning life on most roads is uneventful. It is a monotonous and a simple life.

I continue on. The road is downhill to town and more strenuous on the return. This is the second day I am traveling this road, so I am not making history. The morning is cool. My only mistake that I am living

with is that I left my gloves in San Francisco. My hands are cold and destined to endure this mistake.

One does not know what one will encounter when one leaves ones
home. Yesterday my wife and I and two friends from San Francisco
traveled along the Donner Pass and onto Truckee and Donner Lake. I
stayed up into the night discussing and reading about the Donner family
and the journey they took with a party of eighty nine persons in coming
from Illinois to California in April of 1846. They described it as a
pleasant and beautiful journey as they traveled on to Wyoming. They
then tried shortcuts and struggled through the desert harshness in Utah
and made their own roads. They became mentally and physically weak,
distrusted each other, fought and killed each other. In late October they
reached the Lake (now called Donner Lake) near Truckee. They
struggled through what was to be the worst winter in these parts for
more than a hundred years. The snow was as high as twenty feet.
Members of the team starved to death, ate the dead, and desperately
fought to escape. Forty seven of the eighty nine members of the party
survived. When John Donner and his wife Tamsen left home in Illinois,
how could they know the death that would destroy their journey and
dream and that I would be thinking about their ordeal? Indeed, how
deeply have their lives and journey cut into my thinking? In leaving their
Illinois home they never could have imagined that one hundred and fifty
years later a lake would bear their name and that millions of people
would hear of their journey and their tragedy. Certainly many other
people left their homes and made it to California and their achievements
and failures died with them. What awaits me now that I have left my wife
at the mountain lodge? I do not know, am unable to know.

Up the road before me I see the body of a dead animal. My mind
struggles with the lessened life in our world. I see myself dead and life
continuing on without me. Life and death seems so clear, so ordinary.
The animal seemed unlucky. Is life not a gift given to us all? The earth
is a wasteland of matter and bodies! When I reach the body of the

disintegrating animal, I see only crumbled paper. My mind from a distance had constructed an illusion of an animal form. I had seen a body, a life, and a death that were never there. I continue to run and to think other thoughts. I see a dog at a nearby house. I think about what I might do if he comes to attack me. I never know until I am into an encounter. Last week I was running along the sea in San Francisco and was bitten by a wild, barking dog. I was not hurt. The dog at this nearby house hardly notices me as I run by.

I reach the town center and turn around. It is now light. It is as though darkness never was. I know that I am fortunate that I am still able to run these roads. I have been running for more than ten years and I am running as hard and as strong as I ever have. I know that running hills such as these and running long distances enables me to run beyond my thoughts. I once read about a professional football kicker who was struggling in his performance. He sought advice from an older player who had retired. The player told him to kick against the wind. It transformed his game and his life as a player. He achieved his highest level of performance. My running life was as great as it ever was. Running hills in the high altitudes pushed back the illusion of barrier and previous impossibilities. This life on the road is a hard life, a good life. I was nearing the end of the run. Running in the cold morning adds energy to my existence and to the days of my life. Some days I am dead tired when I am finishing a run. Today I am finishing strong.

There is a final hill to climb in reaching the lodge. As I thoughtlessly cross the road to the hill, I am amazed that I run into a bear who stands on the other side of the road, observing me. It is a spectacular moment that I do not know how to process. I am shocked, surprised. I feel no panic because I had seen this bear from a distance the previous night. I had studied his actions and behavior for thirty minutes before he ran away into the night. So he is not a stranger. He had found human food in a trash dumpster and had run away with it into the wilderness. I have never been this close to a wild animal in my life. I had traveled among giraffes, zebras, wildebeest, and an occasional lion in Kenya and Tanzania, but I had seldom been this close, and alone. For me nothing surpassed the moments in human existence than those where wild animals ran free in the wild. It greatly uplifts my spirit. The black bear that stands before me is a magnificent animal. I shall probably never pass this close to such a creature again.

How rare it is to be here. I had traveled through much California wilderness, always wondering about bears, wondering what I would do if I ever came upon one. When we camped we stored our food in places away from them. They never came. In all of my expeditions they never came. I had read about black bears (Ursus americanus) wandering into campgrounds. The smell of food would attract them, or their own natural curiosity would lead them to human places. It is the responsibility of humans to prevent them from becoming a problem by keeping human food away from them. So I have read. The taste and the availability of human food can condition them to an easy and an undisciplined life where they abandon their struggle for natural food. I respect his presence. I never stop running or change my course. He follows my motion. What will he do? One hears many theories and stories as to how one should act in the presence of a bear. My mind was empty. I had no thoughts. I continued to run. His eyes followed me up the hill to the lodge. He remains motionless along the road. I told my wife and friends and others at the lodge about the encounter. When they left to see him he was gone. He lived a life unknown and a mystery to us. I had lived through the morning without harm or tragedy. I am the person I am because of all the mornings I have lived through. The adventure of an unknown morning awakens my soul.

Running the road and the hills, I think about black youth in the classroom who reach a wall and who feel defeated. I know their world is my world also. When I run I understand the change in the state of energy needed to overcome obstacles. I know it takes self-discipline for us to go deeper into life, and I learn from running that life is a challenge and an adventure. School must challenge our personal and collective learning. Such learning involves personal discovery in our way of life. What I find is that school and running can be adventures from which one is able to see life for oneself.

CHAPTER 37

Summit

A mountain is a strong challenge for me. Mountains are places of great beauty and they speak to our deepest feelings. When one ascends to a mountain summit it is a significant journey. When we struggle to ascend the face of a rock or a mountain, we are absorbed in life and surrounded by adventure. The climb teaches us about life in real terms.

I awoke early on Tuesday, July 9th, prepared for the climb to the summit of Rainier. Paradise, the mountain town where my wife and I were staying, is located at 5,400 feet above sea level. The first destination of the climbing team was to reach Muir base camp which was at 10,000 feet above sea level. It was a six-hour journey across the snow fields. There were seven climbers and two instructors or guides. We all introduced ourselves and shared what had brought us here for the summit climb. The six other climbers included an engineering couple who worked for the National Aeronautics and Science Administration (NASA) in Houston, a mathematics professor from Stanford, an Outward Bound instructor from North Carolina, a visitor from Sweden, and a mountaineer from New Hampshire. The most interesting of our group was Albert who was an engineer from NASA. This was his third attempt and everyone was curious as to why he had not made it on the two previous attempts. We also wanted to know how had he prepared differently this time. He and his wife had worked hard together and had done some rock climbing and a lot of bicycling. His wife was certain they would both make it this time. The previous two times he had become dehydrated and had not been able to negotiate the high altitudes. He had not been married on the two previous attempts. At 10:00 AM we left for Muir. It was a rigorous journey over the snow fields. We all had our snow boots, ski poles, backpacks, and most of us were dressed in shorts. It was a warm day. We stopped approximately every hour to drink water and to eat along the way. We made a total of three stops before reaching Muir. I was exhausted when we got there. We arrived at Muir at 3:24 PM. The instructors made it clear that we were all being continuously evaluated as to our ability to persevere and to go on. We were all told that we had done well until this point and that we would all be proceeding to the summit climb the next day. I had also learned from the journey to the base camp that one of the guide instructors (George) had completed a summit climb to Everest. He had made it on his third attempt. He was asked if he used oxygen to reach the summit and said that he had. We had also met Lou Whittaker, the brother of Jim Whittaker, on our journey to the base camp.

I attended an Outward Bound meeting several months earlier in San Francisco and heard a presentation by Jim Whittaker, the first American to climb Mt. Everest. The presentation was about an international peace expedition with climbers from the USA, China, and the USSR. They had made practice climbs at Rainier to prepare for the Everest climb which they successfully completed. Afterwards, I discussed with him the possibility of climbing Rainier. He told me about his brother who ran Rainier Mountaineering Incorporated (RMI) and suggested I write and enroll with them.

Seeing Lou Whittaker was a highlight to several of the climbers. One of them referred to him as "the legend." He was a concerned and humble person when he greeted our group as he appeared as a traveler on the road heading back to Paradise. That evening we examined our gear and heard the plan for the journey. We went through the proper use of the harness, ice axe, crampons, head lamp, helmets, and the necessary clothing.

I have been told that Mount Rainier is referred to as the California Killer and that it is a much tougher endurance climb than the California mountains. My wife and I arrived in Paradise on Sunday, July 7th. We walked to the RMI building and saw climbers entering from just having completed the summit climb. They seemed exhausted and several commented on the unusual ordeal they had encountered. My wife was amazed that so many of them had achieved the climb. They seemed young for the most part. It was deceptive because it seemed a very ordinary feat to accomplish because a number of persons had made the climb and the next day there would be another group, and the next day another, throughout the summer. Was climbing to the summit as simple as it appeared, as common an exercise as we were witnessing? The answer was yes. My wife later learned from a ranger talk that of the approximately eight thousand persons who attempted the summit about half successfully made it.

We went back to Paradise Inn and I slept until the mountain climbing school began the next morning (Monday). Fourteen of us attended the school. There were two instructors and we all walked across the snow fields to approximately a mile away. I was not used to walking in the snow and it was probably more of an ordeal for me than the others. At the school we learned what it would require to successfully make the summit climb. Each item of clothing was discussed. The equipment was discussed. We spent time on the use and importance of our equipment. The ice axe, crampons, and ski poles were thoroughly demonstrated, and we had extensive practice in falling in the snow and recovering. We involved ourselves in the detail of how to walk in a biorhythmic pace in the snow to be productive at the high altitudes. I was not surprised at how cold my hands had become while falling and moving in the snow and ice. They were numb and wet. We also learned to walk in teams in our harnesses and roped together in groups. As we worked I learned that two of the students had climbed Mt Shasta. One student had just recently climbed to the base camp on the south side of Mt Everest. The chief instructor had just completed reaching the summit of Everest. He had much to tell us about mountain climbing. The school lasted for five hours. Everything I had learned would be used. It was a special school to me because it had a mission, also each of the students had a mission, the total focus was on everyone reaching the summit. We all shared this vision.

We made it to the base camp and now rested and waited to attempt the summit climb. We discussed our team assignments and then we all rested until it was time to begin. We were awakened at 12:30 AM by Aaron the chief instructor and guide. I did not feel strong. I had hardly slept. I knew that I had not eaten well or wisely. I had existed mainly on raisins. Those around me were filling themselves with more bulk liquids and solids. I knew also that I had not trained very hard for this expedition. I talked to a ranger when I first came, and he told me how important it was that one strengthen ones quadriceps muscles in the upper leg. I had given no attention to them. None. What was there for me to do but to leave with a clear mind? I did not fill it with confusing ideas of questioning my readiness. All that I had not done up until that moment did not matter to me now. I leave with no thoughts, and I am too serious to be held back by doubt or fear. It was Wednesday, July 10th at 2:15 am when we all set out with our head lamps guiding us through the darkness and the ascent. We left in two groups tied by rope into one team of four led by Aaron and the second team of five led by George. I was with the second team. It was a six hour climb to the summit. It was as difficult an endurance climb as I had ever faced. For me it was an endless journey of snow and ice and an effort in every step. My hands became colder and colder as the climb continued. My breathing rhythm was uneven and it was a struggle to maintain the pace.

We stopped at 11,000 feet and then at 12,300 feet. It was at the 12,300 foot mark that Albert told George he did not feel he could make the summit. George told him that we would make a decision at our next stop. At each of our stops we drank water, ate what food we packed, put on warm parkas, and tried to keep warm. At 13,500 feet (the third and final stop) Albert told George that he could not make the summit. He was physically and mentally exhausted and could not go on. He was left behind in a sleeping bag and George told him we would be back in two hours as we descended from the summit. Albert's wife said that her father had climbed Rainier and that it was probably in her blood to make the summit. She was born in the Seattle area. The two teams climbed on and we reached the peak at 9:30 am.

We were exhausted and elated to have made it. The climb made us know ourselves better. I was so glad that I made it and would be able to tell my wife that somehow I endured the struggle to get here. The 14,400 foot summit demanded more from me than I realized. I do not know what drove me on, but I was able to work harder and move myself to an inner and a physical level to make the top. It was a mission deep in me to get there. During the entire ascent the biorhythmic walking pace had remained a pattern that I was unable to master. In the final struggle to the summit, however, I found the power of this motion and it had helped me to the top.

We remained on the summit for thirty minutes where we enthusiastically talked and listened, ate, took pictures, and viewed the world that surrounded us. We left at 10:00 am. We descended and collected Albert at 13,500 feet and continued on. It was still a challenge in the descent. The sun softened the snow and the downward trek made falling a constant possibility. The sun was relentless with its penetrating force that diminished our strength. It took us four hours to reach the base camp at Muir. We arrived at 2:15 PM. We left Muir at 3:15 PM for Paradise. It was a three-hour journey over the snow fields. Surrounded by a world of snow, sun, heat, and light, we struggled down the slope. For me it was not routine. Energy was drained from my body and I was in this immense paradise of snow and ice that was everywhere I moved. It was a world of grandeur and beauty in which we could not rest. Our total effort was moving through it.

Several things were evident to me in the return from the summit. All of the emphasis on forcing oneself to drink water materialized into a real situation. By the time I had struggled to get back to Muir base camp I was noticeably weak and dehydrated. I did not drink enough water nor eat enough food at the high altitude.

This fact communicates to me a fundamental truth about learning and freedom. To go from **A** to **B**, our thought constructs an imaginary connection between them. The summit of Mt. Rainier was point A and the town of Paradise was point B. Why had my mind invented an ideal return and assumed that I would descend without obstacle and not die from a mistake or some other unknown? Why had I been so elated in reaching the summit that I had idealized and underestimated the return? Reality had not followed the path that my mind had contrived. There are other examples of worlds that our thoughts invent. A person's race is point (A). Human thought says that person (A) is Black and connects this being to a world (B) of underachievement, violence, and fear; or human thought says that person (A) is white and makes a connection to a world (B) of power and dominance. Humankind is imprisoned by the idea that it can invent connections between any two points, A and B. Freedom exists in what we discover and find as we leave A and travel on a new journey or adventure to B which does not exist. In our arrival there "B" is created or discovered. Illusions and other unreal images lie outside of the present state. There are also battles out there for us to die in. Freedom does not follow known paths or connections. It is the creation and discoveries along the way that deepen our lives. I was so exhausted at Muir that I longed for my wife to drive up and collect me, but the only way down was by foot or helicopter. I set out with the others. I was so weak and dehydrated that I continuously fell as I moved along with my ski poles. Aaron assisted me during the entire journey back. There was so much energy within me from making the summit that nothing would stop me from getting back to Paradise. But God, it was hard. I was so impressed with Aaron's knowledge of life in these mountains and his concern for getting me back. He loved his work and was an inspiration to me and the others.

He got us back to Paradise at 5:30 PM. We had accomplished the mission we set for ourselves. No one was more deeply moved than I was to have made it and to have been a member of the team. It was a serious and trying three days for me. My wife was there to meet me. She was glad to see me and to hear that I had made it to the summit. It was a great day for us both. I drank a cold root beer from Paradise Inn. It seemed like the greatest drink I ever tasted in my life.

The climb is significant to me because it is the most rigorous mountain climb that I had done. That made it a powerful personal experience. As an educator and a teacher I had encountered new learning experiences. And in facing hard times such as climbing a mountain which can appear so impossible to conquer, one is moved to a depth of energy and attainment.

CHAPTER 38

California Road

I am on a road to Mount Shasta which is north of San Francisco. I drive past small, rural mountain towns that may have stood for a hundred years. There is a saneness to countryside places. They are unsophisticated and parochial. They are enclosed and isolated yet seemingly boundless. The world's towns and villages are diminishing because of the disordered extension of its cities. Some cities are so overcrowded and deteriorated that they imperil the earth and its inhabitants.

When my wife, daughter and I lived in a small Kenyan village we were not able to obtain firewood from the countryside where we lived. There were no more nearby forests. The world's cities act as destructive parasites on the surrounding countryside, which become the diminished societies of the world. Deforestation of the earth causes massive erosion and the loss of an area's watershed. In Kenya we bought water from a Somali and we stored it in metal reservoirs and rationed its use. We were disciplined, cautious, and deliberate with it at all times. **We were programmed to use the least quantity for the greatest good.** Massive urban air pollution causes global warming, and our planet decays and struggles not to become another abandoned and lifeless body in space. In the modern era, people have continued to move to the cities. They have been lured to Lagos, Mexico City, New York, Chicago,

Los Angeles, Rio de Janeiro, Shanghai, and Bombay. What will stop us is the limited resources of the planet or an unknown catastrophe.

Mount Shasta is not visible in the dark but is a spectacular site in daylight. It is a glacier and has quietly existed through earthly transformations. Its Ice Age ridges and peaks still exist. After an eternity of perpetual cold, the earth warmed and humankind found this planet to be a great and a friendly home. In the human journey life moved out of the caves and the cold to other adventures and to invent ways to express itself in written languages, to construct tools and objects, to make charts of the world and the skies, and to discuss the meaning of our uniqueness as well as our connection to the world. The break from the cold gives us new life. The warmth is a great gift. The earth remains warm, livable, and habitable for us.

It is still warm. We continue to celebrate. Some say, however, that we are between ice ages. A new ice age will come and devastate life as we now know it and our cities and towns and villages will be destroyed and crushed and animals will become extinct as they become frozen out of existence. The equatorial region may be the only habitable place on earth and humankind may begin a journey again in Africa. The universe itself may at some point contract and begin again. Who knows? Who can know?

Our youth in our cities and in our towns face equal barriers to learning. The obstacles are therefore beyond the places from which we come. No youth learns when he or she is being told what to do or is subjected to forced instruction. We learn when we discover things for ourselves. The joy of learning comes from our own internalization and understanding of the world that we discover.

When I lived a village life in Nigeria, I learned to live alone, independently, and in a socially organized society. Walking to town to buy food, or a mosquito net, to find a kerosene lantern in a town thirty miles away, to get clothes and shoes, and to cook one's meals were all overbearing tasks. I discover much about life and living in the world.

I am fortunate to have lived that life. It was a hard and a lonely life and a rich life. I understand that most of the world does not come to me through the guidance or teaching of someone else. I find that some things are new and unpredictable, and some things are surprising. It is not results that I search for in my mind. It is my observation and discovery of the world as it is revealed to me that I am able to understand it.

Life is contrived when most of our problems are difficult and beyond us or when they are easy and beneath us. In actual life youth face the easiest problems and the very hardest problems. By discovering that life requires our attention to handle both the simple and the complex we are not overwhelmed to face any challenges. Many youth never understand challenges. They never understand that there are easy days and there are hard days. They become bored and say things are too hard, and they quit. Later they wished they had learned to stick it out and move deeper into life.

Students need to pursue those things which interest them, regardless of the obstacles. They can increase their abilities and become both competent and creative at what they are doing. They can learn how discipline and freedom increase their capabilities. I learn new things in living in Africa and in living in the mountains. It is a joyous time to come to the mountains. Right now being here and traveling here is as great a life as I can live for this moment.

I am to meet an expedition in Shasta City tomorrow morning. I do not know how many others will be there. It is an Outward Bound expedition.

I find learning in wilderness and adventure programs to be a profound experience. It is also true for others I know who have had the interest to pursue such programs. Our capabilities are strengthened through our living a strenuous life.

The night is filled with travelers on the road, and we are all strangers to each other. And what can impact our lives and the worlds we exist in more than the meeting of a stranger or a traveler?

As I travel along I am aware of all the other people moving up and down this road. Sometimes when one stops and talks to a traveler one learns of unbelievable adventure. One day I stopped and talked to a man on the road in San Francisco. He slowly passed me on a bicycle as I ran along the road which followed the Pacific coast. The beach along the ocean is fascinating because of its rich, momentary, monotonous, and unpredictable life. One day I ran along the sea and saw a dog madly chasing seagulls which always flew away. The dog ran in exhaustion. It was an incredible act. When I was young I read a poem. It was about a man chasing the sun.

Round and round they sped.
I said, "You can't..."
He said, "You lie." And he kept on running...

It is not possible for me to communicate with the dog. He is determined to do what he is driven to do. I run beyond him and his mad journey. The man on the bicycle has stopped riding and is now walking his bike. He sees me and greets me. He seems interested in starting a conversation. There are other runners, but he is intent on communicating with me. Is it because I am the only black person on this road? I stop and I talk to him.

He seems well-traveled. He tells me that he is traveling down the coast to Los Angeles (five hundred miles) and beyond. His accent seems different; I am unable to discern its origin. As I talk with him I find that his journey is profound. He began in Canada on this long and winding road that now brings us together at this particular moment. He is from Toronto, and I suppose that is the slight accent in his speech that I am noticing. He gives me a newspaper article that was written about him and it has his picture and it has a picture of his riding his bicycle heading north along a highway. He autographs the newspaper article and gives the copy to me. I never asked for the article or his autograph. He wanted me to have them. I had nothing to give him to help on his journey. He said that he had a bad tire and that it needed replacing. I had to run another seven miles to get back to the car, and I had nothing there that I could give him. A young couple came along and they had five dollars which they donated to him. This showed that if you are generous (as he was to me) that you will be paid back in return.

This expedition made his life interesting. The death of his wife had brought him grief and loneliness which inspired him to begin a new life and to take to the road. It speaks to the greatness of the human spirit. His journey across North America was in its fifth year. He had been married for twenty seven years and his wife died of leukemia. His life hit rock bottom. He gained more than fifty pounds sitting around his home thinking about his life and drinking whisky. He said that he was a disaster. He was told that he would likely die of a heart attack. He decided to run away from life. That is why he started the journey and instead he found himself right in it.

He has traveled over 55,000 miles and has a story of the world and life from his own point of view. He has many stories to tell and he is writing a book about the people that have formed his journey. He says that there have been poor people who have struggled to find room to accommodate him in their houses. He has been bitten by a rattlesnake, robbed at gunpoint, and attacked by wild dogs. He continues on his journey, traveling sixty miles a day. His odyssey is living the life that is within him. We all have within us journeys that we can make up and down roads that we have not seen, friends we have yet to meet.

Life is filled with fascinating journeys. Recently I learned about a foot race from Hunington Beach in Southern California to New York City. It was a three thousand mile race and the runners ran for sixty miles a day. They ran for more than two months. Some of them reached the destination which was Manhattan in New York City. I ride on.

At last I reach Shasta City, and I sleep until morning. The next morning I connect with the other members of the expedition. Are we the individuals who can match these mountains that stand so rugged, so strong, and so mysterious?

CHAPTER 39

Shasta

Day 1 Friday

We assembled at the Fifth Season mountain shop in the town of Mount Shasta at 10:00 AM as scheduled. We acquainted ourselves with each other and were fitted for boots and crampons. An Outward Bound vehicle took us from the town of Mount Shasta to the North Gate Access and the foot of the mountain. It was about a two-hour drive over a back dirt road. We arrived at the North Gate Head at 3:00 PM. We are a group of four students and two instructors. The instructors assisted us in the distribution of individual and group equipment. We learned the anatomy of the backpack (lumbar pads, hip belt, shoulder straps, extensions, sternum strap and other parts). We assembled as a group to express what motivated each one of us to come for the ascent of Mt. Shasta (14,162 feet). We had all come for the physical and mental challenge as well as the spiritual quest and inward personal journey. We all looked forward to an unknown adventure and to the profound journey of a climbing expedition.

In the journey to our campsite we each participated in determining locations through map reading skills. We arrived at the campsite at 8:15 PM. We were aware of the minimum impact on the area by our predecessors. Our altitude was at 9,500 feet. During the night the assistant instructor pointed out the Northern Lights to two of us. All others were asleep. It was cold but a comfortable night.

Day 2   Saturday

We were all awake by 5:15 AM. We completed our morning chores and were instructed in the use of crampons as well as techniques for walking in snow and ice. The view of the mountain from the campsite with its vastness and the effort and perseverance to ascend it was unbelievable and awesome. There were expeditions which had already begun early in the morning and we could hardly see and recognize them inch along the enormous mountain. They were black specks on the wall of white snow. It fascinated us all to follow their slow and endless journey to the summit. Over time their minute movement seemed evident. They were ascending the mountain, barely, but certainly. They all possessed a great spirit of adventure, determination, and wonder. What they were accomplishing hardly seemed within possibility to us. The instructors stated that on Sunday morning we would be on the same journey we were witnessing. We gave no further attention to anticipating the challenge of this seeming awesome ascent.

We left camp at 9:00 AM to establish a high campsite from which we would ascend to the summit of Shasta early Sunday morning. We arrived at our new campsite at around twelve o'clock noon. The altitude of the camp was 10,800 feet. We all participated in map reading exercises. At 3:00 PM we all went to snow school. We ascended about five hundred feet above our campsite in order to learn how to survive the multitude of situations we could encounter. It was emphasized that safety was paramount. The safety of the team depended on each individual being responsible for his or her own safety. We practiced for hours on how to walk in snow, how to fall and how to use our ice axes to self-arrest and terminate our falls. We worked and worked until we were all good at what we had to be prepared to execute. We then roped ourselves together for safety in two teams of three which would be how we traveled in our ascent to the summit. We then spent an hour or so on roped team travel. We returned to campsite, discussed our plans for the summit ascent on Sunday morning and went to sleep early that night.

Day 3   Sunday

We were awakened at 3:30 AM. After hurrying to prepare and after a speedy breakfast, we left camp at 4:40 AM. Under ideal weather conditions, we began by initially ascending a slope of fifteen to thirty five degrees of mixed terrain. We walked in hard morning snow that would be soft corn snow in the afternoon. Dawn came as the sun arose at around 5:15 AM from the hills beyond us. We slowly but steadily made our way through the igneous rock formations and up continuously steep terrain. The crevasses were being exposed by the melting rays of the sun. It was a hard climb, but we had a good team. We worked the mountain slowly, struggling in a winding switchback trail. Amy, who walked ahead of me, was determined and tireless. She had just completed a New York City Outward Bound course where she had been paired with a student from a New York public housing project, and the two of them had walked across tall ships, lived in shelters and existed on a small fixed budget. What stands out in this climb is how minute and insignificant we seem.

The height that we ascend is overwhelming to my mind and body. It would be a frightening feeling to be in such a precarious position on this enormous and grand mountain if only I had the energy to look down. It is a dizzying height that takes your breath away. It takes my total attention, though, just to make the small and endless steps that must be made to get us up the mountain, otherwise the perilous drop would distract my mind. We are driven to make the summit. Higher up on the mountain we passed loose scree slopes. We reached the upper plateaus where the sulfur springs were active. We ascended the last five hundred feet to the pinnacle summit (14,162 feet) following the Hotlum-Bolam route. We reached the summit at 11:00 AM and experienced the immense feeling of reaching the top. We took photographs, ate lunch, and we descended at about 11:30 AM. In the descent we utilized the skills we learned in similar situations we had prepared ourselves for. I slid down the mountain and self-arrested my fall with the ice axe. It accelerated the laborious and trying descent which seemed endless. Nothing is simple in the descent. In climbing to the summit, within you is a determined focus but once you have completed the mission you are not at the same energy level when you descend. You are not as focused, and Shasta is such a vast world, it is easy to go off in a wrong direction, and there is sometimes the possibility of a drop off or a crevasse. That had happened to climbers on Rainier who had fallen to their death into a crevasse shortly after I had been there. In the end we made it back to our campsite and quickly continued the descent. The soft corn snow had been difficult to travel in.

We stopped and visited two sacred Indian sites near the end of our descent. One sensed that the quietness, fresh running water, rock formations, and patterns of light, were symbols to the Indians who dwelled in these places.

The places were significant to me as well. They may well have been discovered hundreds of years ago, though I see no evidence of prior dwellers. I then thought about the meaning of this mountain to me. These quiet places did not resemble the mountain as a whole whose great mass at the higher elevations was a world of snow and ice. There were no streams nor warmth there. It was a world where other forces governed your existence as your mind and body struggled in desperation. Gravity and a diminishing atmosphere dominated that world, as did the weather and wind and the restlessness of the volcano. Climbing the mountain had provided us with another view of the earth and changed us from the lives of our normal state of existence of breathing and moving about on earth in crowded cities and prosperous highway towns.

We reached the camp at 2:45 PM. We arrived at North Gate at 7:00 PM. It was a great expedition and deep adventure for us all. Each one of us learned new things about ourselves and completed his or her mission.

CHAPTER 40

Kilimanjaro Highway

We are now back traveling in Africa again. My wife and daughter are on the road traveling through game reserves in Tanzania, and I am here to climb Mount Kilimanjaro.

I first saw Mount Kilimanjaro more than twenty-five years ago when I visited here from Nigeria. It was an unbelievable encounter. It was a world of unexpected greatness that appeared before me. I was immersed in a place of endless wildlife that was dominated by the mountain, yet free. I was struck by the mountain and the life it sustained but I never had penetrated into its world.

Getting started. I read as much as I could about the mountain. I searched the internet for all that existed. A colleague told me about a California adventure and travel company. The company informed me that if I were in Africa and made the Kilimanjaro expedition alone it would cost me three thousand dollars. If five other people were on the team then it would be two thousand dollars each. I decided to make my own arrangements once I got to Africa. My daughter and I attended a Mountain Club of Kenya meeting in Nairobi on Tuesday but found little information about the climb. They knew much however about Kenyan expeditions and especially about climbing Mount Kenya. They were not very interested in Kilimanjaro, which is in Tanzania, because it cost too much to climb was often said. There were mostly Europeans and several Americans present. There was a South African who was bicycling from South Africa to England whom we met. He had just climbed Mount Meru in Tanzania. He said that he was caught in the rain and that instead of dressing to protect himself he had stripped himself to a pair of shorts only and sealed all of his clothing in his pack to keep them dry. When the rain stopped everything was dry but the shorts. He seemed happy to share this philosophy that had worked for him.

We needed a ride back to Nairobi and there was a British climber who said that he could give us a lift there. He said that he had climbed Kilimanjaro more than seventy times and talked for thirty minutes about how to make the climb. He told me that I would be smart to take six days to make the climb and not try for five. He told me that I could go to a hotel in Moshi, Tanzania and that they could completely prepare me for the climb in a day and that it would cost seven hundred American dollars. He had been a good person to talk to because he loved sharing all that he knew about the mountain. As I was leaving Nairobi an American living in Tanzania told me not to pay more than three hundred dollars. We got to Arusha and I met an African to whom we had talked to about the climb and game safaris. He had arranged for a guide and two porters. This is a Tanzanian requirement for a single climber. I would pay thirty dollars to the guide and twenty dollars to each of the porters for the five days. I went to the Arusha market and spent twenty American dollars on food for the expedition that Wednesday, and that Thursday we were at the Marangu Gate ready to climb. I had spent a total of three hundred dollars for a five day climb. This included the salaries of the guide and porters, the food, the hut fees, the accident insurance, and the nonresident fees. I had brought my own climbing gear.

What surprised me most in the beginning were the number of persons looking for work, who were in line to join expeditions up the mountain. Before coming here mountain climbing had always been a white man's activity in my mind. How amazed I was at seeing all of the

Africans who are here for jobs in climbing the mountain. They were mainly Chaggas who have lived in this area for hundreds of years.

We enter the gate and we begin the climb to Mandara Hut. It is the rainy season and the mountain itself has never been visible. Our destination is a summit we cannot yet see. It is the rain forest area and as we walk Richard, the guide, points out movement in the distance. I see several monkeys on the ground and in the trees. I also see a baboon. Probably at one time there was an abundance of wildlife in this rain forest. I think this because when we lived in Kenya twenty years ago there were numerous giraffes and other wildlife on the road from Kenya to Tanzania. Now there are none. It is an easy walk in the beginning and the climb up the mountain seems almost effortless. The forest is green and lush, and I am unable to realize that we are climbing a great mountain. Richard is twenty-two years old but knows this mountain and understands its barriers and secrets. He emphasizes that I move slowly, slowly. Pole. Pole. He reminds me, "There is no rush in Africa."

I know these are more than words and must be internalized in my motion for ascendance to the summit. He is telling me that I begin to live now so that I can get through the hard times.

From the very beginning I know that I am a curious stranger to some. Once the first African of the many who are working this mountain realizes that I am an African American, there never dies some interest in my presence on the road. I am told by Richard that the news of my presence has spread up and down the road. There are those who are shocked that I am here climbing the mountain. To some Africans I am just another African passing on the road. Some hardly notice me. I am absorbed in the climb and seldom interact with them beyond a passing greeting. Occasionally I am asked where my country is.

"United States. I am a black American."

They all know about black Americans. The world is more of a global village than it was when I once lived in Africa. I am amazed at the American T-shirts, sportswear, caps, and other garments the Africans display ascending and descending the road. (The most enthusiasm and curiosity I had encountered about news, clothing, books, and conversation about Americans, and black Americans especially was at the Kenyan-Tanzanian border. They were particularly obsessed with getting American objects. My wife calls it the Americanization of the Africans.) The many white people who are climbers, in my mind, have no idea that I am not African. Why would they assume otherwise on this road?

It took us two hours to reach Mandara Hut which was at nine thousand feet. The weather is cooler, and I am not as enthusiastic as when I began the journey. I hiked to Mundahi Crater alone. I decided that I would work the mountain as hard as I could each day. I would carry heavy loads and push myself to my physical limit. I then felt good about being here. After reflecting and working out my own philosophy on how I am to approach the climb, again I am on fire with enthusiasm and my spirit soars.

I left the crater, which was quiet, inactive and desolate. I am surprised at the dining hall where the other climbers are from Germany, Denmark, United States (New York, Utah, and California), England, and other places. I am the only black person among the twenty other people there. One's distinctiveness matters everywhere among humankind. I have never been to a place where race does not matter. The presence of black people in America has never ceased to be a profoundly significant event. A Norwegian woman on the bus ride from Nairobi could hardly believe that my wife did not know which tribe or region in Africa her ancestors had come from. Each group had its meal prepared and served separately. The food was fresh and delicious. (Dinner consisted of mushroom soup, bread, cabbage, carrots, potatoes, peppers and an orange. I am a vegetarian.) My main conversation had been with the German group, three students who spoke and understood English profoundly. They knew about America globally and locally. They had traveled there and amazed me with their depth of knowledge. They talked of San Francisco history and San Francisco sports, Oregon geography, and the federal prison system. Their names were Volker, Ingo, and Thomas. My roommate was Martin from Denmark. He is a quiet, thoughtful, and kind individual. To my surprise he would one day write to me in America. We all use pit toilets in weather that grows cooler as the day darkens. It is cold the next morning when we awake. I eat breakfast (bread, butter, jam, avocado, peanut butter, milk, tea, porridge, eggs, tomatoes, and cucumbers) and we leave at 8:00 AM.

Day 2

There is impressive scenery along the way. For the first time we see the Kibo peak of Kilimanjaro. I had not seen it since I was last in Africa. Its wonder and greatness have not diminished. It took five hours to reach Horombo Hut. It is located 12,340 feet above sea level. Steven, the group cook, asked for an advance in his salary of a thousand Tanzanian shillings ($2 American) to buy cigarettes. A number of porters and guides are observed smoking up and down the road. He says that he has been smoking for nine years and that he has climbed Kilimanjaro to the summit many times. The road we are traveling is the tourist route. One of the Germans tells me that it is called the Coca Cola Route. I had bought a coke at Mandara for 400 shillings (eighty cents). It costs 500 shillings at Horombo (one dollar). This popular Marangu route takes five days for the round trip. Day One is from Marangu Gate to Mandara Hut. Day Two is from Mandara Hut to Horombo Hut. Day Three is from Horombo Hut to Kibo Hut. Day Four is from Kibo Hut to the Kibo Summit to Horombo Hut. Day Five is from Horombo Hut to Marangu Gate.

I am surprised and impressed at the solar energy that is present in each of the huts which allow them to provide electrical power. Water is pumped from springs that provide flush toilets at Horombo. At dinner I talk to the Germans about San Francisco, and then I speak with an American lady who had surprisingly joined me at the table. She was interested in knowing how I was doing. It seemed like she already knew me. I was surprised at her energetic and concerned presence. She wanted to know about my family whom she said she had seen on the bus from Nairobi to Arusha. I told her they were on safari in Tanzania. She seemed to be one of the most genuine and sincere individuals I ever met. She wondered why my wife and daughter were not climbing. I told her that my wife's health (asthma) would not allow her to make the climb. My daughter though had just turned twenty three and was very healthy. Several people had asked me why she was not climbing. She was at the perfect age and time in life. I had asked her about the climb but she was not psychologically driven to attempt it. I told the lady, "Maybe another time," for my daughter.

The dining hall is filled with many persons because of the people who are on their way back from the summit climb. Horombo is the location where the night is spent after attempting the summit. It is also the place where people spend two nights when they take six days for the climb.

Day 3

It is Saturday. I arise at daylight. We leave at 8:30 AM. The weather is cold, and for the first time in my life I am aware of possible blood in my urine. I travel on. The view from this altitude becomes grand, vast, and otherworldly. There are only five or so of us on the same schedule from Horombo to Kibo Hut. Many are taking a six day climb and have therefore remained another day at Horombo. They will remain there and some will take the climb to Mawenzi to further acclimatize themselves. On the road is a couple from England. The fellow had become ill at Mandara and they had spent two nights there. They only had five days for the expedition and would therefore have to turn back at Kibo Hut and not attempt the summit. It was unfortunate because he is now well, and his climbing seems so spirited. They are happy in this world. They are not disappointed about not going to the summit, but are grateful that they are climbing together and that they have come as far as they have. Around the saddle, area between Kibo and Mawenzi peaks, on the road to Kibo Hut he turned around to see Mawenzi peak (17,562 feet). He was moved and thrilled. He said," I am so glad just to be here."

Before I left California I had read a report from a British climber. I had read his account of the climb. He had chosen Kilimanjaro because of the opportunities it gave to learn of altitude climbing without technical skills. I especially remember his account of Day Three in the saddle area where they had come across a Tanzanian youth on the same schedule as his team. The youth had trouble breathing and within five minutes was dead. He was fourteen, with a group of scouts, and he never understood the sickness he had received from being at this altitude. He had died from a pulmonary edema. A memorial service was held for him on the mountain and a wooden cross was placed where he died. I learned also that ten to twelve people died a year on Kilimanjaro from Acute Mountain Sickness (AMS). The incidence of headaches, loss of appetite, nausea, and vomiting begin to occur in this area.

It had been hard work finally reaching Kibo Hut. I was the first to struggle in. The Germans usually were.

"Who is the blue man?" a German had remarked as I moved along the road in blue climbing attire. Today was one of my best days of climbing. Kibo Hut is at 15,520 feet and in entering the site one takes no step for granted. The higher we travel the more vulnerable we are to this mountain world and its lifeless elements of altitude, rocks, sand, and freezing wind. They all cause us to move in slow motion, and they are the elements that wear on us and slowly destroy us. Inside the hut it is damnably cold and impossible to bear. The wind is so strong that it blows right through the hut and the body. The only warm place is outside in the sun. I join the three Germans as we all fight to sustain a life in a place that is cruel and unforgiving. One of the Germans is bleeding from the nose and is affected by the altitude. We all are dominated by the wind and the cold.

"What do you think the temperature is here?" I am asked.

"I think that it is just about the freezing point."

"What's that, about 32 degrees Fahrenheit?" the German asked as he converted from centigrade. "They seemed to be filled with technical information. I remark that the solar panels should be generating heat in the huts."

"What they need up here are windmills," the German remarked. I agreed.

There is a team of Japanese who have an injured team member. They stay until evening and then travel on to Horombo Hut for the night.

It was too cold to sleep. I am glad to be here at this point. I consider the interesting events that bring us to the mountains. In climbing Mount Rainier I had met a person who said that he was going to climb the mountain because he lived in Tacoma and he could daily see this mountain from his window and all of these years had motivated him to come for the climb. I do not know if he ever made it to the top. I asked Richard, the guide, if African women ever climbed the mountain. I am told that school girls climb this mountain as part of school field trips. Would it not be a serious expedition for an American youth field trip? It would be a great learning place for those who wanted to be here. They would enter into an unknown place, exploring and learning about themselves and others in a new world. A great diversity of people share this mountain world. Here we are in a totally new place and we must set ourselves free from what we have always known, possessed and been taught.

Day 4

We arose and began the climb at 1:00 AM. There is still blood in my urine. I never learn why. It is hard work from 15,000 feet to the summit through the scree, darkness, and the battle to acclimatize. It is a grueling and inhuman struggle for more than five hours.

I always felt that I was to climb this mountain. It was a momentarily significant event, reaching the summit. I had been so devastated though at a point in the climb that I had struggled to reach Gilman's Point (18,700 feet). I did not go on to Uhuru but descended from Gilman's. We had passed the altitude where the oxygen present was half the amount as at sea level. My body became strengthless. I had joined the two Germans there. They strongly impressed me because they had accomplished their mission and gone on. They too had returned from Gilman's. The youngest German student who had felt faint at Kibo hut did not look strong. He was forced to turn around shortly after we started the ascent to the summit. The others were helpless in moving him on. In the end the guide took him back down to Kibo Hut. In the short time that I know him I realize that he is a good person and he came to climb this mountain and how important it was for him to accompany his colleagues to the summit. I hope this day does not alter his great spirit. Yesterday I met an Irishman who was walking back down the road to Marangu Gate, and he said that he had been too sick to reach the summit but that his wife had made it to the top. He said it was a problem that he had to live with, though it bothered him. This can become a road of failure and loss. We come to this world for a great journey and a deeper life. There is achievement and there is tragedy. In the end all of our adventures are just stories along a Kilimanjaro highway.

At the summit, I thought about the Germans. They brought great energy to the mountain. They were youthful, with keen minds, and seemed such competent climbers. They were individually independent and had an unbreakable bond of friendship. And as invincible as they were the mountain had severely tested them. Though the youngest and most spirited of the group could not overcome the destructive force of the earth's altitude, the focus of the team had been total dedication in their effort to assist him and then to have him safely return with the guide to Kibo lodge.

The other two had gone on to the top. They cheered for me to reach the summit. A new wave of energy came to me, and I joined them there. They had not intended to stay there for long. They talked about the severity of life at this altitude, the lack of oxygen, the risk to brain cells. They calculated their time there, wished me well, then descended. The mountain had tested them, but did not change their collective strength.

We reached Kibo Hut again in a quick descent, sliding down the loose scree and gravel. It took an hour to return. We traveled on to Horombo. I spoke with the woman who wondered about my wife and daughter. We passed briefly on the road.

Day 5

We left Horombo early and reached Marangu Gate at 11:00 AM. Along the way I had conversations with the guides, porters, and with Martin from Denmark. My wife and daughter were there to greet me. They were glad to see me and to hear that I had made the climb. My wife has been with me everywhere and supports me always.

This had been a great African challenge for me. The guide, the Germans, the Africans, and the mountain deepened my life.

Richard, the guide, was as competent as any person I met in my mountain travels. When I had met him in Arusha he looked like a fourteen-year-old who was too young to guide a mountain expedition. He understood Kilimanjaro in-depth, and I was proud of and amazed by, his ability to lead and manage the five day expedition. I was also impressed with the other Africans throughout the journey. They all knew mountain life well and worked the mountain expertly.

One concern I had on this African mountain was the influence of the Europeans. There were several monuments commemorating them. The first person to climb the mountain is credited as being a German climber in 1889. The Africans who work the mountain have no serious problem with European recognition in contributing to the prominence of the mountain. They find in many ways it is good for the country. I saw graffiti throughout the expedition. Everyone wants to leave his or her mark. European names and nations for the most part marked beds, rocks, walls, doors, and other surfaces. Perhaps in the African quarters of the guides, porters, and other staff there were also such writings and symbols. No one is perfect. But it is evident that the Africans in their years and many journeys to the summit have left few marks to show that they have been here.

We are fortunate when our individual and collective quests get us over our barriers. I experienced a special time being on a team with Richard and the others as we worked to ascend the mountain. The Germans as a team and as individuals were unbothered by the world. They demonstrated individual strength and an unbreakable team spirit that knew few bounds. Being on Kilimanjaro provided them a time to be on a great team. In any climb it may always be our last time to live with such a profound challenge. I personally commended them on the spirit they all gave to the climb.

The mountain itself is a remarkable place. It is a volcano with glacial ice fields arising from tropical rain forests. It is a quiet place. Still. Unique. I had climbed almost nineteen thousand feet and walked more than fifty miles in five days. Though my wife and daughter never saw the summit of the mountain because it was always hidden in the clouds, this Kilimanjaro expedition had been a special event in Africa for us as a family. Indeed, many people would be greatly interested in the mountain and the climb and would seriously want to know about the expedition. We know individuals living in Africa and America who will ask from genuine fascination about the Kilimanjaro journey.

After the climb we left the Marangu Gate where others now enter this mountain highway. I am told by Tanzanian officials who work here that sometimes as many as fifty people a day pass through this gate on the road up the mountain. To me Kilimanjaro is not a distant and external world but a place on which to find insight into oneself.

In the Kilimanjaro world I find that it is important to have a philosophy in moving through it. I do not wonder about why men or women climb mountains. I only know that I am fortunate to be here now, to have the opportunity to climb Kilimanjaro, and to face such a deep challenge. I am moved to discover how hard I can work each day and see where such a life leads me. It is important to do profound things as our lives vanish and we move on. I observe from the Africans the freedom and discipline in them from the countless journeys up and down the mountain. The totality of a climb is an overwhelming venture that is done step by step, camp by camp, day by day in life along the Kilimanjaro highway.

CHAPTER 41

Epilogue

Reflections

How momentary my stay on Kilimanjaro had been. As hard as the climb had become in the end, I found that it was an ordinary day on the mountain. I was fifty-one years old when I made the climb, but I was so surprised because the person who had signed the climber's log ahead of me was a sixty-nine year old from Switzerland. My wife, daughter, and I were excited when we were reunited at Marangu Gate. This part of our journey was complete. We left and traveled back to Kenya just as we had done years ago.

I have learned from marathon runs, mountain climbs, and wilderness hikes that such experiences are not to be held onto. When our lives depend on things that have already happened we give away our freedom to time and objects. They can never liberate us.

Having finished running the San Francisco Marathon, and in excellent condition and quietly confident, I had played basketball with high school players for the first time ever, but the nature of rapidly running up and down the court quickly exhausted me. My past marathon running seemed meaningless. I was unable to sustain the pace, and I left the game.

If our lives depend on objects and events **out there** in space or in time we are their prisoners. The things that matter most to us are as impermanent as is all else.

Often I preferred being alone in the dining halls of the lodges as we climbed the mountain. But people came to talk to me. I was the only black climber and some of them deeply wanted to be a friend. Others were not used to a black presence. I have heard humankind described as individuals with stone age minds living in a space age world. Most evident of ancient thought was the colonial view of the Africans by the white travelers. They wanted to see me as different, but I observed the violent thoughts they brought with them, evident in their attitudes of white superiority.

For many the Africans were less than human. Some of them learned that I loved Africa and the people deeply. And as American Africans did we face the greatest oppression of humankind from the slave trade days? Possibly. Possibly not. But why dwell on a second class or remainder status? Acknowledge it. Move deeper into life. Don't collaborate in our own oppression. We make the oppressor greater than he is.

It is difficult to counteract this because some people desperately seek an explanation for their suffering. The thoughts of the white people on the mountain road are from an ancient life burdened with racism and oppression. They become attached to their assumptions. They do not question their world. Their minds and thoughts perpetuate inequality, and they are unable to change its course. Sometimes the human course is changed with purpose and design, sometimes not. On a day after the climb we were in Nairobi, discussing a trip to Mombasa, a Kenyan city on the Indian Ocean. My daughter had been excited about the journey, but my wife had severe migraine headaches and was unable to travel anywhere else in Africa. Our life in Africa ended. We had to leave and return home to California. We changed our course and immediately left. How unexpected and unplanned it had been.

There is also great energy in those who come to climb the mountain. Different interests and passions attract the climbers. I learn this because after I climbed Mount Kilimanjaro I wrote about it and shared it on the internet. Those who wanted to climb, as well as those who had already climbed it, communicated with me. I learned about them and their energy through their questions, experiences, doubt, wonder, and high enthusiasm. Persons of different races and nationalities communicated with me from the United States, Europe, Australia, and South America. I became acquainted with a person who had met the South African bicyclist and I had even met a person whom the British climber at the Mountain Club of Kenya had visited and stayed with in California. I met Americans who had been teachers in Tanzania. They had climbed the mountain several times with groups of African students. They had climbed from the Marangu route and the Machame route. I was so impressed that as teachers they had passed through such an environment of beauty, challenge, and adventure and that they and the students had completed such expeditions.

The information highway is changing the world. Life has been to move the atoms of our bodies and other objects throughout the world at the speed of thought and physical movement. Now by moving electrons (bits) at the speed of light, traditional communication barriers no longer exist and digitized bits of information change the world and human capability.

Nothing is ever more devastating to me than a death in the mountains. The death of the Tanzanian youth on Kilimanjaro and a recent death of a San Francisco youth on a nearby California mountain affect me at the deepest level. The power, adventure, risks, sanity, and healing of the wilderness frees us, but freedom does involve us in the life and death matters of our existence. If all things die—people, trees, the planets, and the stars —then whatever is great, perfect, ordinary, or tragic will at some point cease to be. Only from death comes rebirth.

It is useless to fear death. In climbing a mountain we are here and not there (a place yet to happen). We are here and deep into the climb. Here is the place we always are. A restless mind wants to be elsewhere. It becomes an effort to get through the climb because of not living in the moment. To climb without consciousness, limit, or boundary, to not be a prisoner of time, distance, and thought liberates us and enables us to go beyond ourselves.

CHAPTER 42

Final Notes

From Within

Why do we struggle on the sea, hike in the wilderness, and climb mountains? They are ways to empower us. They engage us and give us strength from within. The universe struggles and unwinds to express itself, as does life. In climbing a mountain each person is on his or her own quest to do what is in that person to do. I find it is profound to climb with no image of self-achievement but to understand how hard I can work, how far I can go. What is the significance of the summit, the finish line, or the destination? They get one started and bring energy to the quest. The sea, Africa, the world of running, and the wilderness school got me started in a life of self-discovery. For others it may be religion, technology, school or the environment.

When I allow superficial thinking to follow from a conclusion or a belief and prevent inquiry I am not living profoundly. When I live in chaos and destroy the existing world I do not live a creative life. In such times I am limited by the permanency of ideas, place, time and objects.

The illness I lived through in Africa was devastating at the time. I have been challenged to live a healthy and fit life and am therefore seldom ill. The one serious health dilemma that I have encountered resulted when traveling in Africa. I was never again hospitalized. For many years I lived a healthy life. I have had occasional backaches over the years that never last.

Recently they have been more intense, and I find myself in the emergency room of a San Francisco hospital, unable to stand up from the pain. The medical staff is mystified at the cause of the problem, since I had run marathons and climbed mountains and all the tests and examinations revealed nothing. They sent me to another hospital for further tests which revealed that I had gallstones. The doctor reported that it was a serious problem and required surgery. I was referred to a surgeon for the operation. He discussed types of surgery that included a new method and a traditional open surgical procedure. I did not qualify for the newer recent surgery because of the physical condition that still existed from my operation in Nigeria. In the end I refused to undergo surgery. I understood the results of the examination and the certainty of the diagnosis. The doctors were very concerned about my condition and they talked with me on several occasions. One doctor drew a picture of how the gallstone was blocking the duct to the gall bladder and all the known details of the situation were explained. Thinking, comparing, and evaluating are the things that the mind does best. Still I refused the surgery. I am disinterested in past cases and beliefs or images of my condition and I know that it is in me to overcome the current condition. I am in severe pain just as I was when sick in Africa where determined doctors operated and saved my life. These San Francisco days, though, are as the days of life in Africa. I am determined not to have any further surgery if an alternative treatment is possible. They are new days in my life, and I see them as a time of adventure in an uncertain world. It is a quest and a struggle from inside and within me that I face.

The Concoction

My wife has had continuous and serious problems with her migraine headaches. She is currently being treated by an acupuncturist who is able to help her condition. He is an inquiring Chinese physician. She told him about the gall stone condition. On a torn sheet of paper he wrote the following by hand:

1/2 lemon (juice)
2 tablespoons of olive oil
1 glass of water
mix it and take four times a day

I was told that the mixture may treat the gallstones. I took this concoction and felt its effects immediately. I never had another backache. I take it every day for one year and my body feels good with no symptoms of gallstones. After the second year there is no trace.

On the Road

I have started to run again. Recently my wife, daughter, and I went to Mexico and climbed two small mountains. The mountain towns of Mexico are a new frontier for us and not unlike those of Tanzania and East Africa. Humans have ventured out of Africa into voyages and ages of discovery throughout the earth. How deep do we now move beyond the earth into space, into human existence? Freedom and adventure stir our souls.

In the villages and towns life is lived moment by moment. The villages and the poor who live in them are isolated and cut off from the flow of material wealth in the cities and from the affluent classes.

When we cross the border and travel to Mexico, the uncertainty of unknown Mexican towns and mountains drives us. Poverty is everywhere in almost every African and Mexican village we have ever passed through. We know that freedom exists as energy within us. It is why the earth's poor (los pobres de la tierra) are not rescued by outsiders. We cannot control and dominate the lives of those whom we wish to help. From deep inside a person, a village, or a school is the energy that liberates existence from the oppression of past worlds and permanent things.

Final Passing Comment

One's life is more profound when one enters a world where one is able to figure out things for oneself. One inquires into a world and penetrates it, driven by knowing what one does not know. In schools and in conventional society we focus on what we know or are supposed to know and are left unprepared to deal with the things we don't know. We are enclosed in the world of the known. To inquire deeply we must move beyond the boundaries of our knowledge. Children liberate themselves when they go fearlessly beyond these limits and encounter new questions, observations, and investigation.

The year I made an unexpected expedition into the Sierra wilderness in California was as powerful a form of learning as I had ever encountered. It changed the meaning of the world for me and others with whom I journeyed. In life we discover such expeditions in schools and the wilderness, which renew us. The deep adventures we encounter are no less than that of humankind which emerged from the East African world of Kilimanjaro to learn and discover the profound life we can make of this earth.

About the Author

Hoover Liddell worked as a mathematics teacher in Nigeria, Kenya, and San Francisco. He worked as an educator in San Francisco public schools for thirty years.

9 780595 004874

6612643R0

Made in the USA
Lexington, KY
03 September 2010